University of Nebraska-Omaha Football

On the Front Cover: Gerald Gardner, pictured at age 20, was a six-foot, two-inch, 215-pound tackle. He was the largest member of the 21-player Cardinals team of 1936, coached by Sed Hartman. (Courtesy of the University of Nebraska–Omaha, Criss Library Archives & Special Collections.)

On the Back Cover: The 2010 University of Nebraska–Omaha football team was the final squad to represent the Mavericks. (Courtesy of the University of Nebraska–Omaha, Criss Library Archives & Special Collections.)

Cover Background: The Omaha University football team defeated Morningside 34-0 in 1955, extending its school-record winning streak to 16 games. (Courtesy of the University of Nebraska at Omaha, Criss Library Archives & Special Collections.)

University of Nebraska-Omaha Football

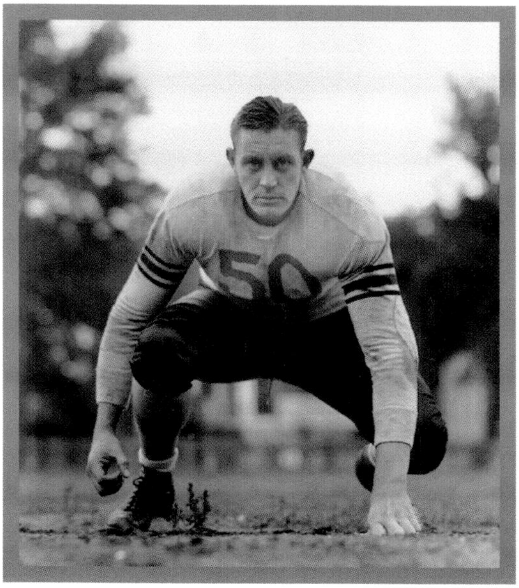

Darren Ivy

ARCADIA PUBLISHING

ISBN 978-1-4671-1461-5

Published by Arcadia Publishing
Charleston, South Carolina

Printed in the United States of America

Library of Congress Control Number: 2015934793

For all general information, please contact Arcadia Publishing:
Telephone 843-853-2070
Fax 843-853-0044
E-mail sales@arcadiapublishing.com
For customer service and orders:
Toll-Free 1-888-313-2665
Visit us on the Internet at www.arcadiapublishing.com

This book is dedicated all of the players
who made the program what it was over the years.

CONTENTS

ACKNOWLEDGMENTS

This book is provided as a compilation to showcase the memories of UNO's football program, and it could not have happened without the efforts of Les Valentine, who has spent countless hours making sure that the football program's stories and history are preserved as a valuable part of UNO's archives. Unless otherwise noted, all images appear courtesy of the University of Nebraska–Omaha, Criss Library Archives & Special Collections.

Hopefully, the images in this book will tell the story of the players and coaches who brought life to the program for years to come.

INTRODUCTION

University of Nebraska–Omaha archivist Les Valentine and business manager Beau Malnack organized a reunion of the undefeated 1954 Omaha University football team on April 12, 2014. The attendees watched a video synced with the radio broadcast of the 1954 Tangerine Bowl. Valentine and Malnack were impressed with how many people came out.

The remaining players, their families (Malnack's father, Wayne, had been on the 1954 squad), and close to 200 other people attended the special showing at UNO's Criss Library. Those who were in attendance to watch a replay of arguably the biggest game in the program's history left with an even greater appreciation of what the undefeated 1954 squad had achieved and what football in general had meant to the school from 1911 to 2010. *Omaha World-Herald* columnist Erin Grace wrote about her experiences at the event in her Sunday column. She had high praise for all the former players she had met.

"It was really something," the late Rudy Rotella said after seeing the tape at a private showing in 2013, before his death. "I was proud to be the captain of the team." Nearly every person who had the opportunity to play for the UNO football team would probably express similar sentiments and look back fondly on their years of collegiate football for OU and, later, UNO. They would probably choose to remember the good times, but media reports throughout the program's history touched on the underlying financial and school-support issues that the University of Nebraska–Omaha, Municipal University of Omaha, and Omaha University football teams faced.

Outside of a few seasons, football teams played before relatively small crowds, and the program struggled to stay afloat and be relevant in a state where the Cornhuskers were kings. UNO was a commuter campus for many years, and students had to drive to the campus on the weekends to show their support for the team. In later years, students could walk from their dorms, a few blocks from the stadium.

Most players participated in football for the love of it, as athletic scholarships were not available until the 1960s. And, even then, they were not as readily available as at other schools. Still, the school captured numerous conference titles, won a couple of bowl games, qualified for the NCAA playoffs multiple times, and produced its fair share of professional players, like Marlin Briscoe, who became the first African American starting quarterback in the NFL. Coaches came to UNO and invested years of their lives into the program, helping mold students into not only great football players, but great people. However, in the end, the high cost of maintaining and growing the football program to a Division I level as an independent school was one of the reasons that the sport was discontinued following the 2010 season.

At the time of this book's publication, in 2015, UNO is in its fifth year of not fielding a football team. University officials cite what they call the new economics of athletics, which do not allow for millions of dollars in subsidies to support football, which is not offered conference-wide in the Summit League. The former Al Caniglia Football Field and Track, which seated nearly 10,000 football fans, has been converted to a soccer-only facility of the same name. The old football goalposts have been replaced with soccer goals. Most of the undergraduate students who walk by today do not know what it was like to attend a Maverick football game on a fall Saturday afternoon or evening.

Many Maverick players from the 2010 team finished out their football careers at other schools, while others chose to drop the sport altogether. A few even made it to the next level. The players moved on following the vote by the University of Nebraska Regents on March 25, 2011, to move forward with joining the Summit League and ending the football and wrestling programs.

In these post-football days, UNO is pouring the majority of its athletic budget into its Division I programs, with men's hockey being the main draw. Men's and women's basketball and women's volleyball also will call home the new $75 million UNO Arena, slated to be completed in 2015.

The thousands of men who played for the Mavericks (1971–2011), Indians (1939–1971), Cardinals, and Maroons should be remembered and honored for the years they poured their hearts and souls into the Omaha football program.

Football will always be a part of the history of UNO. It is hoped that when people look back years from now in the collections that have been preserved in the school archives, they will appreciate what the game meant to the school and its role in putting Omaha University on the map.

1

The Beginning

With 12,248 full-time students according to the 2014 report to the NCAA, the University of Nebraska–Omaha has come a long way from when the school was housed in one building and barely had enough boys to field a football team.

Omaha University classes opened on September 14, 1909, in the old Redick Mansion at Twenty-fourth and Pratt Streets, with 29 students. Men's basketball preceded football by one year as the first sport at the school. Football barely got off the ground in 1911. According to an *Omaha World-Herald* article, "The team was not organized or any practice held until the last week of September. No regular practice was started until a week later when Andrew Dow of last year's Omaha High School team was elected captain. The team had no coaching until a week before its clash with Creighton when [Howard S.] Maxwell took charge of the men. Later in the season, Maxwell was assisted at times by 'Tate' Matters, F.C. Currens and other former football coaches in the city. At no time during the season, was there more than 15 men on the field, and these were light in weight."

In 1911, Creighton University was the top football program in Omaha, having been built up since starting in 1900. The Bluejays even took on mighty Notre Dame in 1915. Down the road in Lincoln, the University of Nebraska was under the direction of first-year coach E.O. Stiehm in 1911. The Cornhuskers would go 35-2-3 and 14-0-1 in conference play from 1911 to 1915, with five Missouri Valley Conference titles. The Shetlands, as Omaha University's team was known that season, opened with a 25-0 victory over Nebraska Deaf at the school field at Twenty-fourth and Pratt Streets. It then lost 57-0 to Creighton, 13-6 to Peru State, and 59-0 to Hastings College.

The 14 men who earned "O" sweater letters that inaugural season were Neal Parsons (left end), Stanton Salisbury (left tackle), Victor Jorgenson (left guard), Charles Frandsen (center), Peter Strehlow (right guard), John Selby (right tackle), Ray Reel (right end), George Parish (quarterback), Almet Solomon (fullback), Paul Selby (right halfback), Neal Doren (center and guard), Willard Flor (right end), and David Larsen (left halfback).

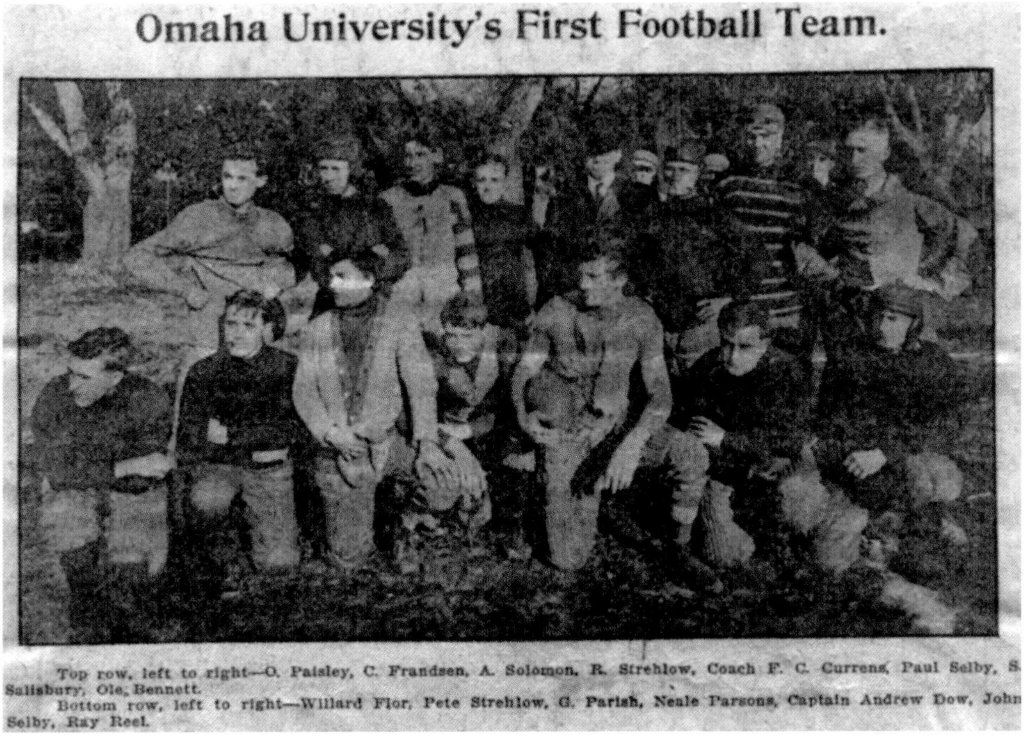

Omaha University's First Football Team.

Top row, left to right—O. Paisley, C. Frandsen, A. Solomon, R. Strehlow, Coach F. C. Currens, Paul Selby, S. Salisbury, Ole, Bennett.

Bottom row, left to right—Willard Flor, Pete Strehlow, G. Parish, Neale Parsons, Captain Andrew Dow, John Selby, Ray Reel.

The first Omaha University football team is pictured in the October 15, 1911, *Omaha World-Herald*. The players are, from left to right, (first row) Willard Flor (right end), Pete Strehlow (right guard), George Parish (quarterback), Neal Parsons (left end), Andrew Dow (quarterback), John Selby (right tackle), and Ray Reel (right end); (second row) Oldham Paisley, Charles Frandsen (center), Almet Solomon (fullback), R. Strehlow, F.C. Currens (coach), Paul Selby (right halfback), Stanton Salisbury (left tackle), "Ole", and ? Bennett. Not pictured are Victor Jorgensen (left guard), Neal Doren (center), David Larsen (left halfback), and Harold Haaker.

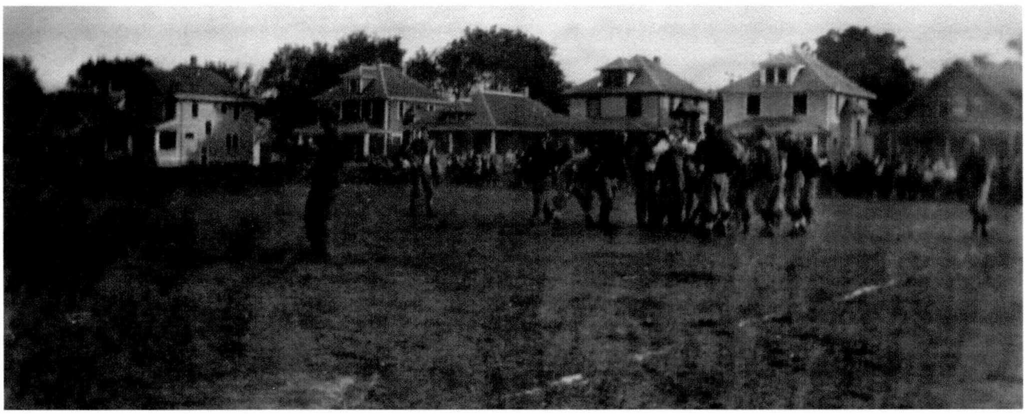

Omaha University student Beulah McCaw captured the first official game, against the Nebraska Deaf team at the school field in Omaha. Andrew Dow is at the far left, behind the Omaha University line. Directly in front of him is Ray Reel. The Shetlands, as they were known that season, opened with a 25-0 victory.

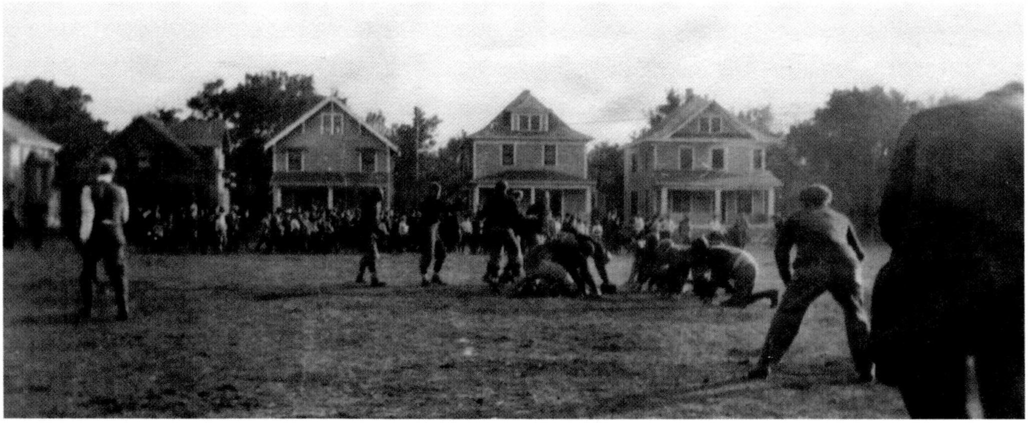

The 14 men who earned "O" sweater letters that inaugural season were Neal Parsons, Stanton Salisbury, Victor Jorgenson, Charles Frandsen, Peter Strehlow, John Selby, Ray Reel, George Parish, Almet Solomon, Paul Selby, Neal Doren, Willard Flor, Ole Bennett, and David Larsen. After defeating Nebraska Deaf, the 1911 OU team fell 57-0 to Creighton, 13-6 to Peru State, and 59-0 to Hastings College.

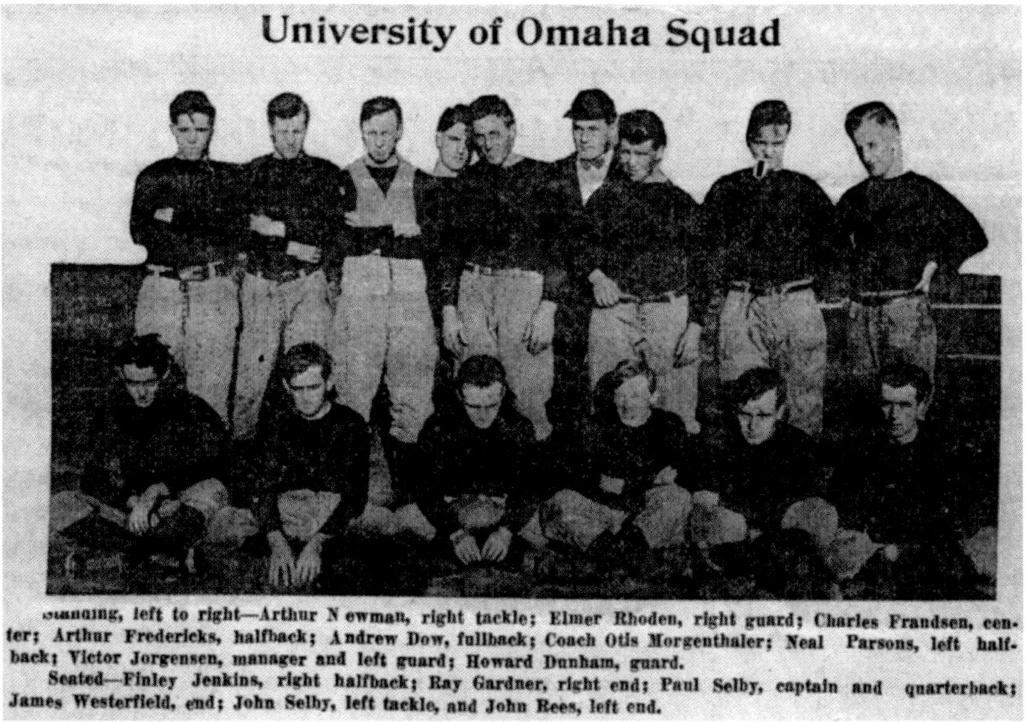

University of Omaha Squad

Standing, left to right—Arthur Newman, right tackle; Elmer Rhoden, right guard; Charles Frandsen, center; Arthur Fredericks, halfback; Andrew Dow, fullback; Coach Otis Morgenthaler; Neal Parsons, left halfback; Victor Jorgensen, manager and left guard; Howard Dunham, guard.

Seated—Finley Jenkins, right halfback; Ray Gardner, right end; Paul Selby, captain and quarterback; James Westerfield, end; John Selby, left tackle, and John Rees, left end.

The 1912 Omaha University team included, from left to right, (first row) Finley Jenkins (right halfback), Ray Gardner (right end), Paul Selby (captain and quarterback), James Westerfield (end), John Selby (left tackle), and John Rees (left end); (second row) Arthur Newman (right tackle), Elmer Rhoden (right guard), Charles Frandsen (center), Arthur Fredericks (halfback), Andrew Dow (fullback), Otis Morganthaler (coach), Neal Parsons (left halfback), Victor Jorgensen (manager and left guard), and Howard Dunham (guard).

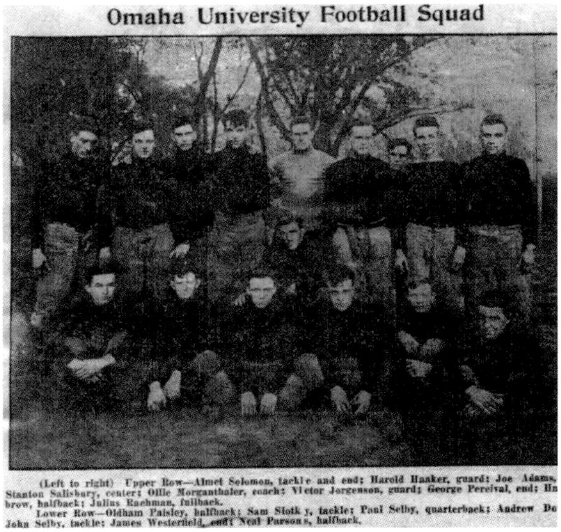

Omaha University Football Squad

(Left to right) Upper Row—Almet Solomon, tackle and end; Harold Haaker, guard; Joe Adams, Stanton Salisbury, center; Ollie Morganthaler, coach; Victor Jorgenson, guard; George Percival, end; Hn brow, halfback; Julius Rachman, fullback.
Lower Row—Oldham Paisley, halfback; Sam Slotk y, tackle; Paul Selby, quarterback; Andrew Do John Selby, tackle; James Westerfield, end; Neal Parsons, halfback.

In another photograph of the 1912 team, the members include, from left to right, (front row) Oldham Paisley (halfback), Sam Slotky (tackle), Paul Selby (quarterback), Andrew Dow (end), John Selby (tackle), James Westerfield (end), and Neal Parsons (halfback); (back row) Almet Solomon (tackle and end), Harold Haaker (guard), Joe Adams (tackle), Stanton Salisbury (center), Ollie Morganthaler (coach), Victor Jorgenson (guard), George Percival (end), Harry Disbrow (halfback), and Jullius Rachman (fullback).

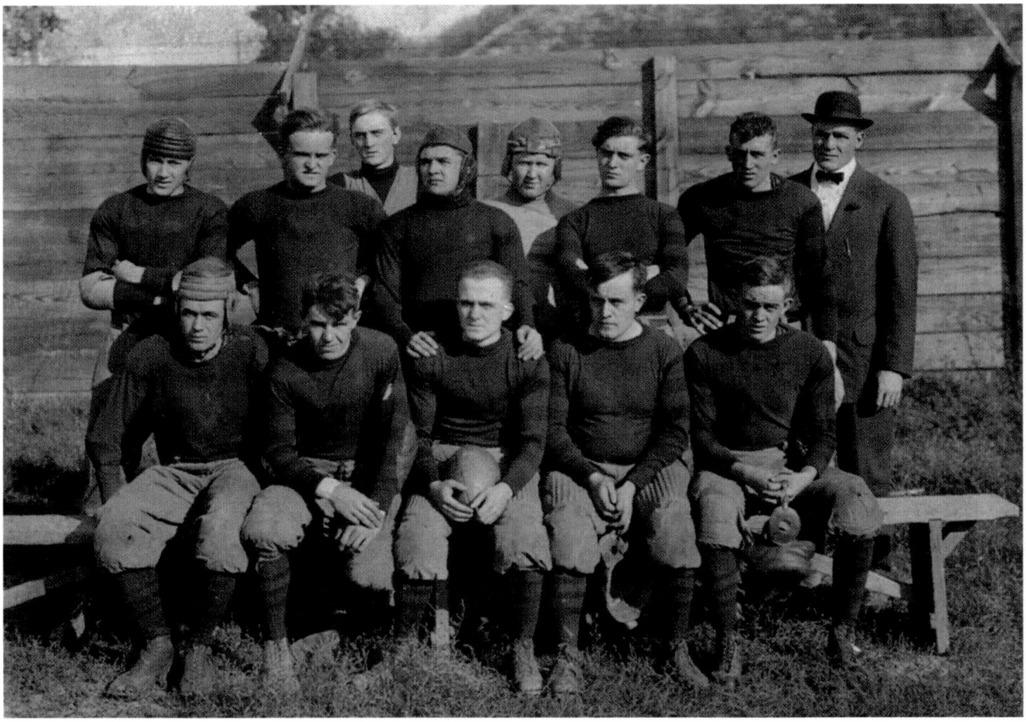

The 1912 team poses for a photograph. Shown here are, from left to right, (first row) John Reese, Neal Parsons, Paul Selby, John Selby, and Finley Jenkins; (second row) Elmer Rhoden, Victor Jorgenson, Glen Reeves, George Parish, ? Morris, Arthur Fredricks, Andrew Dow, and Coach Morganthaler. The team went 2-4, with wins over Cotner College (7-6) and Peru State (6-0) and losses to Creighton (34-14), Western Iowa Vocation (26-7), Nebraska Wesleyan (36-6), and Tarkio College (6-0). George Parish and Stanton Salisbury were the first players to graduate, in 1912. The former Omaha High teammates were standouts on the 1912 Omaha University squad that finished 2-4.

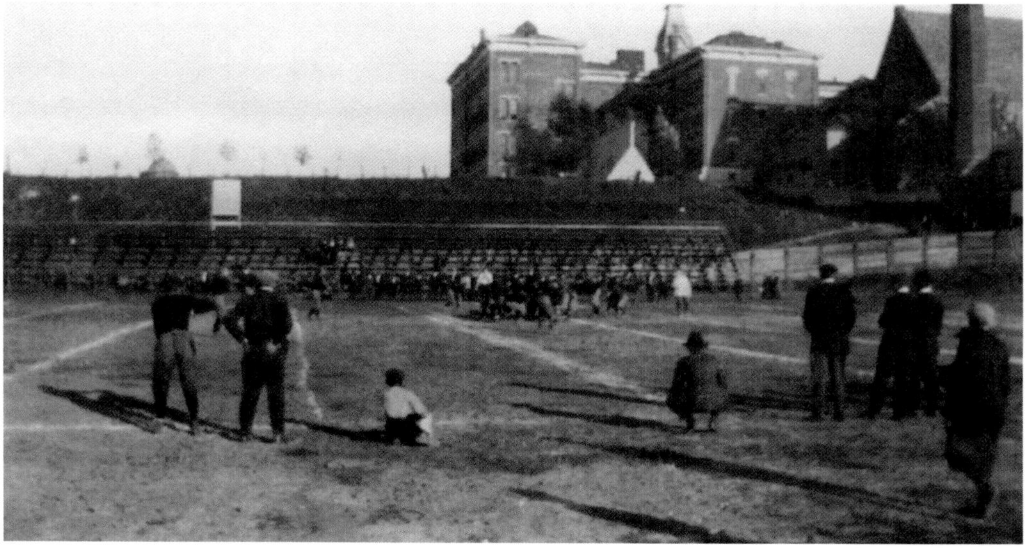

Omaha University opened the 1913 season against Doane College on October 11, 1913. According to UNO history books, Omaha dropped the game 13-6, but the *Omaha Bee* reported the score as a 14-0 loss. "The invaders played a clever and clean game of straight football, making all their down on line plunges with no intermixture of open playing or forward passing." Omaha University ended up going 0-4 in 1913, with a 13-7 loss to Cotner, a 128-0 setback to Creighton, and a 53-0 loss to Nebraska Wesleyan.

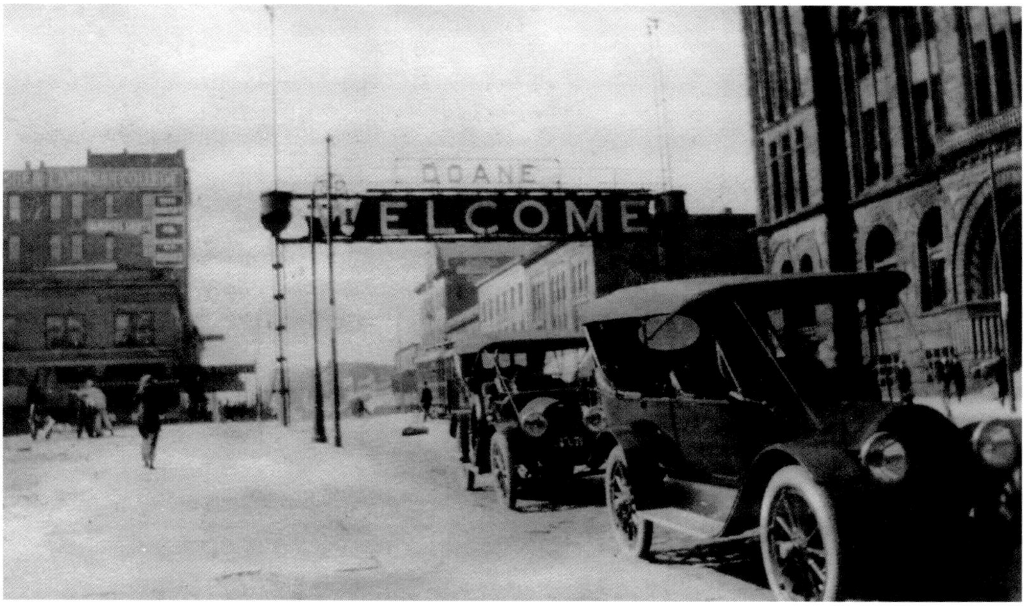

October 11, 1913, was a big day for the city of Omaha, as OU met Doane College at 3:00 p.m. at Creighton's field. This was the first meeting between the schools, and the *Yellow Sheet* reported that at least 200 tickets needed to be sold to cover the costs of bringing Doane to Omaha for the game; the cost of entrance to the contest was 50¢. A small parade was held before the game in downtown Omaha.

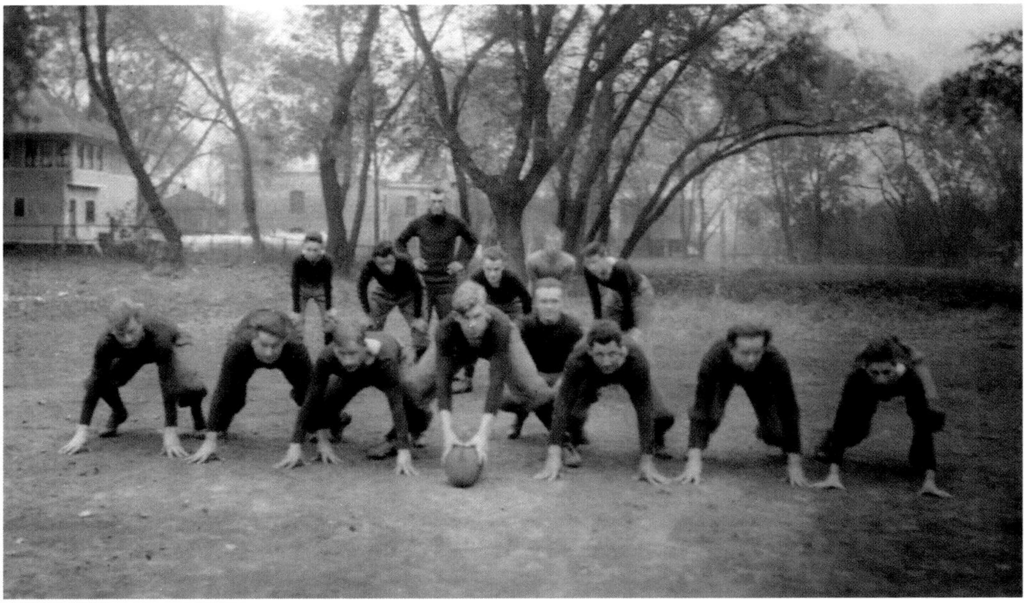

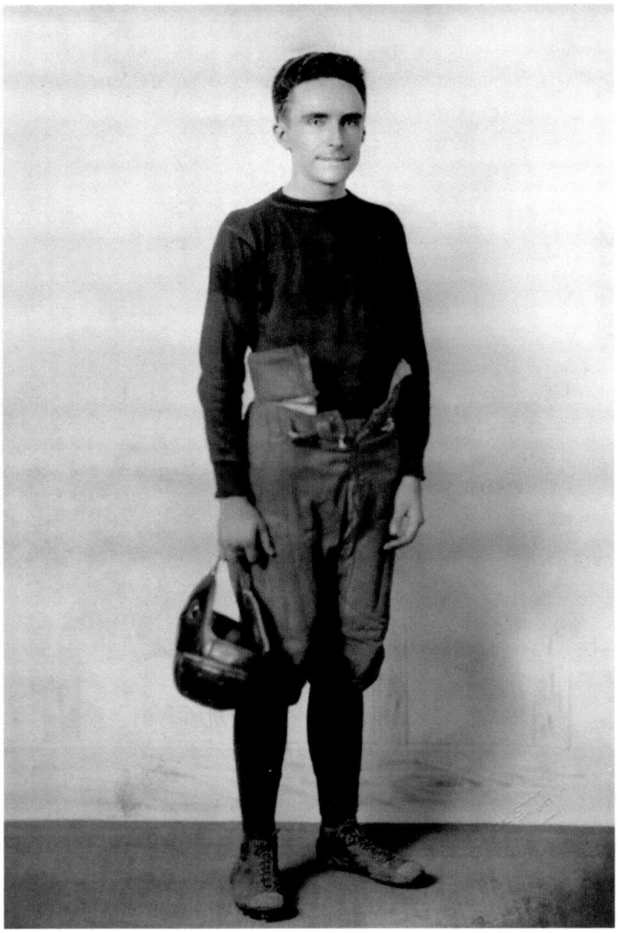

Coach Andrew Dow's 1914 squad only played three games, suffering a 21-13 loss to York, a 26-0 setback to Wayne State, and a 14-0 loss to Cotner College.

William Thompson graduated from Omaha University in 1917 but was only able to play on the football team in 1915 and 1916, as the school did not field a team in 1917 and 1918 due to World War I. He returned as the athletic director in 1931 and was head of the psychology department. The alumni center was named for him in 1981, shortly after his death.

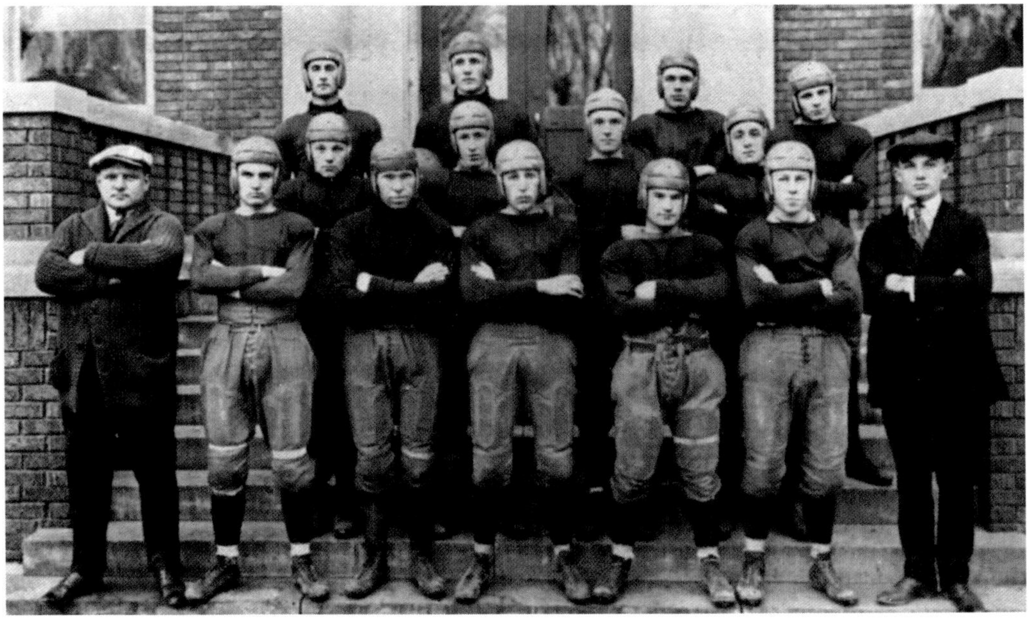

The 1919 Omaha University football team was the first squad fielded after a two-year absence for World War I. Coach Frank "Iron Major" Cavanaugh's squad went 3-2-1, with wins over Palmer, Missouri (14-7), Fort Omaha (7-6), and Trinity (20-0). Cavanaugh, a member of the National Football Foundation Hall of Fame, had coached at Dartmouth and Holy Cross before service in the war, where he was seriously injured. On October 23, 1918, Cavanaugh was wounded in combat in France. He later went on to coach at Boston College (1919–1926) and Fordham (1927–1932). He died on August 29, 1933, at age 57. In 1943, he was depicted in the movie *The Iron Major*, with Pat O'Brien in the lead role. The movie extolled Cavanaugh's "love of God, love of his country, love of his family."

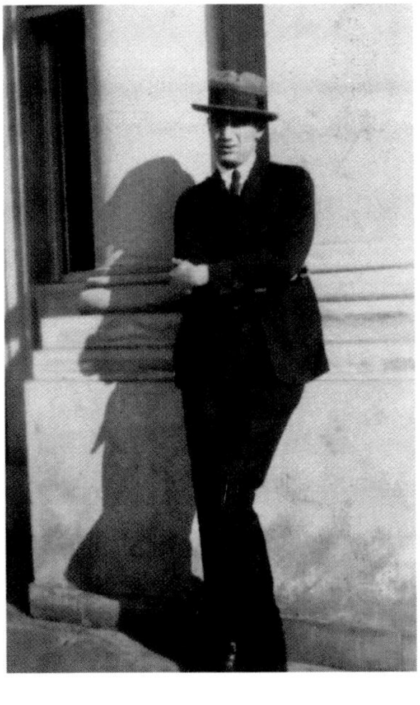

The first athletic board, formed in 1920, appointed Ernie Adams, a former Omaha University student and athlete, to coach and head the physical education department. Adams coached through the 1925 season before being replaced by L.M. Bradfield in 1927.

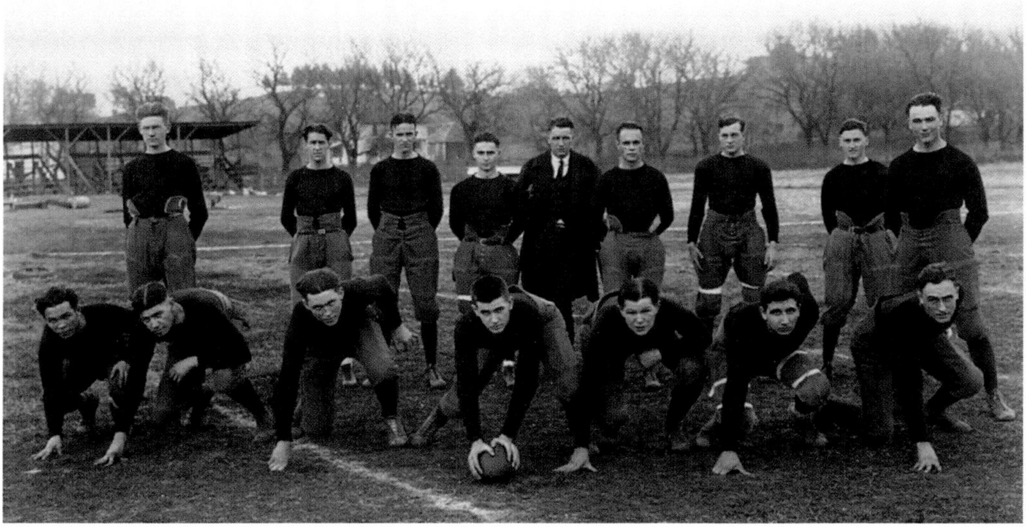

Omaha University boasted an overall enrollment of 702 students in all sessions; just 18 bachelor's degrees were given at its June commencement that year. The 1922 football team, under the direction of Ernie Adams, went 2-3, with wins over Tabor, Iowa (26-0) and Western Union (23-0). An 11-game schedule had been planned, but as happened in those days, quite a few were canceled for various reasons. Here, members of the team pose for a photograph prior to the road game at Tarkio, Missouri. Shown are, from left to right, (first row) Paul Konecky, Bill Flynn, Tex Pratt, Fletcher Slater, Alfred Kastman, David Chesneau, and Merril Russel; (second row) Wilbur Erickson, Harold Ackerman, captain Edwin Wilmarth, Leo Konecky, coach Ernie Adams, Charles Poucher, Glenn Hesler, Bill Christy, and Ben Shurtleff.

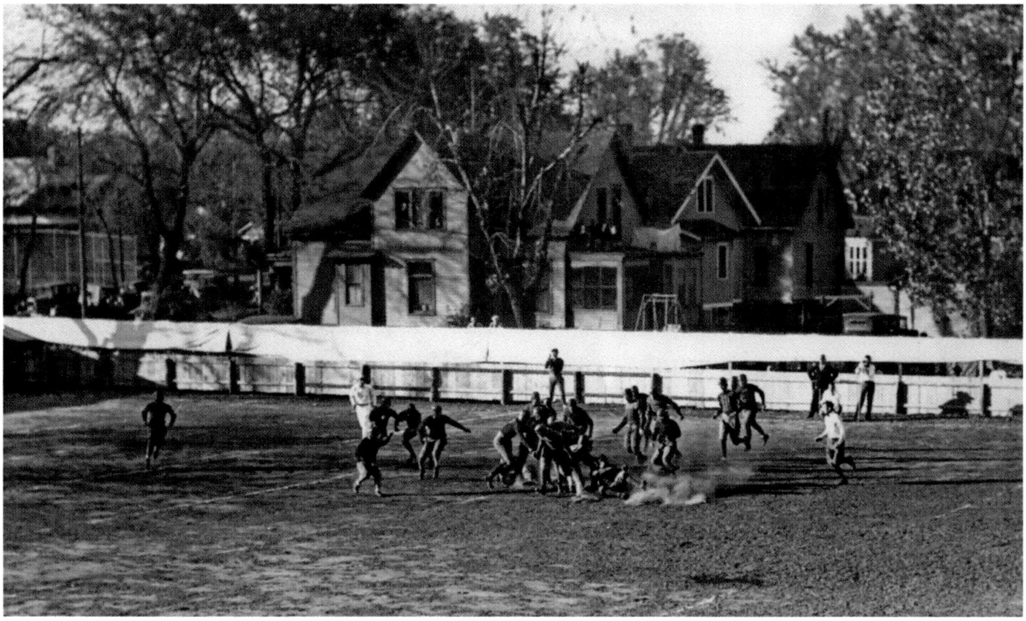

The Maroon Warriors took on Grand Island College on October 22, 1927. Coach L.M. Bradfield's squad suffered a 20-0 loss at the Saratoga Park field.

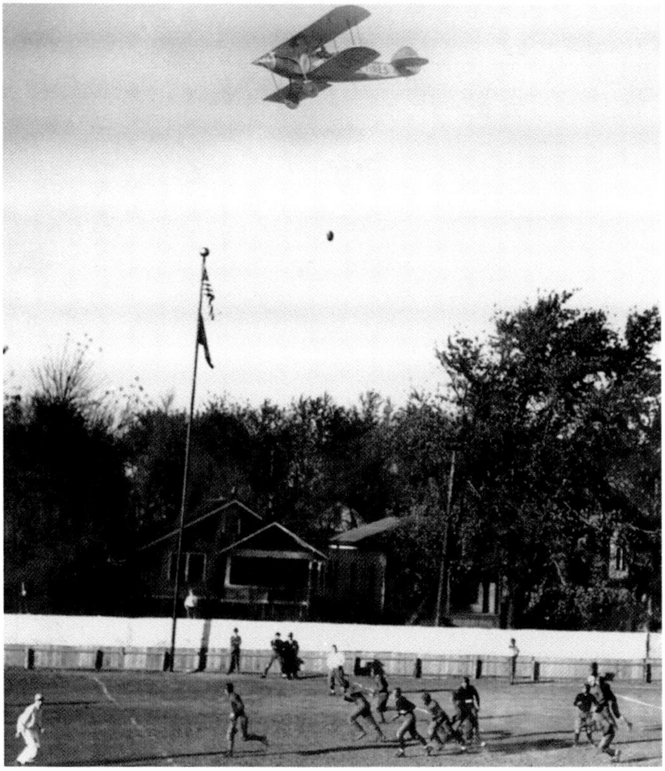

When Omaha University debuted its new football field at Saratoga Park (Twenty-fourth Street and Ames Avenue) in 1927, sponsor Overland Tire Company began a game by dropping a football from a low-flying airplane. North Omaha may seem like a good distance from the current UNO campus, but the original Omaha University campus was located at Twenty-fourth and Pratt Streets, about five blocks from this field. Omaha businessmen formed the North Omaha Activities Association in order to redevelop Saratoga School's playing field into a football field.

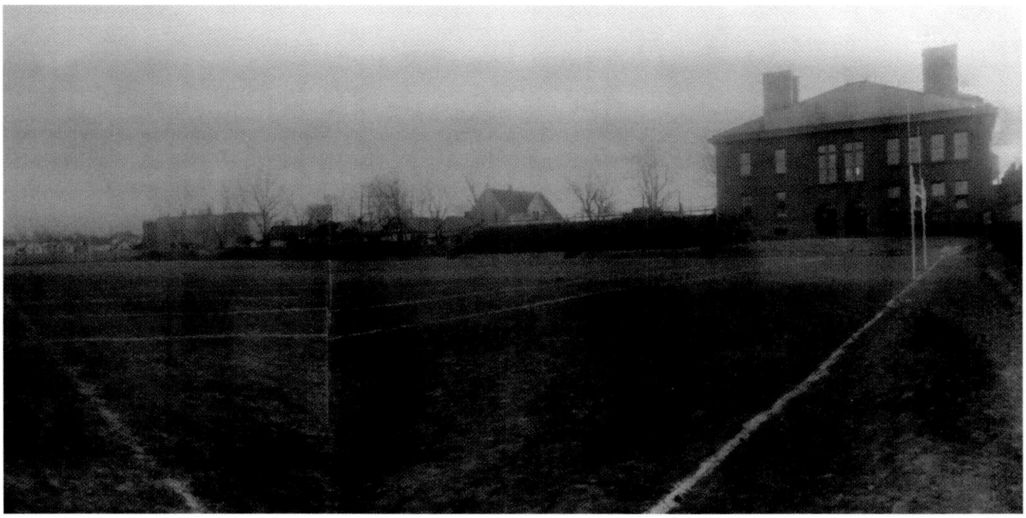

On November 24, 1928, OU football player Gilbert Edwards died in an automobile accident after suffering a broken skull. Freshmen Frank Threadgill and Robert Streitweiser and sophomore Ralph Kahn were injured. Earlier that day, Omaha University celebrated its first homecoming "in a manner that gave promise of what future homecoming will bring forth." A parade was held for the first time. The football team lost 37-0 to Peru, which held a 30-pound-per-man advantage. The *Gateway* reported that the parade "did much to arouse interest in the University and was good advertising for the afternoon's game," which was attended by 700 persons.

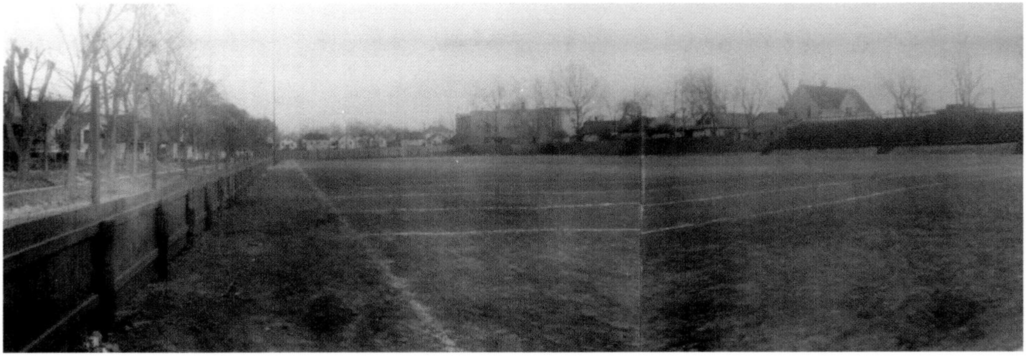

Saratoga Field is shown in 1928, Omaha University's first season in the Nebraska Intercollegiate Athletic Association.

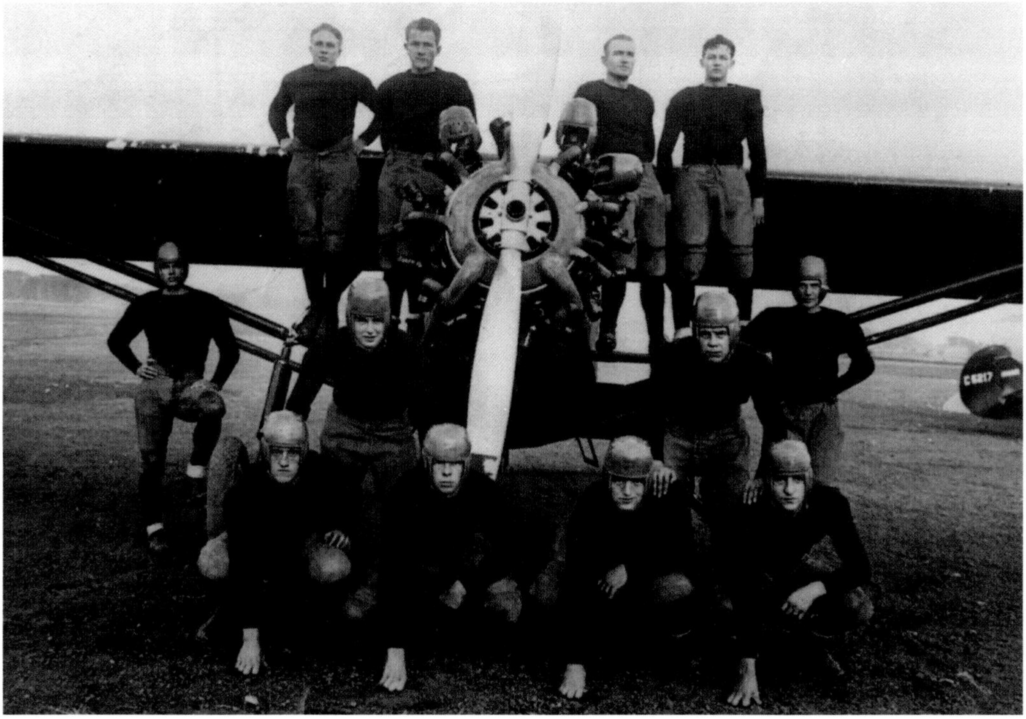

The 1930 Omaha University football team was the first college team known to fly to a game. John Barber, who played center on the team, had this photograph in his possession for many years, but it was not until a chance meeting with fellow Omahan Gary Wiren in 2001 that the image was publicly displayed. It eventually found its way to the College Football Hall of Fame, placed next to a football jersey worn by the great Harold "Red" Grange. In an interview with the UNO Alumni Association, Barber said the trip happened on October 3, 1930, when the Cardinals made the short flight to Fremont to play Midland Lutheran College. The teams played to a 0-0 tie, and the OU team returned to campus by bus. Barber said the team took off from Omaha Municipal Airfield. Because the airplane had limited passenger space, it took three trips to get the team to Fremont, with the plane landing in a field adjacent to the stadium. Barber said it was mostly a "publicity stunt" for a team that would struggle through a 3-4-2 season.

2

Coach Hartman's Teams

In May 1930, the citizens of Omaha voted to establish the Municipal University of Omaha. According to an article in the *Gateway*, "Scarcely had the Board of Regents, appointed by the Board of Education under terms of the state act, begun their administration than an injunction was issued to prevent levying a tax to support the school." However, the District and State Supreme Courts on December 23, 1930, ruled and allowed the new Municipal University to open in January 1931.

According to a January 15, 1931, article in the *Gateway*, OU sports faced an "optimistic era." One reason for the optimism was the hiring of Cecil Leroy "Sed" Hartman as the men's basketball and football coach. The 31-year-old Hartman had been a standout athlete at Lincoln High and then at the University of Nebraska–Lincoln, where he lettered in track and field from 1922 to 1924 and in football from 1921 to 1923.

In the Cardinals' first football season under Hartman, the team went 5-1-1. His basketball team went 20-0. The football Cardinals finished 18-7-5 in the first four years before joining the North Central Conference (NCC) in 1935. The move was a step up in competition, lasting from 1935 to 1942, until football was suspended due to World War II.

Halfback Leo Pearey became Omaha University's first All-American, in 1935, helping Omaha finish 6-3 and earn third place in the NCC, its best finish under Hartman. But over the next seven seasons, Omaha would win at most three games in any year, and Hartman finished with a career record of 39-41-11.

By 1937–1938, the first buildings were being constructed on the current site of UNO. In 1939, the school mascot was changed to the Indians. By November 1942, sixty-seven students had joined the armed forces in the previous few months, and another 192 had left school for jobs in Omaha. In 1943, athletic director William H. Thompson, a former OU athlete himself, as well as former football coach Ernest Adams and former Creighton athletic director Harold C. Linehan, concluded that to pursue intercollegiate football would be contrary to the best interests of the players and the university.

Hartman, who died at age 87 in February 1988, was a lieutenant commander in the Navy during World War II and went into construction and real estate in Omaha after the war.

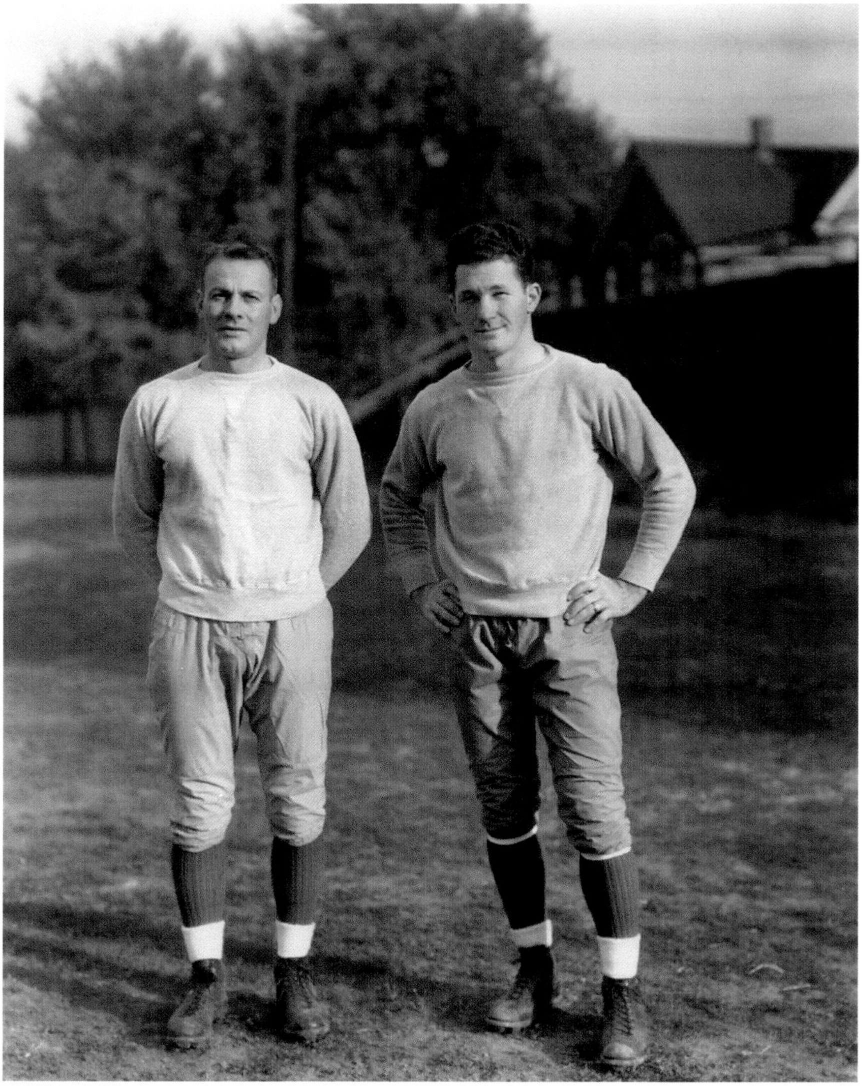

Pictured in 1936, Sed Hartman (left) coached the Cardinals from 1931 to 1942, while assistant coach John Baker (right) assisted him from 1935 to 1937. Baker was also the head basketball coach. Baker had been an All-American in 1931 at the University of California and a head coach at Iowa Teachers College for three years before coming to Omaha. Upon Baker's resignation, Hartman commented to the *Gateway*, "John did us a lot of good in the three years he has coached the line." Hartman had been a standout athlete at Lincoln High and then at the University of Nebraska–Lincoln, where he lettered in track and field from 1922 to 1924 and in football from 1921 to 1923. He played against Notre Dame's "Four Horsemen" in Nebraska's 14-6 win in 1922 and 14-7 victory in 1923. Those were the only losses the Fighting Irish suffered each season. The Cornhusker yearbook described Hartman as "smashing into the line like a battering ram, and with the speed of a bullet." On June 11, 1934, Hartman started an 11-day coaches' clinic with Nebraska head football coach Dana Bible, who was also president of the American Football Coaches Association, and Nebraska track coach Henry Schulte.

Tackle Gerald Gardner, at six feet, two inches and 215 pounds, was the largest member of the 21-player 1936 Cardinals team coached by Sed Hartman. Of the team's players, nine came from Omaha, two from Lincoln, Council Bluffs, and Malvern, and one each from Bloomfield, Wahoo, Walnut, Fort Dodge, Red Oak, and Shenandoah, Iowa. They defeated Morningside and Wayne State, tied South Dakota State and Iowa Teachers, and lost to North Dakota State, South Dakota, and DePaul, the latter by the score of 46-0 at Wrigley Field. Some of the proceeds of that game benefited St. Elizabeth Hospital.

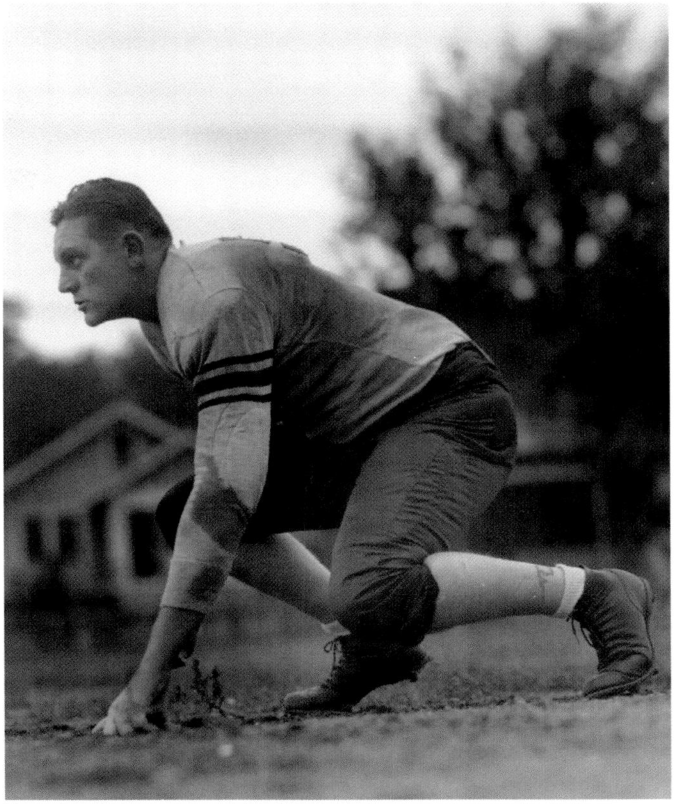

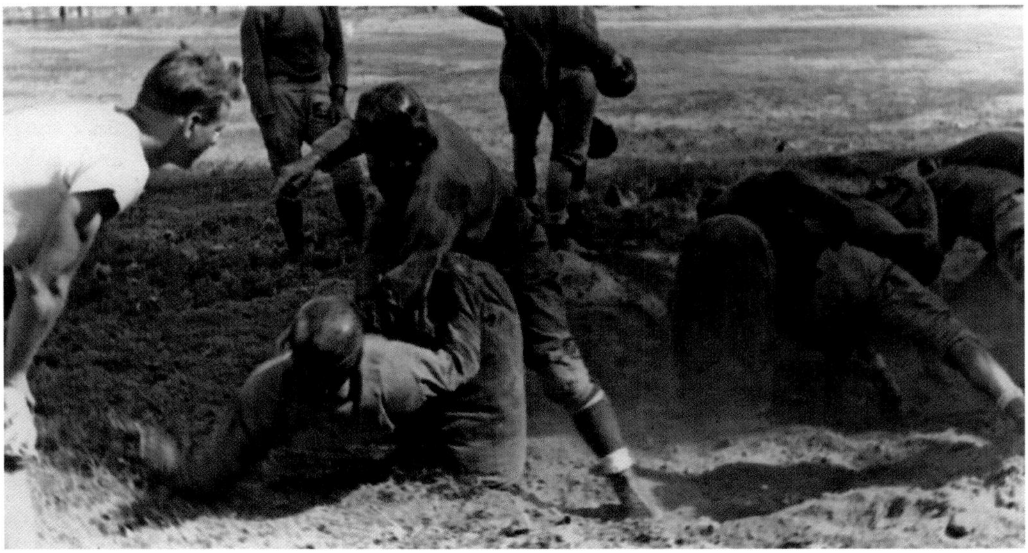

Coach Hartman supervises a rough practice in 1937. The team went 2-6 overall and 0-5 in North Central Conference play. Members of the 1937 squad included quarterback Royce Brown, Hux Bachman, senior Melvin Boldenow, end Ed Kersenbrock, halfback Bill Kulper, center Joe Mazzeri, and Martin Thomas, who played for OU in 1931 and 1932 and came out midway through the 1937 season.

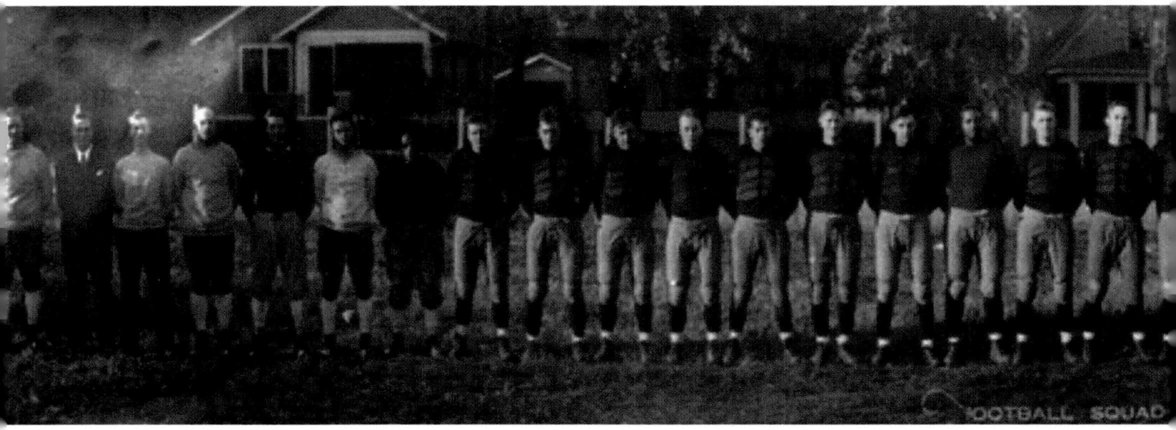

The 1932 team, coach Sed Hartman's second squad at Omaha University, finished 5-2-1.

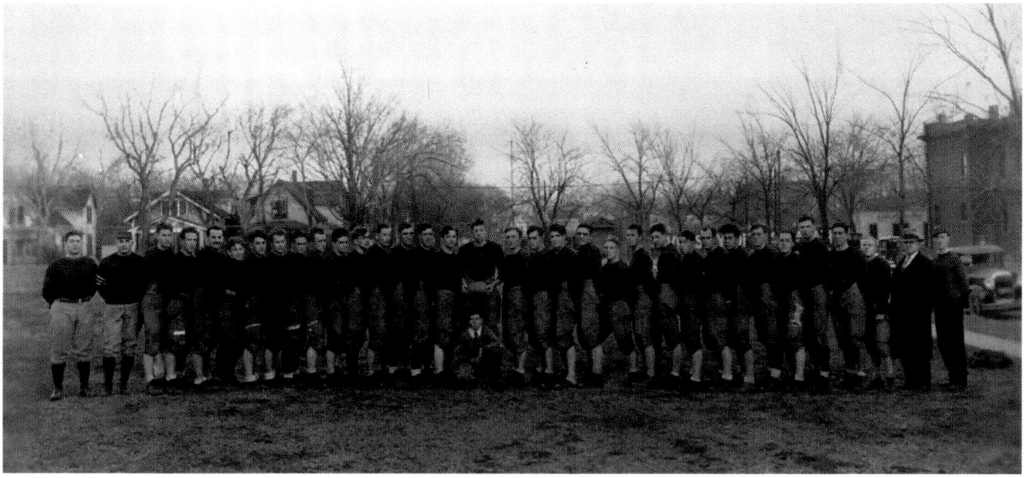

The 1935 Omaha University football team poses for a photograph near the original campus. This year marked the first time OU competed in the tougher North Central Conference while also playing one last year in the in-state Nebraska Intercollegiate Athletic Association. The *Gateway* remarked, "The Cards' rise from the NIAA Conference to the North Central Conference is one of the finest movements the team has made during its years of competitive football." The first-string squad in 1935 included Harold Johnk, Noel King, Lawrence Gammon, Frank Crawford, Howard Sorenson, Norman Sorenson, Royce Brown, Leo Pearey, Morris Loder, Kenneth Turner, Bill Nelson, Bob Fritchoff, Harold Grau, Wilber Adams, Bob Flesher, Stub Riggons, and Bob Frink. The 1935 team started 5-0, but went 1-3 down the stretch to finish 6-3. Pearey and Johnson earned all-conference honors.

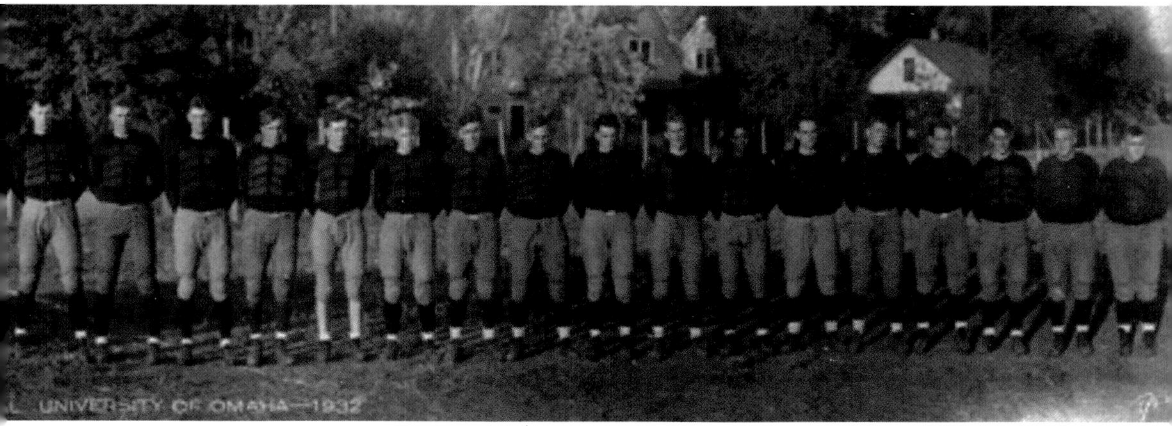

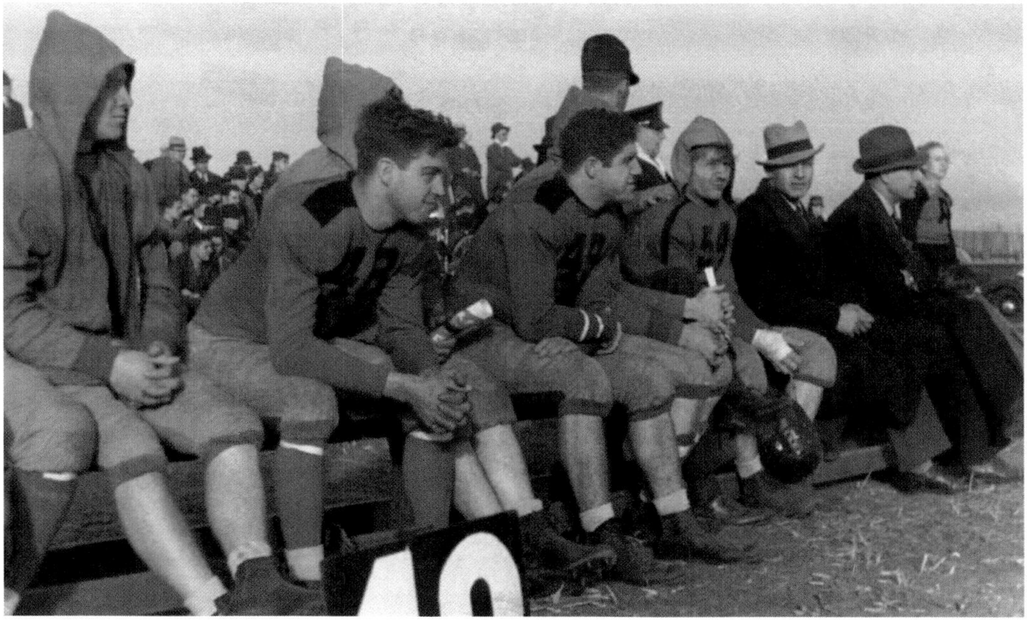

Players take a rest on the bench during a 1937 home game at Omaha Benson High School, where the Municipal University of Omaha played some of its games before the stadium was built on the main campus.

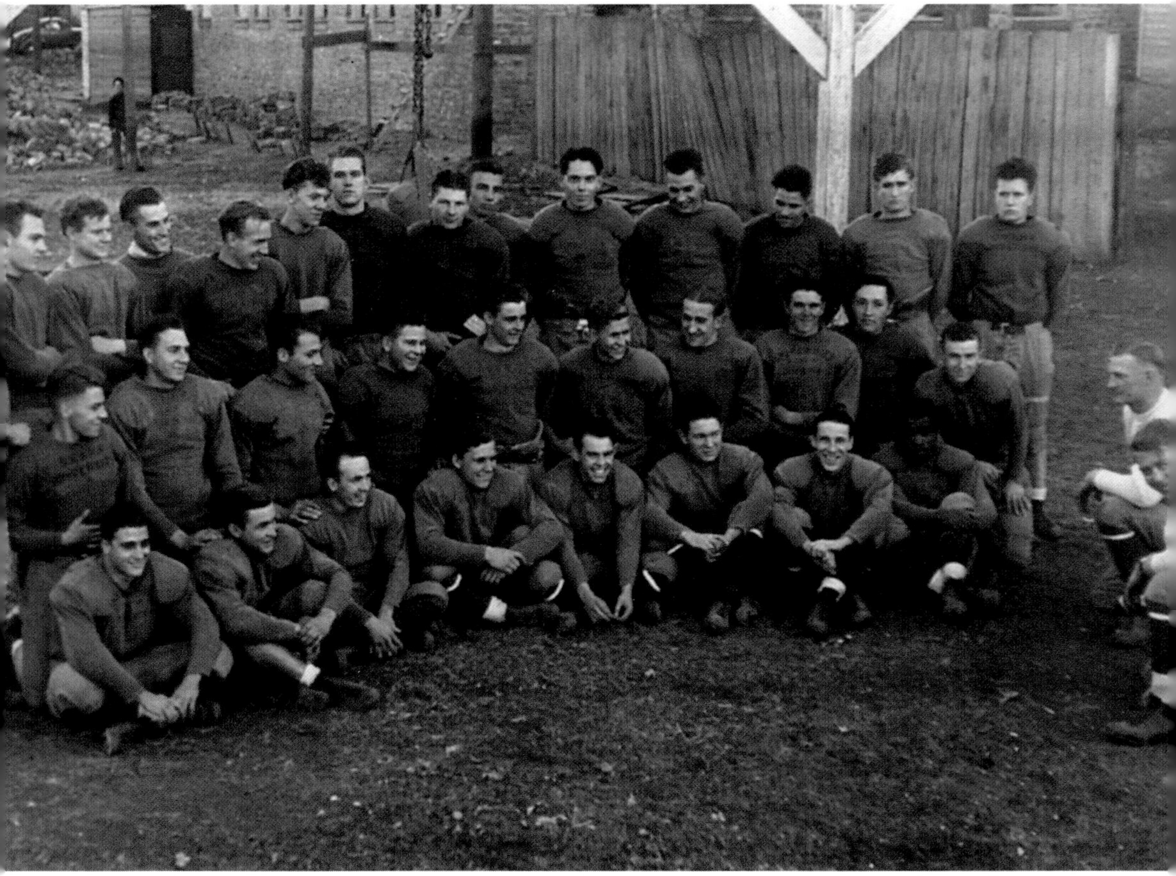

The 1937 freshman football team, coached by former OU athletes Leo Pearcy (far right) and Harold Johnk, a four-time all-conference player (1933–1936), was the largest in school history. On this freshman team, the ends were Cecil Cunningham of Omaha South; Al Hartman of Omaha Benson; Ken Hagarty of Shenandoah, Iowa; Louis Shields of Manilla, Iowa; and Don Zipper of Columbus. The tackles were Stan Skripsky of Omaha South; Laurance Rohde of Charter Oak, Iowa; Austin Vickery of Omaha North; Roy Alley of Omaha North; Denton Dresher of Irvington; and Louis Bendekovic of Omaha South. The team's guards were William Humes of Council Bluffs, Iowa; Louis Profeda of Council Bluffs; Ralph Pickins of Council Bluffs; Dick Lawton of Omaha Benson; Robert Slisesky of Omaha South; and Glen Fay of Harlan, Iowa. Centers were Harold Jacobsen of South Dakota; William Wheah of Missouri; James Henry of Mineola, Iowa; and Joseph Bailey of Omaha. The backs were Don Pflaster of Omaha North; Bobby Vaughn of Omaha Tech; Carl Cook of Pender; Leon Peoples of Omaha South; Vernon O'Neil of Ainsworth; George Talmadge of Omaha South; Frank Vondra of Omaha South; Harold Melcher of Omaha Central; Gordon Christiansen of Harlan, Iowa; Jack Powers of Omaha; Bob Hunter of Omaha South; Olen Newton of Omaha; Len Lavensen of Rushville; L. Lockhard of Omaha; and Bob Dunn of Omaha Central. The team opened with a 19-0 win at Tarkio, but lost 20-0 to Morningside. A NCC rule limited freshmen teams to three games.

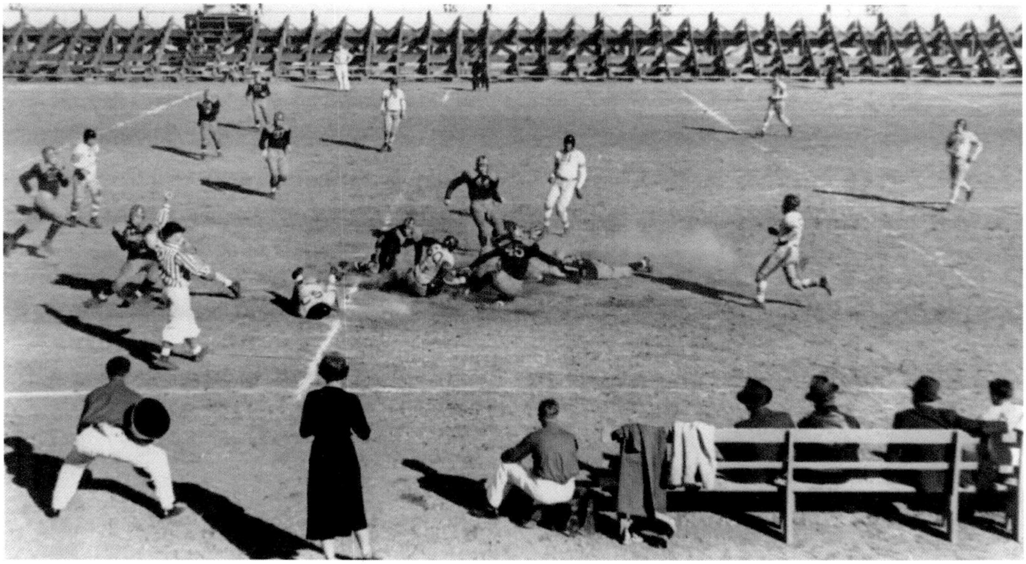

The 1937 Omaha University football team does battle at Omaha Benson's field.

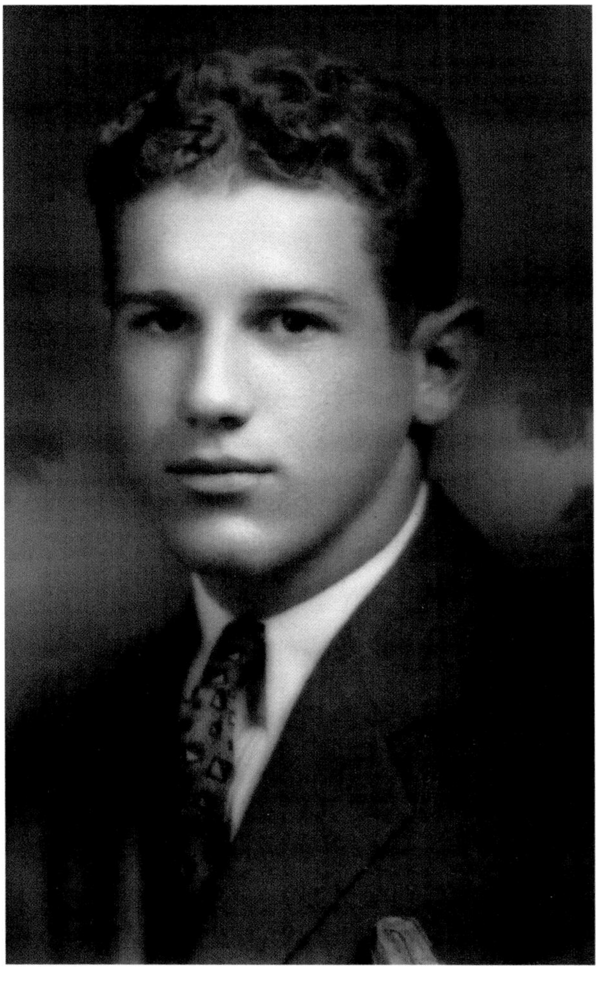

Senior quarterback and defensive standout Royce "Jug" Brown earned All–North Central Conference honors in 1937. The *Gateway* described Brown as "the boy who punts the ball, goes down and makes a tackle, get the punt and then steams down the field for some yardage." Brown was a member of the varsity team all four years. In 1938, Brown played for the Cincinnati Bengals of the American Football League, becoming Omaha University's first professional player. The Bengals finished 7-2-1, including a 17-13 win over George Halas's Chicago Bears. Following that season, Brown went to work for Swift & Co. in Omaha. "It's a great life, but there's no future in professional football," Brown was reported as saying after the 1938 season. "I think I'll string along with the meat packing business."

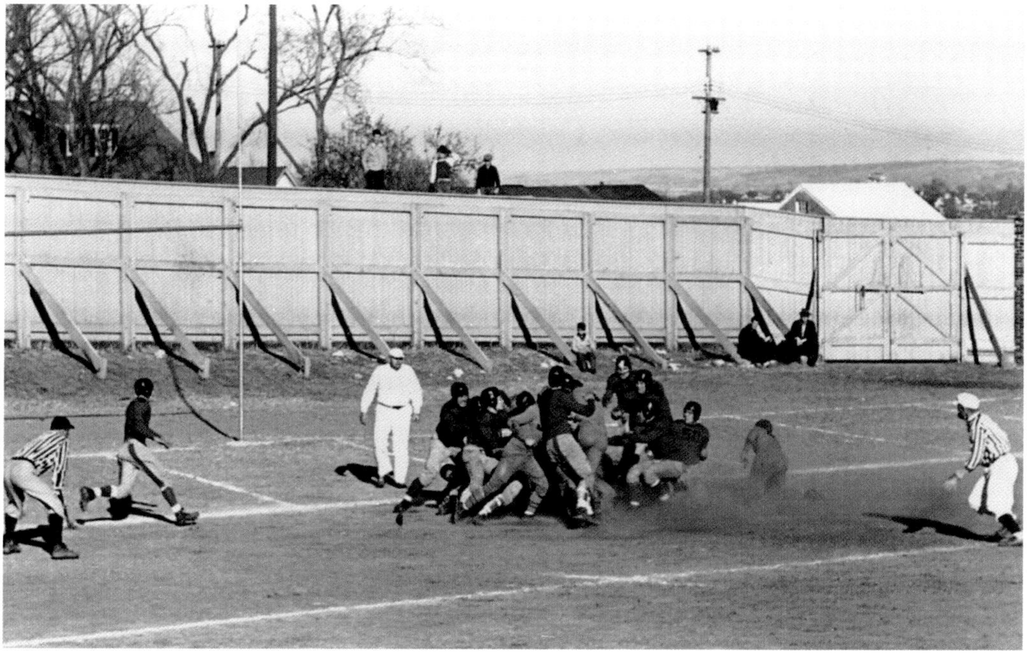

The Cardinals play at Omaha Benson in 1939. OU finished 3-5 that year. Don Pflasterer, Ralph Smeckpeper, and Joe Mazzeri earned All–North Central Conference honors. On October 30, 1939, a group of players asked OU president Rowland Haynes to fire coach Sed Hartman; however, a team meeting with Hartman the next day appeased the players. He remained the coach through 1942, when World War II caused a three-year break from football. He finished with a 39-41 record.

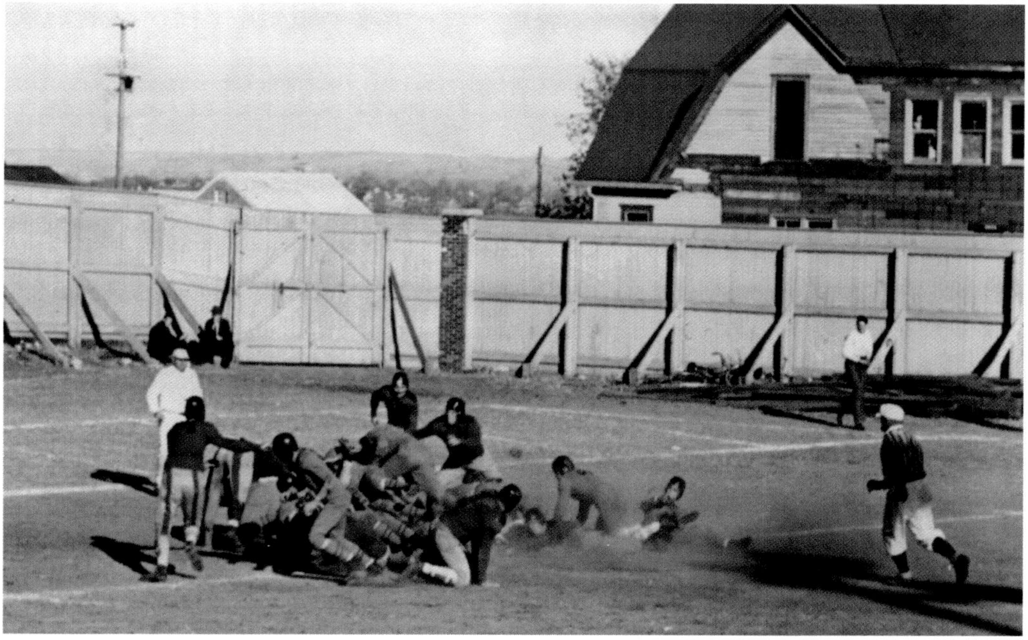

Omaha University continued to play some of its games at Omaha Benson in 1940. Coach Hartman's team went 2-3-2 in 1940, as Pflasterer again earned all-conference honors.

3

Coach Cardwell's Teams

When football resumed at the University of Omaha on September 20, 1947, after a four-year absence due to World War II, the Indians were led by head coach Lloyd Cardwell. Nicknamed "Wild Hoss" from his years of playing football and running track for the University of Nebraska–Lincoln, Cardwell was a sports legend in the state, dating to his days at Seward High School. He lettered for the Huskers in football and track from 1934 to 1936. At 190 pounds, he helped Nebraska win the Big Six track championship in 1935–1936. He also was All–Big Six in football from 1934 to 1936 and earned All-America mention. He scored 120 points in 24 games while earning All–Big Six honors three years and All-American honors two years. He played one of his greatest games in 1935 against Chicago University, scoring three touchdowns, including an 86-yard kickoff return. John Bentley, Nebraska's athletic publicity director, described Cardy as the "greatest outfielder on a football team I ever saw. No one kept account of pass interceptions, but Cardy probably had more than any other man. Foes hated to throw the ball with Cardy on defense because he was such a ball hawk. Only one pass was completed in Cardy's defensive zone in three years of play." Following college, he was the seventh pick of the first round by the Detroit Lions, for whom he played from 1937 to 1942. He was named an All-Pro in 1938 and 1939. In the first All-Pro game, he caught the first touchdown pass from Sammy Baugh.

Cardwell, who had been working at Gates Rubber Company in Denver before coming to the University of Omaha, went to work on August 18, 1947, with a team that included 57 interested players. He installed the single-wing formation for offense, but he had to miss four days of practice during the preseason, as his four-year-old son was hospitalized with polio. His respected staff—ends coach Ernie Gore, a 1933 Nebraska graduate; backs coach Don Pflasterer, an all-conference player at Omaha University; and line coach Harold Johnk, also an all-conference player at Omaha University—were able to run things in his absence.

The first game at what would later be called Al Caniglia Field was played in 1949, although the 9,500 grandstand seats were not installed until 1952.

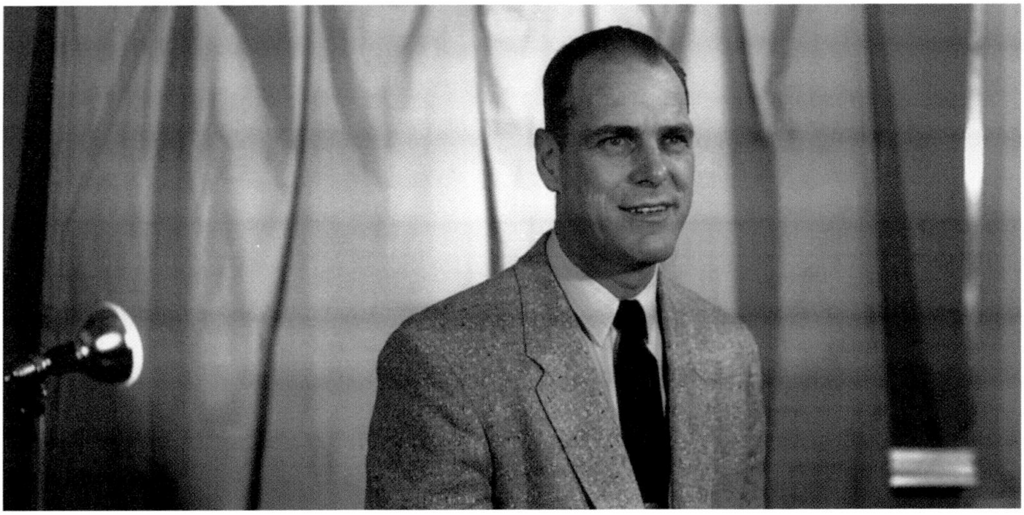

Lloyd Cardwell, another former Cornhusker star, became Omaha University's 11th head football coach in 1947, when the school resumed its football program after World War II. The team benefited from a school-record enrollment of nearly 2,100 students in 1947. However, just one game into the 1947 season, Cardwell and athletic director Virg Yelkin faced a potential problem, as Missouri law forbade "Negro" players from competing against white players in games in Missouri. The Indians were slated to take on Missouri Teachers College in Maryville, Missouri, on September 27, 1947. The African American players on the team—Archie Arvin, Clon Fitz, Ruben Pierce, and N.C. Fitz—ultimately did not play in the game, which Omaha University lost 26-0.

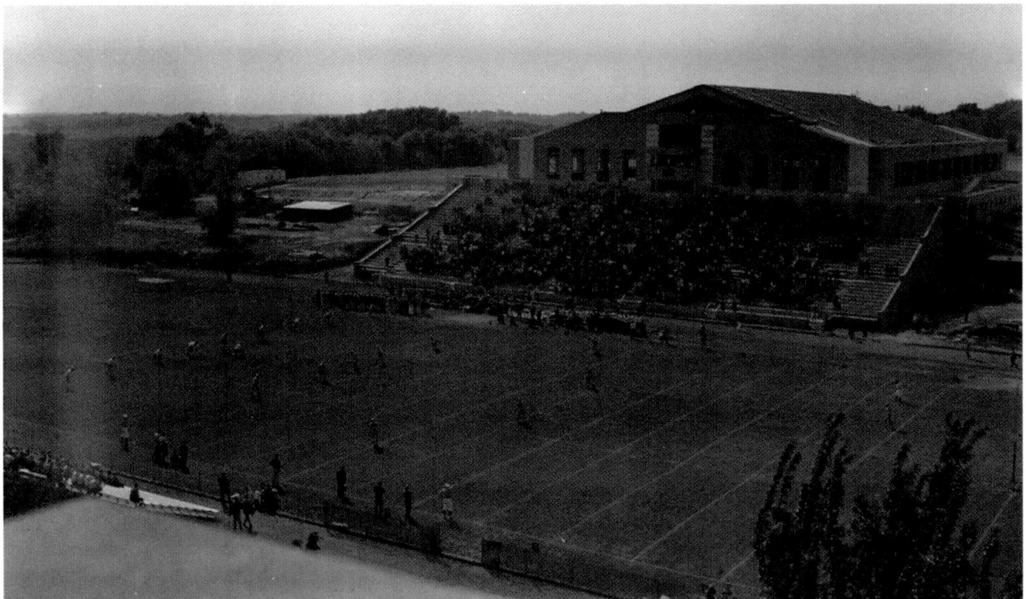

The first game at what would later be called Al Caniglia Field was played on October 1, 1949. Northern Illinois spoiled the debut of the new stadium, winning 27-8. This field would be the permanent on-campus home of the football program until the end.

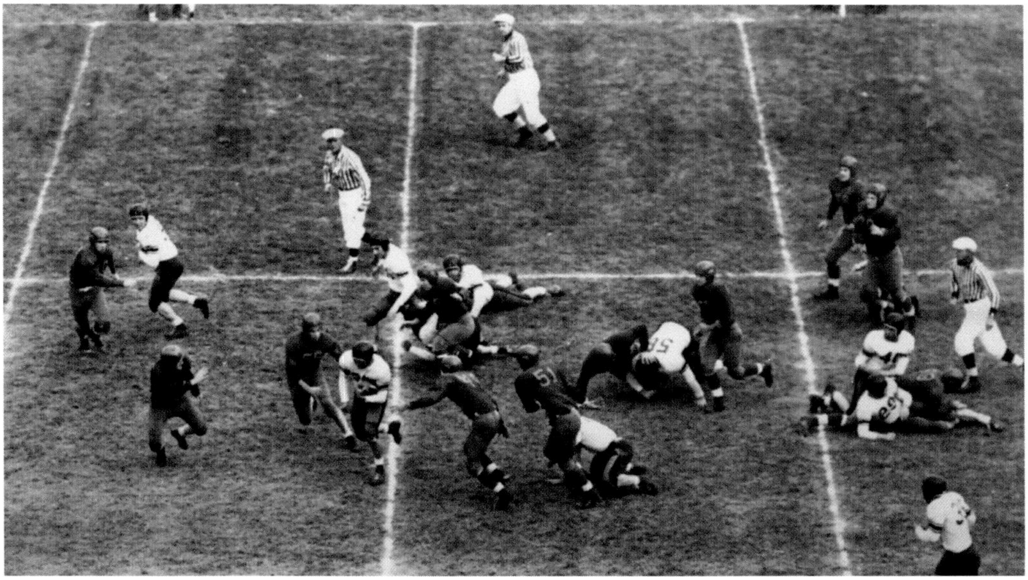

Guadalupe Joe "Lupe Joe" Arenas (no. 32, carrying the ball) came to Omaha University in 1949 at the age of 23. He had been shot in the back in February 1945 during the invasion of Iwo Jima. "What I figured with football sometimes was, 'I've been through a hell of a lot more than this,' " Arenas told the UNO Alumni Association. "It gave me the attitude that 'You can't hurt me.' " He was a member of the 1946 University of Nebraska–Lincoln basketball team, but back problems plagued him, so he transferred to Omaha University in 1947 with no intention of playing football. Lloyd Cardwell convinced him to try out, and Arenas thrived in the single-wing offense, which allowed him to run and pass. He gained 1,612 total yards in eight games in 1949, earning All-American status.

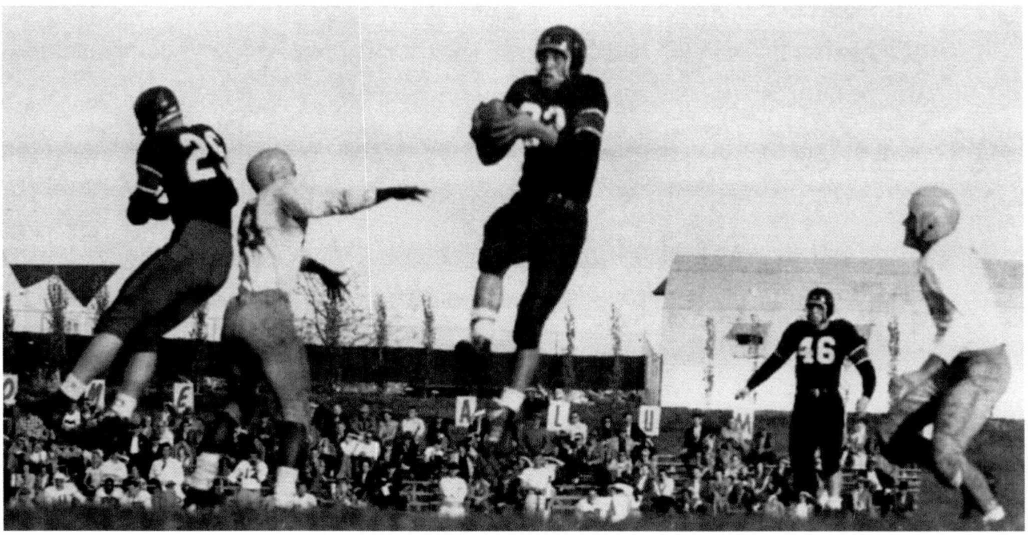

Joe Arenas carries the ball during a 1950 game. He helped the Indians go 6-3 that season. He was the school's second All-American (1949) and its first player selected in an NFL draft. Among football players of Mexican descent, Arenas is considered an icon. He played for the San Francisco 49ers from 1951 to 1957 and was their top punt-return and kickoff-return man.

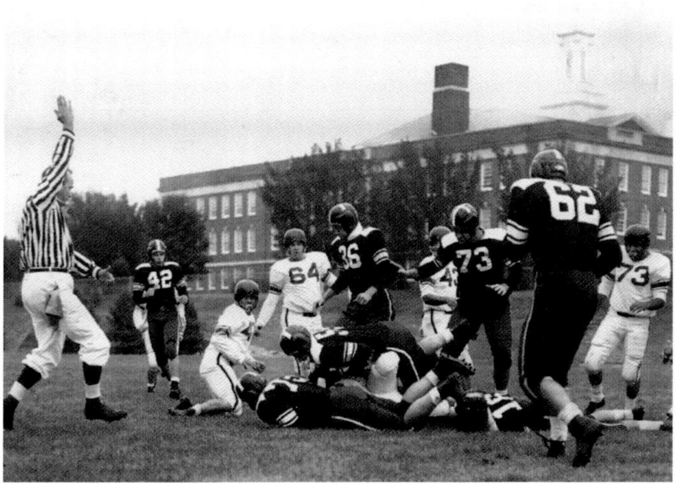

Omaha University defeated Morningside 34-0 in this 1955 matchup in Omaha. Local television station KMTV broadcast the game live on channel 3, the first time this had happened in school history. Prior to this, games had been taped and then shown at a later time. The win marked the 16th consecutive victory by OU, but the streak ended the next week against Washburn.

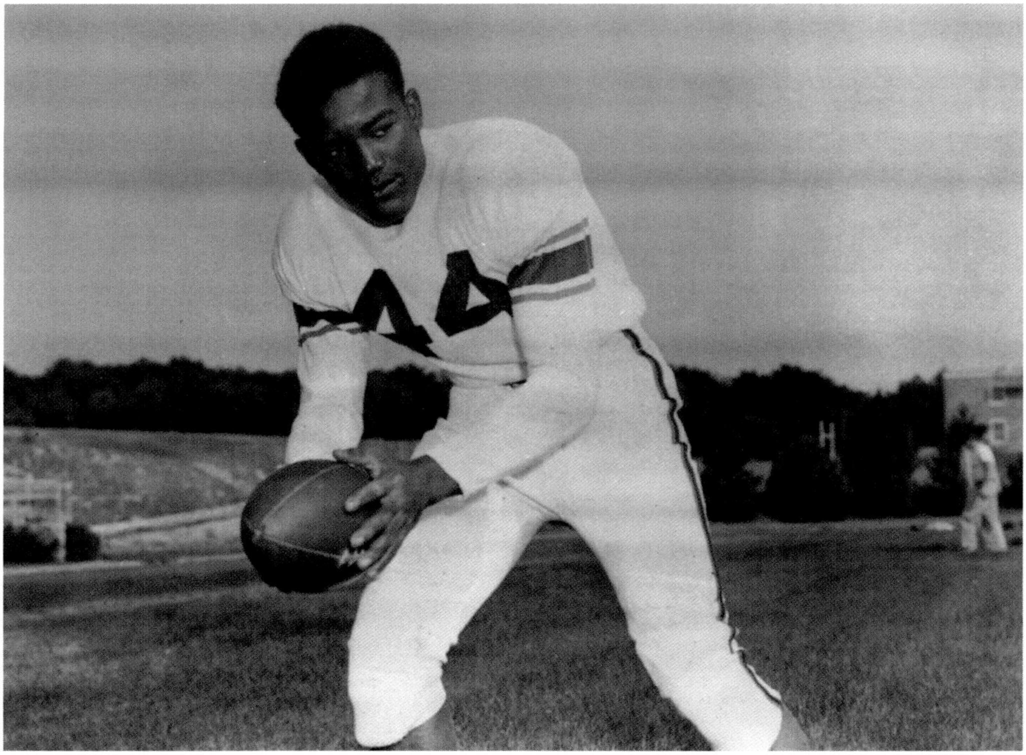

Before he was a legendary wrestling coach at OU, Don Benning was a standout football player who struggled with injuries during his career (1954–1957). In an interview with Leo Adam Biga, Benning said that in his final game at New Mexico A&M he and two black teammates had to stay in a blighted area of El Paso, Texas, due to segregation laws in host Las Cruces, New Mexico. The rest of the squad stayed in plush quarters. Terming the incident "dehumanizing," an irate Benning said his coaches "didn't seem to fight on our behalf while we were asked to give everything for the team and the university." He graduated in May 1958 and returned to the university as a graduate assistant coach in 1958 before becoming the head wrestling coach.

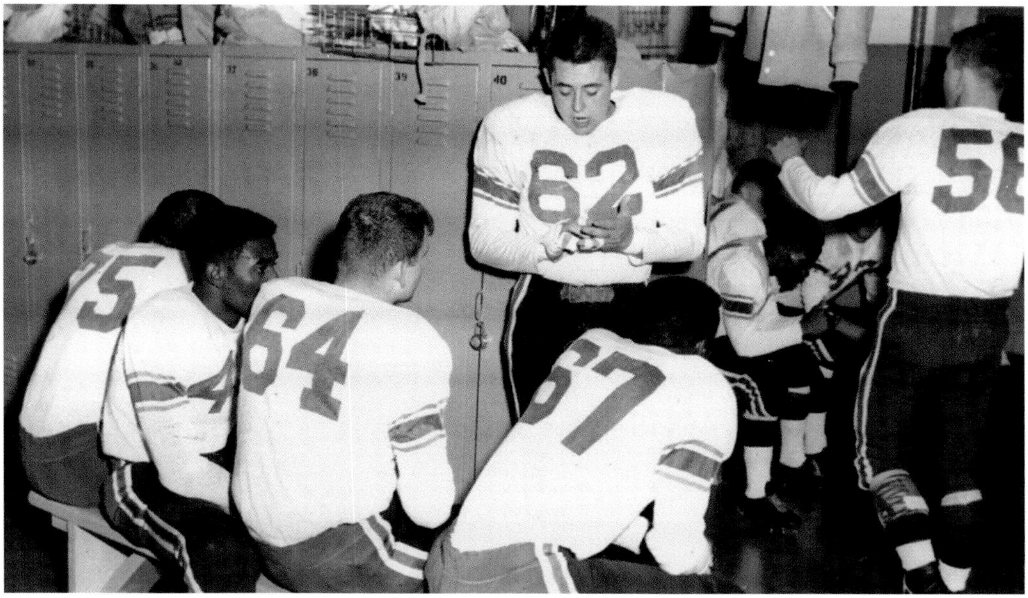

Don Benning (second from left) interacts with teammates before a game in his final season with the Indians.

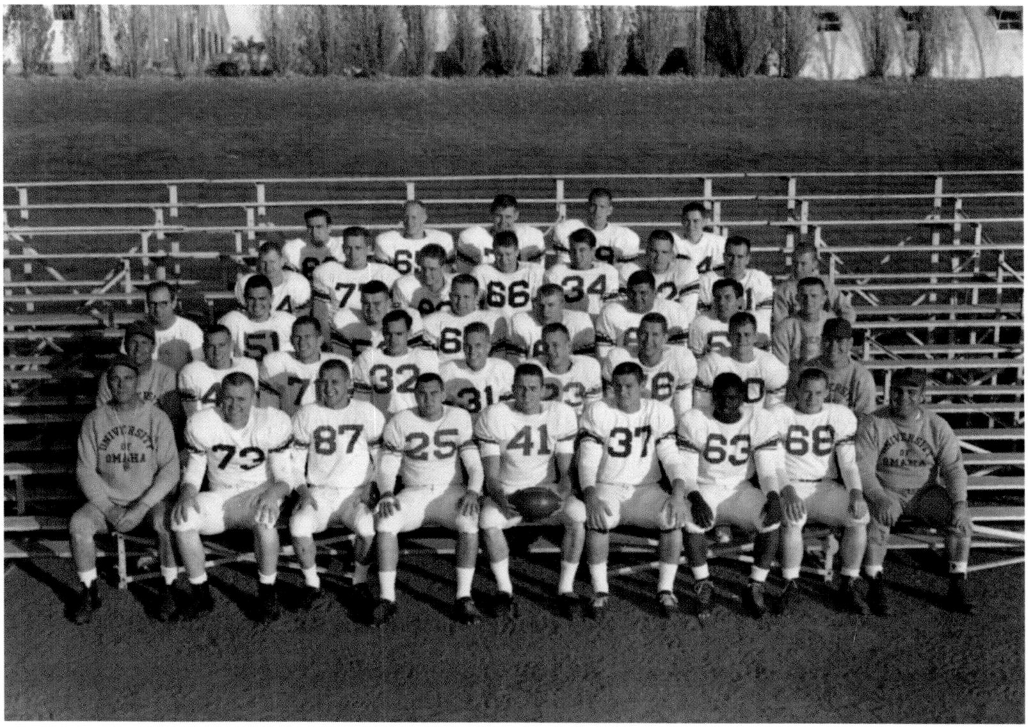

The 1958 squad went winless, part of a 2-22 stretch under head coach Lloyd Cardwell during his final three seasons at Omaha University.

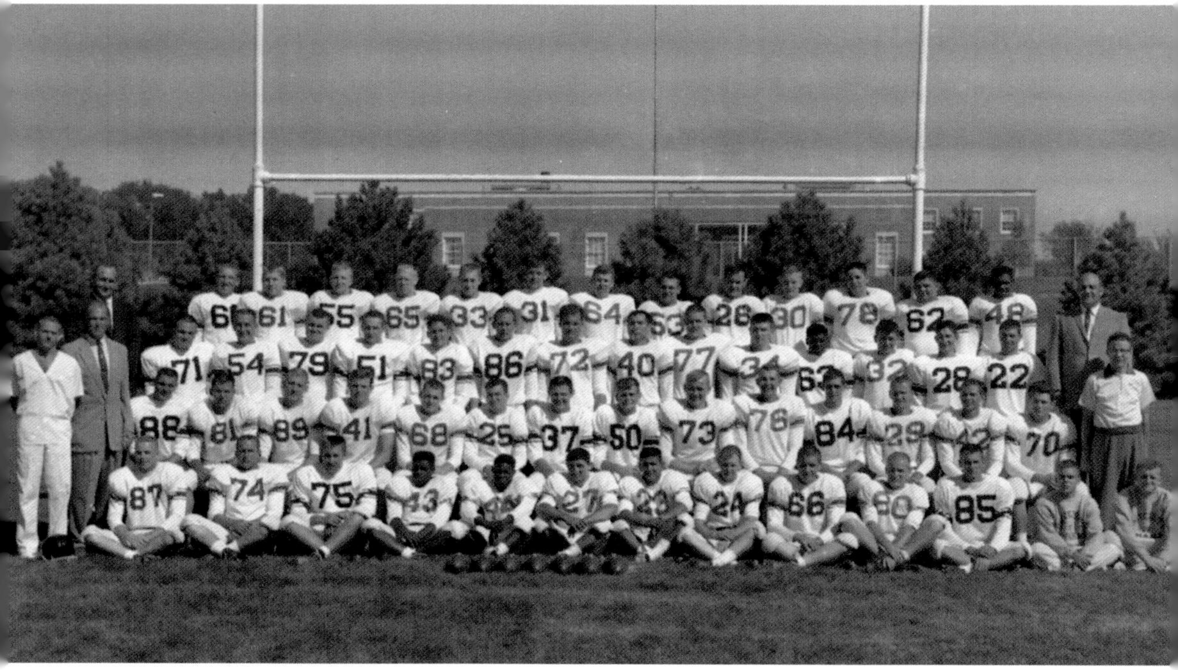

The 1959 Omaha University team was Cardwell's last. The Indians defeated Emporia State for their one victory against seven losses. Center Mick Cochran was a bright spot, earning All–Central Intercollegiate first-team honors.

4

The Undefeated 1954 Team

The undefeated 1954 football team is arguably the shining moment in the 100-plus-year history of the University of Nebraska–Omaha football program.

Coming into the 1954 season, hopes were high, as the Indians had gone 6-2 in 1953, tying the school record for most victories in a season (1935 and 1950). The Indians won their final four games by an average of 41-10 after dropping back-to-back games to Washburn (14-6) and Colorado College (27-6). In the Colorado College game, Omaha led 6-0 at halftime, but five players were ejected in the second half for arguing officials' calls. After that, according to the *Gateway*, "[Coach Lloyd] Cardy [Cardwell] straightened the boys out on bad calls and the Indians went on to chalk up 14-consecutive wins."

The 1954 team photograph shows 41 boys, although newspaper accounts state that the team had 36 boys on the squad when it headed to Hays, Kansas, to open the season on September 18. The Indians were tested right off the bat by Kansas Teachers College, but they hung on for a 27-19 win. A newspaper account midway through the season mentioned 44 boys on the first team, including sixteen Omaha North graduates, eight Omaha Tech graduates, five Omaha Benson and Omaha Central grads, two Omaha South players, and one from Creighton Prep. Also included on the roster were boys from Ralston, Louisville, Valley, Stuart, and Grand Island and from the Iowa communities of Walnut, Griswold, Creston, and Council Bluffs.

"In many cases, OU has united the talent from Omaha area which were once on opposing teams," the *Gateway* wrote in 1955. This closeness was one of the strengths, recalled Lloyd Cardwell in a 1974 interview with the *Gateway*. "I've coaches some real fine teams, but I never coached a team as a whole that stuck together like that bunch," Cardwell said in 1974. "We had a group of young men that really wanted to play football. No one on the team was lured to the school by scholarships or grants-in-aid, as none were given at Omaha University then. Yet, the team had eight to ten players who earned All-State honors at their schools on that team."

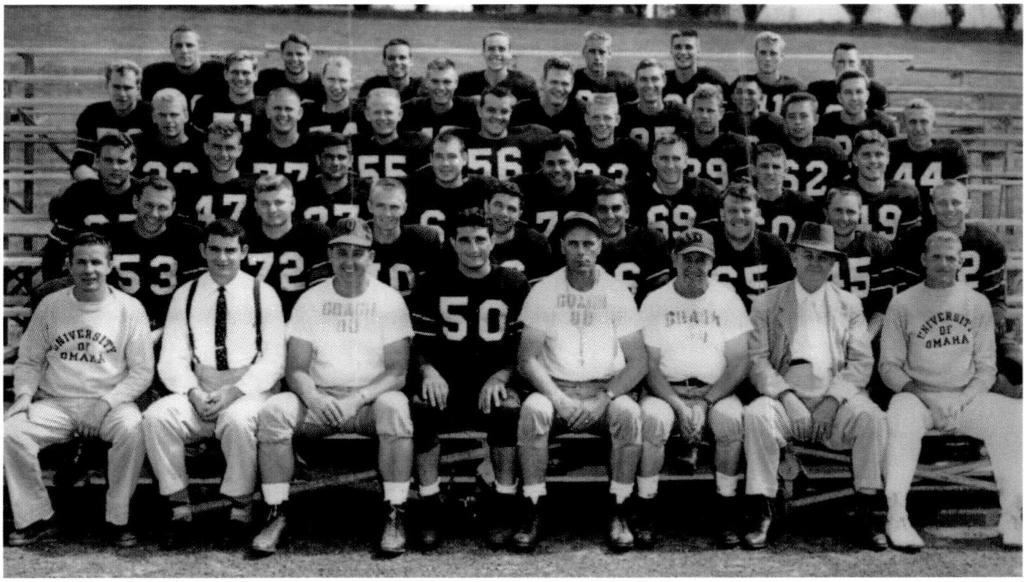

The undefeated 1954 Omaha University football team poses here. Shown are, from left to right, (first row) equipment manager Mike Wolenski, athletic publicity director Lew Radcliffe, assistant coach Tom Brock, Rudy Rotella, head coach Lloyd Cardwell, assistant coach Ernie Gorr, team physician Dr. G.M. McArdle, and trainer Wayne Wagner; (second row) John Welch, Bob Gloden, Dick Cotton, Arnold Smith, Simon A. Simon, Milton Hearn, Fred Adams, and Emil Radik; (third row) Bill Stanek, Dennis Brewster, Frank Mancuso, Frank Hahn, Pete Rigatuso, Hank Goethe, Bob Trumbauer, and Ken Conrad; (fourth row) Clarence Sage, Elwood Mink, Don McMahill, Kenneth Leeper, Robert Wheeler, Howard Baker, Fred Moyer, and Tom Kasun; (fifth row) Bill Engelhardt, Marvin Nevins, Ralph Wissler, Dick Carpenter, Harry Johnson, Chris Salberg, Mike Watanabe, and Jerome Smith; (sixth row) Ed Baker, Jerry Tannahill, Dick Tannahill, Bill Steck, Gary Bieker, Wayne Malnack, Marvin Eatinger, and Darrell Kelley. Not pictured are John Schuetz (38), John Cimino (43), Walt Miller (57), Dave Biddle, and Tom Harper (74).

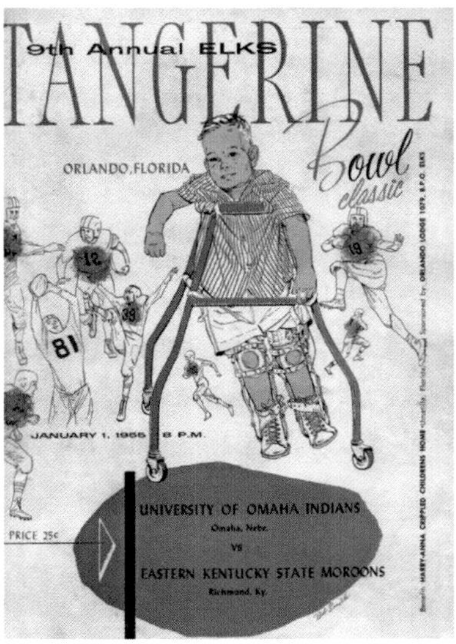

The ninth annual Elks Tangerine Bowl, between Eastern Kentucky State and Omaha University, was held on January 1, 1955, in Orlando. Tickets for the game ranged from $1.50 in end bleachers to $4.75 at the 40-yard line. Greyhound offered students a $43.41 rate for the 38-hour trip. A round-trip in coach by rail cost $77.17, and the 36-hour journey by Pullman car cost $128. According to the *Gateway*, "One girl promised I'll eat bread and water while there if I can just get there." Eastern Kentucky was coached by former Husker Glenn Presnell, who graduated in 1937. OU's coach, Lloyd Cardwell, graduated from Nebraska in 1936. The Tangerine Bowl was known as the "little bowl with the big heart," as it was the only bowl game in the nation devoted entirely to charity.

A few days before the matchup with Wayne State of Detroit, the second-to-last game of the regular season, it was learned that the Tangerine Bowl had contacted OU about its interest in participating. The Indians capitalized on the opportunity, defeating Wayne State 59-7 before what was called a record crowd of 5,200 fans. A season-high 38 boys saw action in the game. After this win, the 8-0 Indians turned down a bid to play in the Mineral Bowl in Excelsior Springs, Missouri, claiming that it was too early to commit. With one game to play, other bowl possibilities included the Tangerine Bowl in Orlando, Florida, the Sun Bowl in El Paso, Texas, the Refrigerator Bowl in Fort Wayne, Indiana, and the Cigar Bowl in Tampa, Florida.

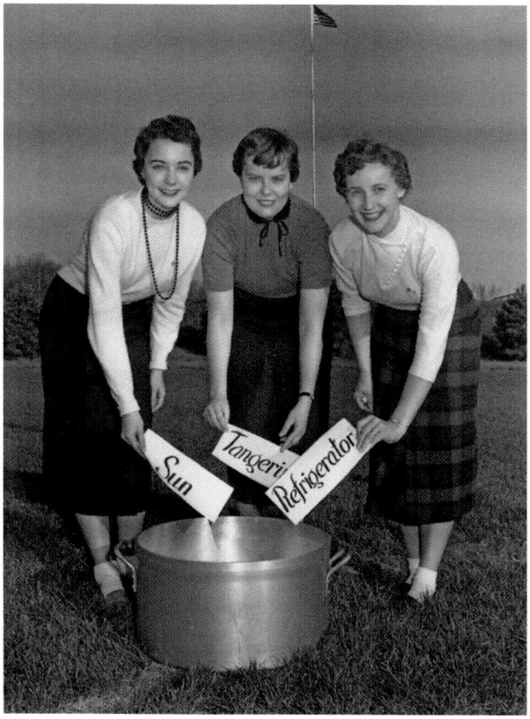

UNIVERITY OF OMAHA 1954 Schedule (Season's Record: Won 9)
University of Omaha 27; Fort Hays Kansas 19
University of Omaha 45; Morningside (S'ux City) 0
University of Omaha 27; Washburn University 6
University of Omaha 39; Bradley University 0
University of Omaha 38; Kansas State (Emporia) 6
University of Omaha 35; Saint Ambrose 14
University of Omaha 27; Northern Ill. State 6
University of Omaha 59; Wayne U. (Detroit) 7
University of Omaha 57; Doane College 2

EASTERN KENTUCKY 1954 Schedule (Season's Record: Won 8, Tied 1)
Eastern Kentucky 19; John Carroll University 0
Eastern Kentucky 26; Middle Tenn. State 0
Eastern Kentucky 25; Murray Ky. State 6
Eastern Kentucky 14; Tennessee Tech 7
Eastern Kentucky 25; Youngstown (Ohio) 7
Eastern Kentucky 12; Morehead Ky. State 8
Eastern Kentucky 13; Toledo (Ohio) U. 13
Eastern Kentucky 21; Western Ky. State 0
Eastern Kentucky 20; U. of Louisville 6

Coach Lloyd Cardwell told the *Gateway* that he was consulted about a bowl competitor and ultimately suggested Eastern Kentucky, which was 8-0-1 coming into the game. "They suggested Florida State University or Eastern Kentucky. Florida State [which had only had football since 1947 and was just starting to become a major college], has lost three games and could lose another before finishing in early December. I feel that we should play a school of comparable class with a good record and to me, Eastern Kentucky fills the bill." Incidentally, Florida State, which featured Lee Corso and future actor Burt Reynolds, lost 47-21 to the University of Texas–El Paso in the Sun Bowl that season. Eastern Kentucky was 8-0-1 and Ohio Valley champions coming into the bowl matchup with Omaha.

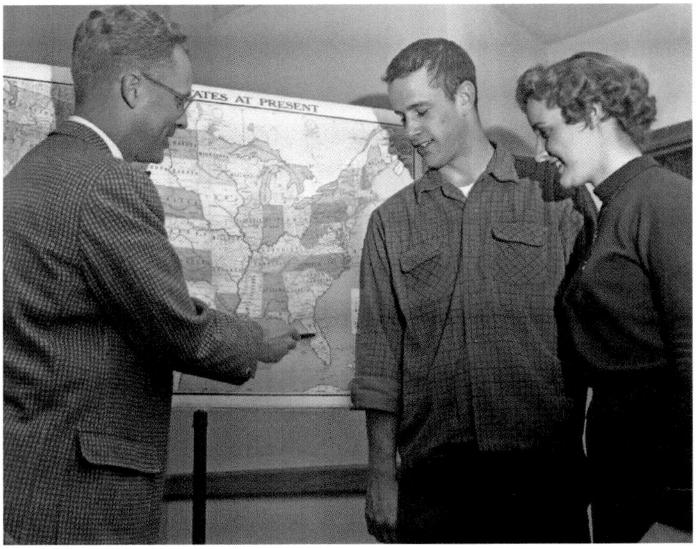

In 1954, many students at Omaha University had never been very far from home, let alone all the way to Orlando, Florida. Here, students are shown where the Tangerine Bowl is on a map by Paul Beck, OU professor of history.

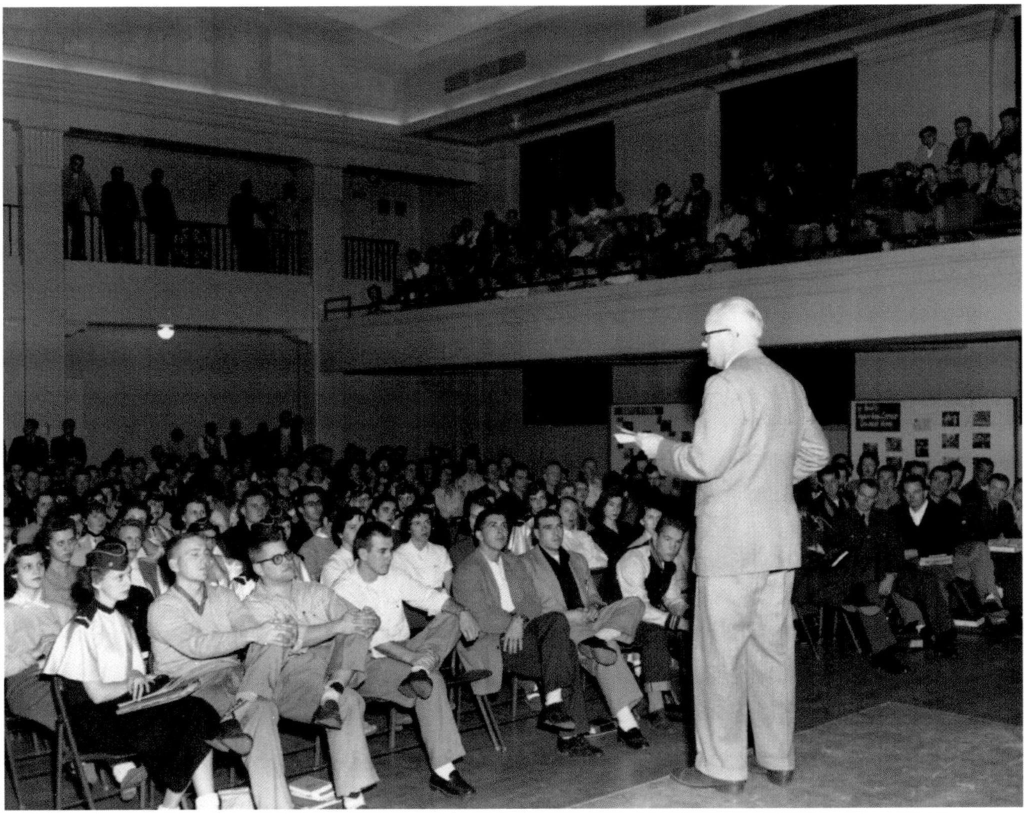

Jay B. McGregor, dean of student personnel, speaks at a pep rally for the 1954 football team before it leaves for the Tangerine Bowl.

Student Charlie Kaipust packs for the Tangerine Bowl. He was among nearly 200 Omaha University students who made the trip to Orlando, Florida.

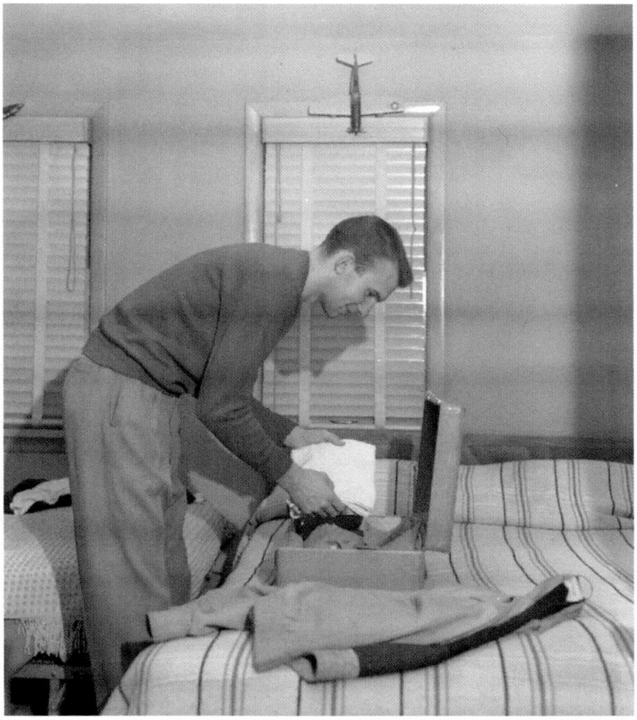

Harry Johnson (left) is all dressed up for the plane ride to Florida as he says goodbye.

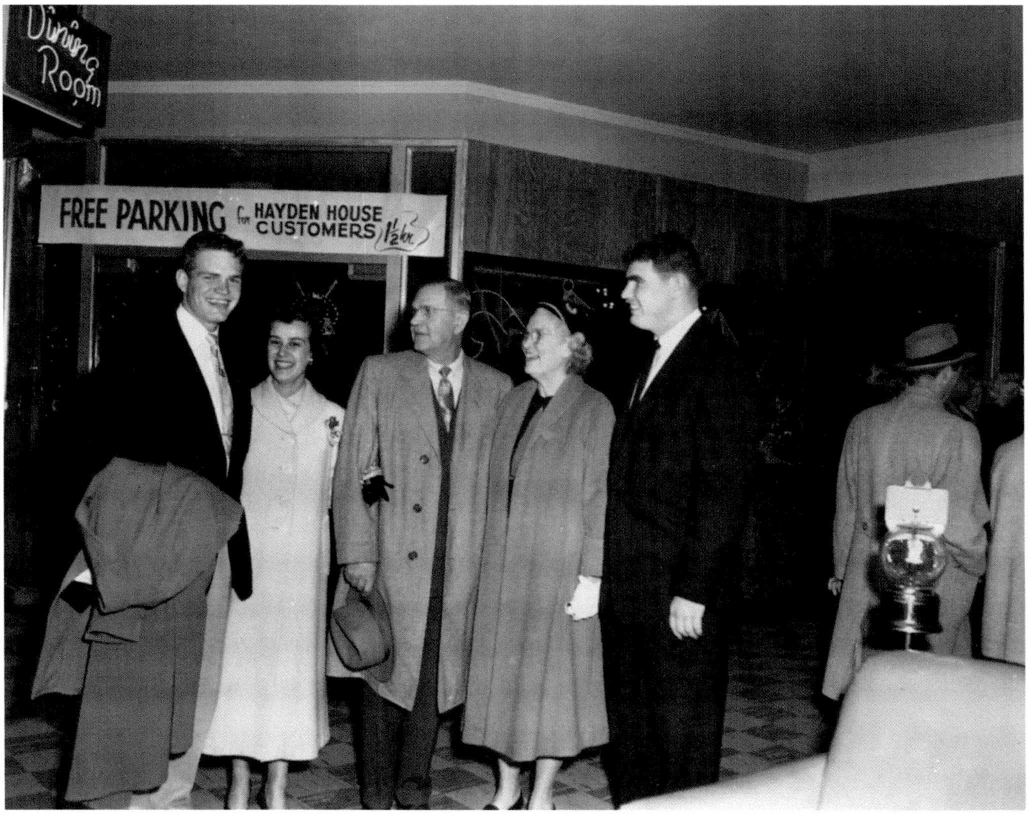

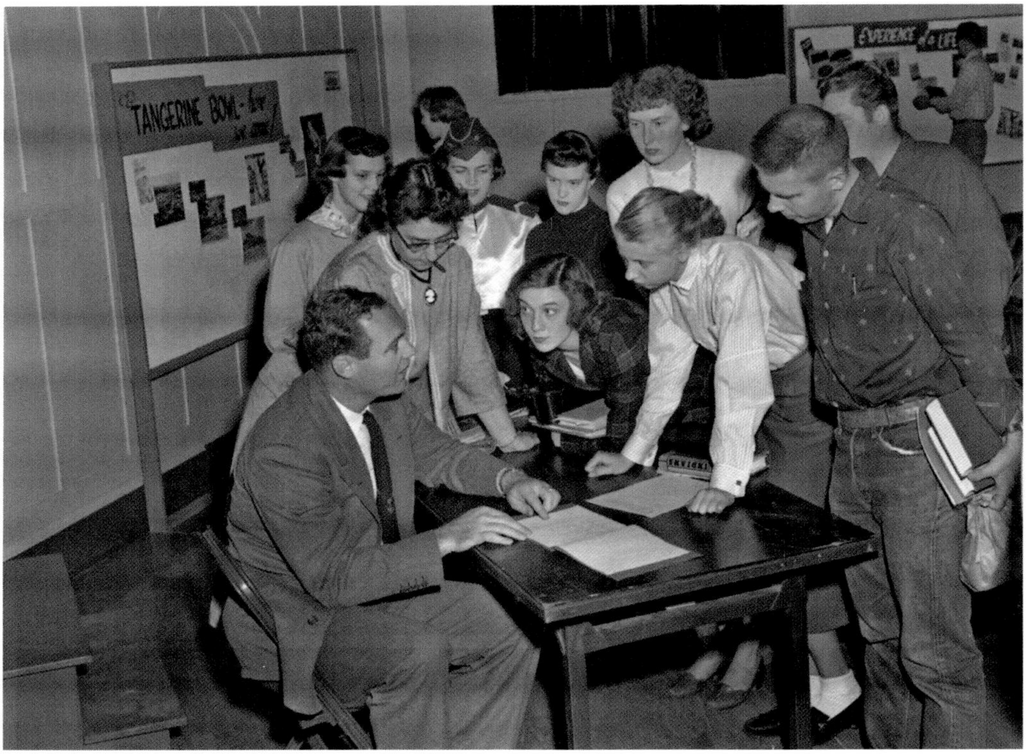

As part of OU's Tangerine Bowl package, free room and board was provided for 100 students. The commission stated that it was returning Omaha's friendliness toward tiny Rollins College's baseball team, which had finished as runner-up in the 1954 College World Series in Omaha. Here, dean Don Pflasterer helps students sign up for the trip. At the last minute, Omaha business firms, associations, and individuals donated $5,000 for the transportation of cheerleaders, ROTC members, band members, majorettes, Ouampi and the Sabres, and the ROTC drill team. E.C. Eppley gave $1,600 so the Marching Angels could also go via Burlington Railroad. All students were required to buy their own game tickets, as it was a benefit game. With so many students making the trip to Florida, second-semester classes were delayed until January 5.

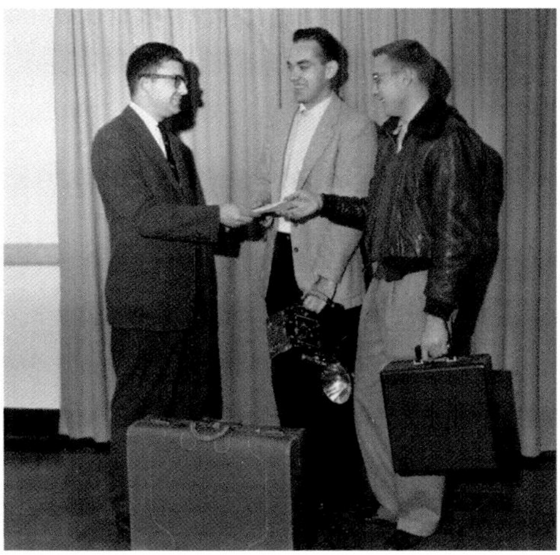

The Omaha University Alumni Association gave $50 checks to Bill Beindorff (center) and Paul Cherling (right), editors of the *Gateway* and the *Tomahawk*, respectively, to make sure the Tangerine Bowl was covered in their papers. Many of the publications' great photographs are included in this chapter.

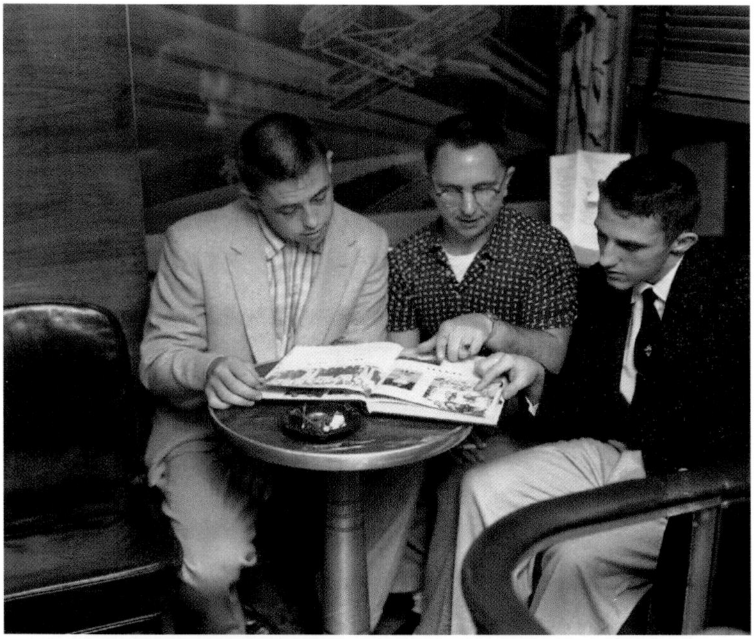

Fred Moyer (left), Fred Adams (center), and Bob Trumbauer look over Eastern Kentucky's yearbook aboard the train.

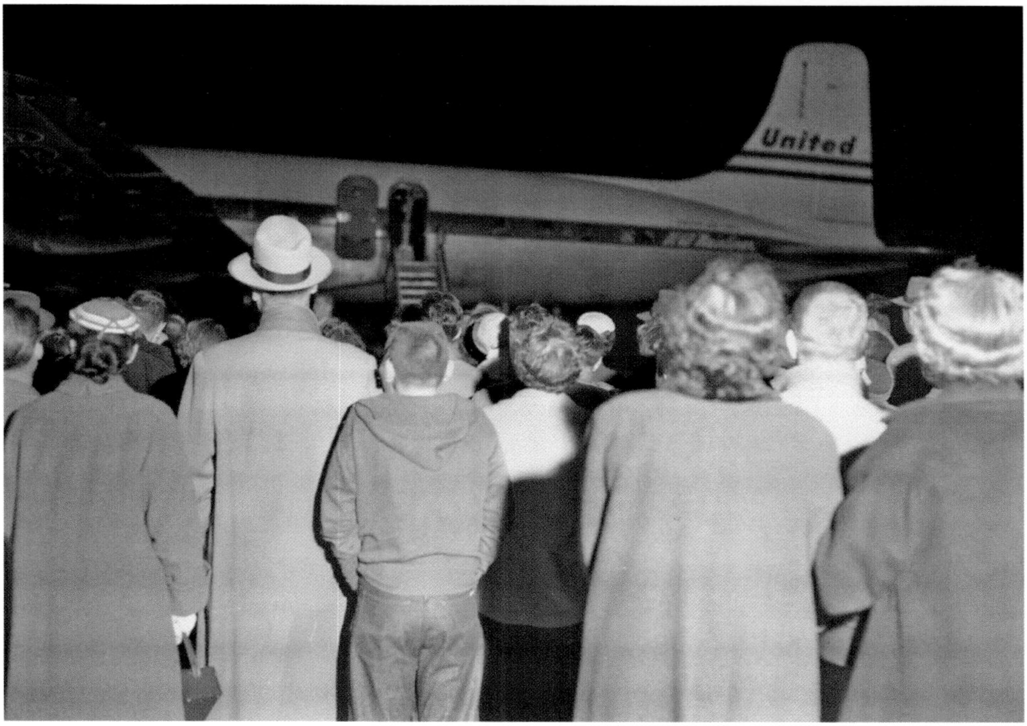

The team of 46 players, coaches, and staff members left by plane on December 26 at 7:45 p.m. and arrived in Orlando at 7:00 a.m. on December 27. "Ninety percent of us had never been on an airplane," Bob Wheeler told the *Omaha World-Herald* in 2014. "Getting into Orlando and experiencing all the fineries—the experience of that was just marvelous. It was something nobody ever dreamed of."

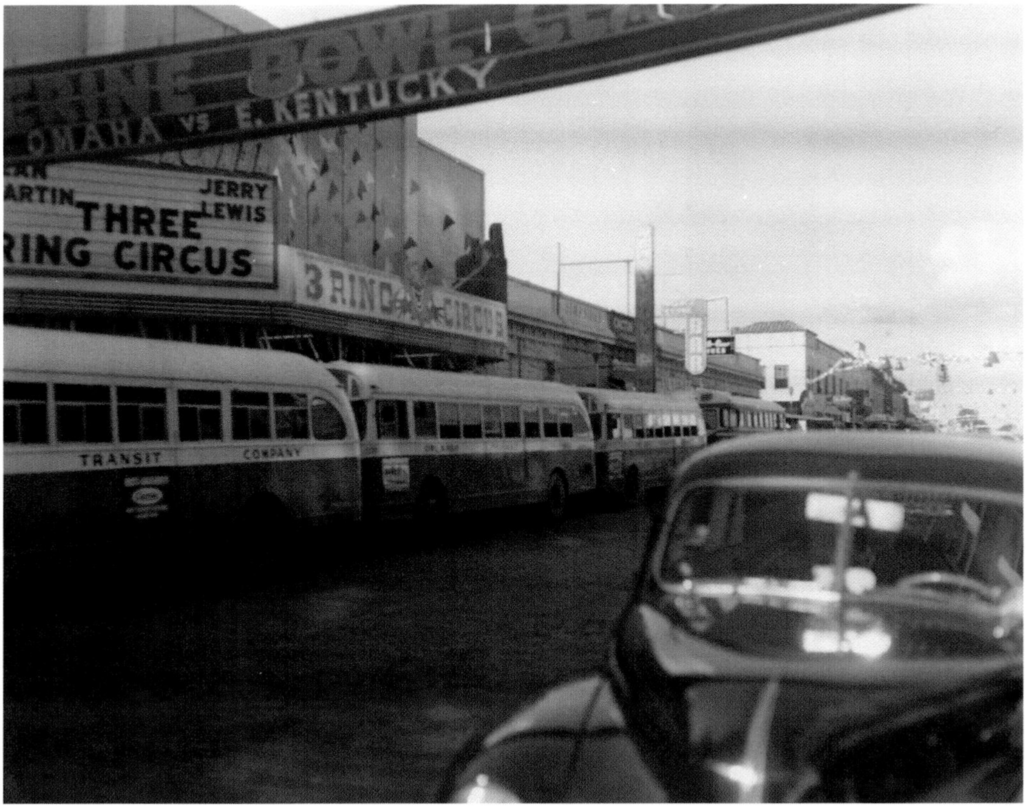

Once the team, band, and fans arrived in Orlando, they were transported by buses to the San Juan Hotel.

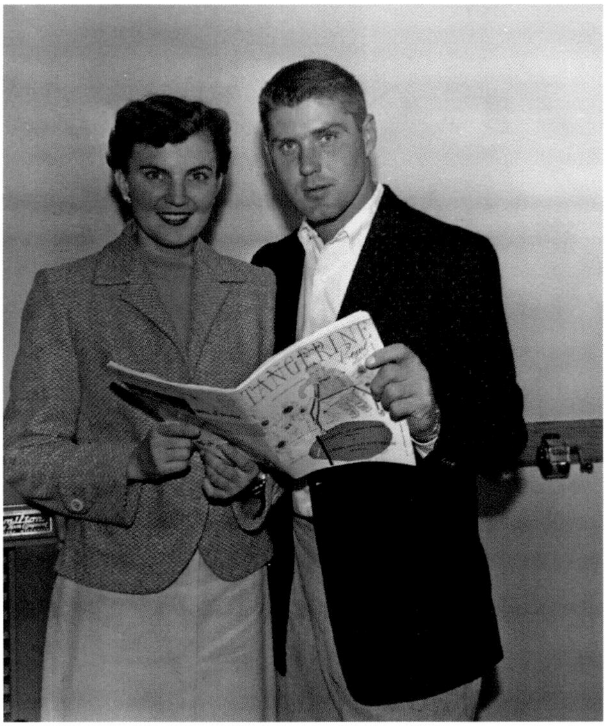

OU Tangerine Princess Jackie Pedersen looks over the game program with football standout Emil Radik.

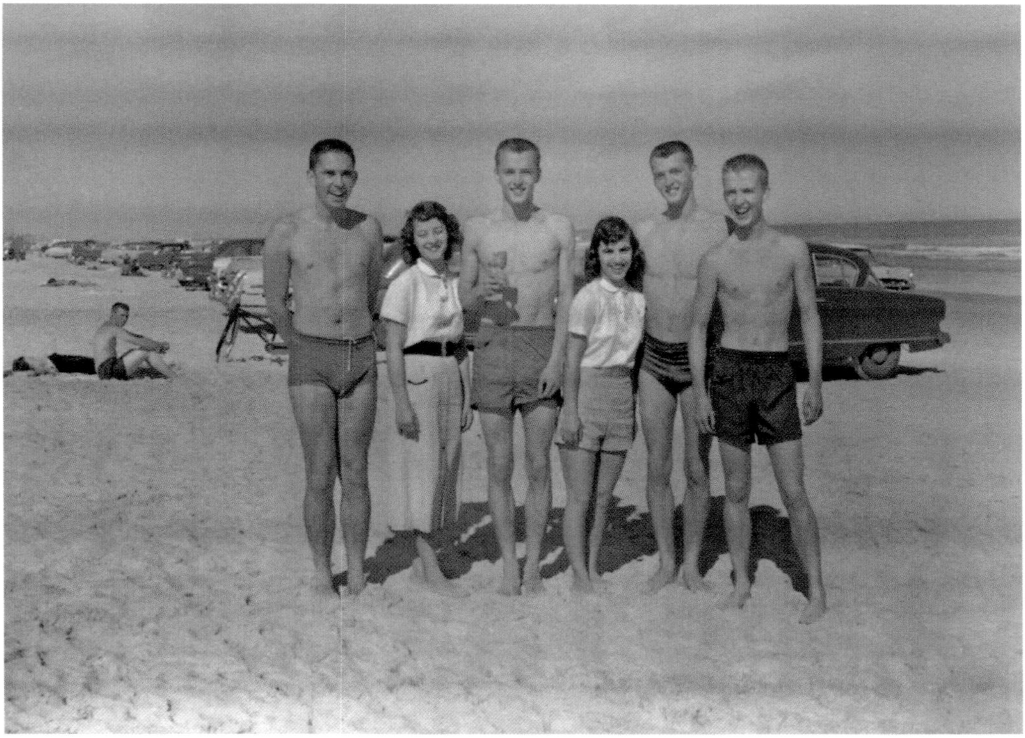

Players and students were able to enjoy the Florida beaches, including waterskiing, while visiting the homes of Elks members, who were sponsors of the Tangerine Bowl. It was a memorable trip for all who attended.

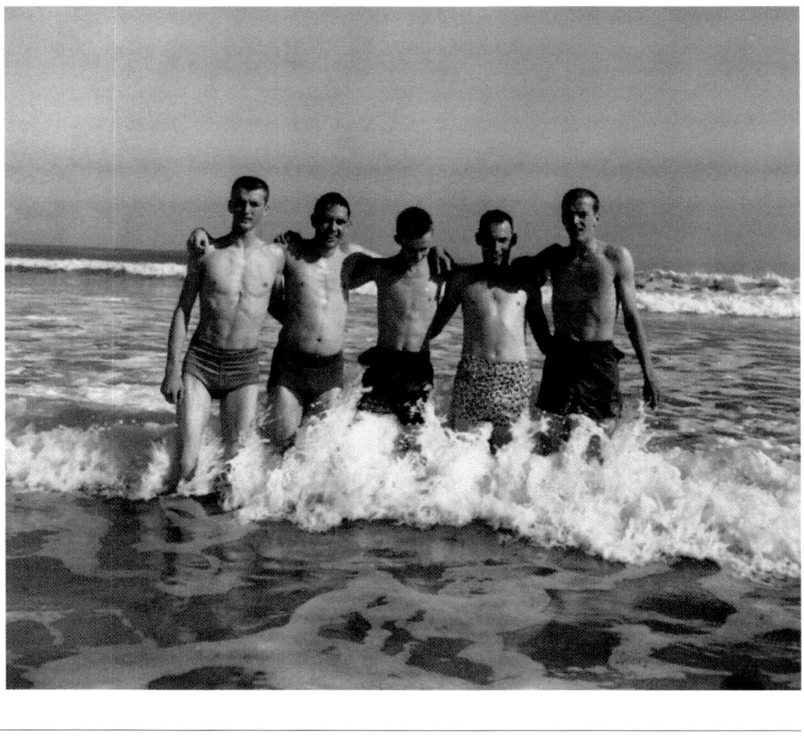

Darrell Kelley, Fred Adams, Dick Cotton, and other teammates enjoy swimming in the ocean.

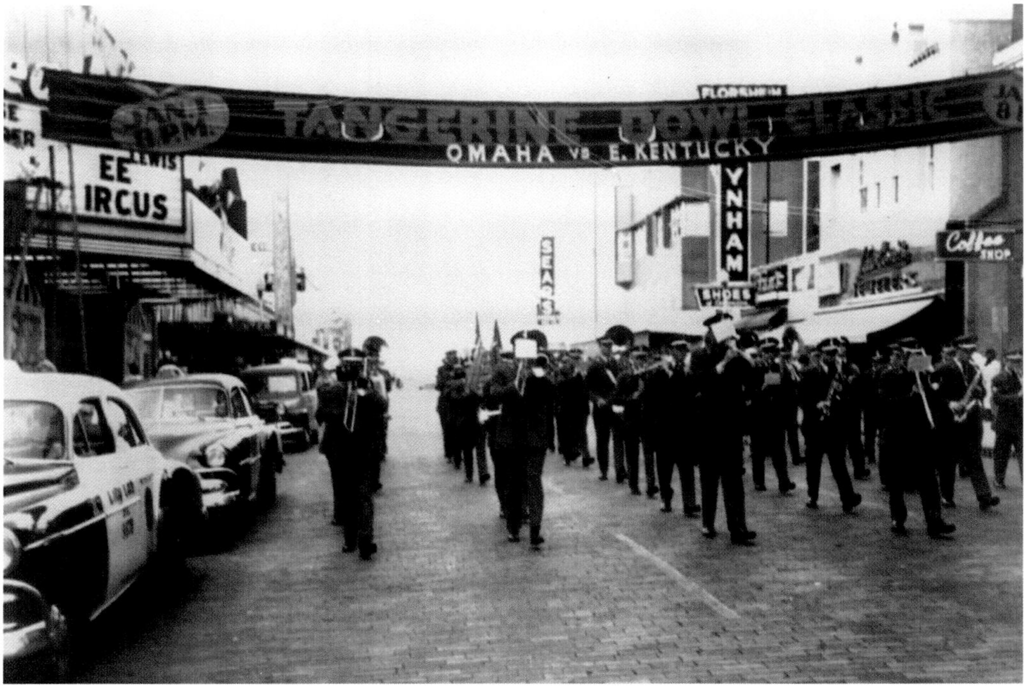

The Omaha University ROTC band performs in the Tangerine Bowl parade. The band was able to travel to the game thanks to generous support from Omaha businesses. At the last minute, local firms donated money that enabled all of the OU supporters to travel to the game.

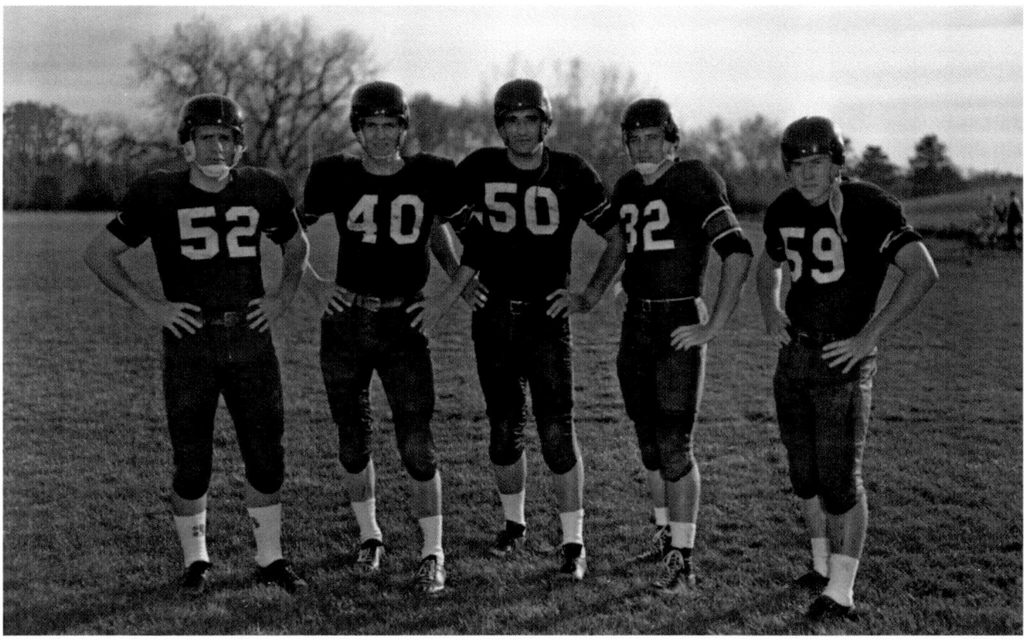

Running back Bill Steck (52), end Dick Cotton (40), end Rudy Rotella (50), running back Emil Radik (32), and quarterback Bill Englehardt (59) pose for a photograph during the 1955 Tangerine Bowl practice. Rotella and Englehardt ended up being named Little All-Americans.

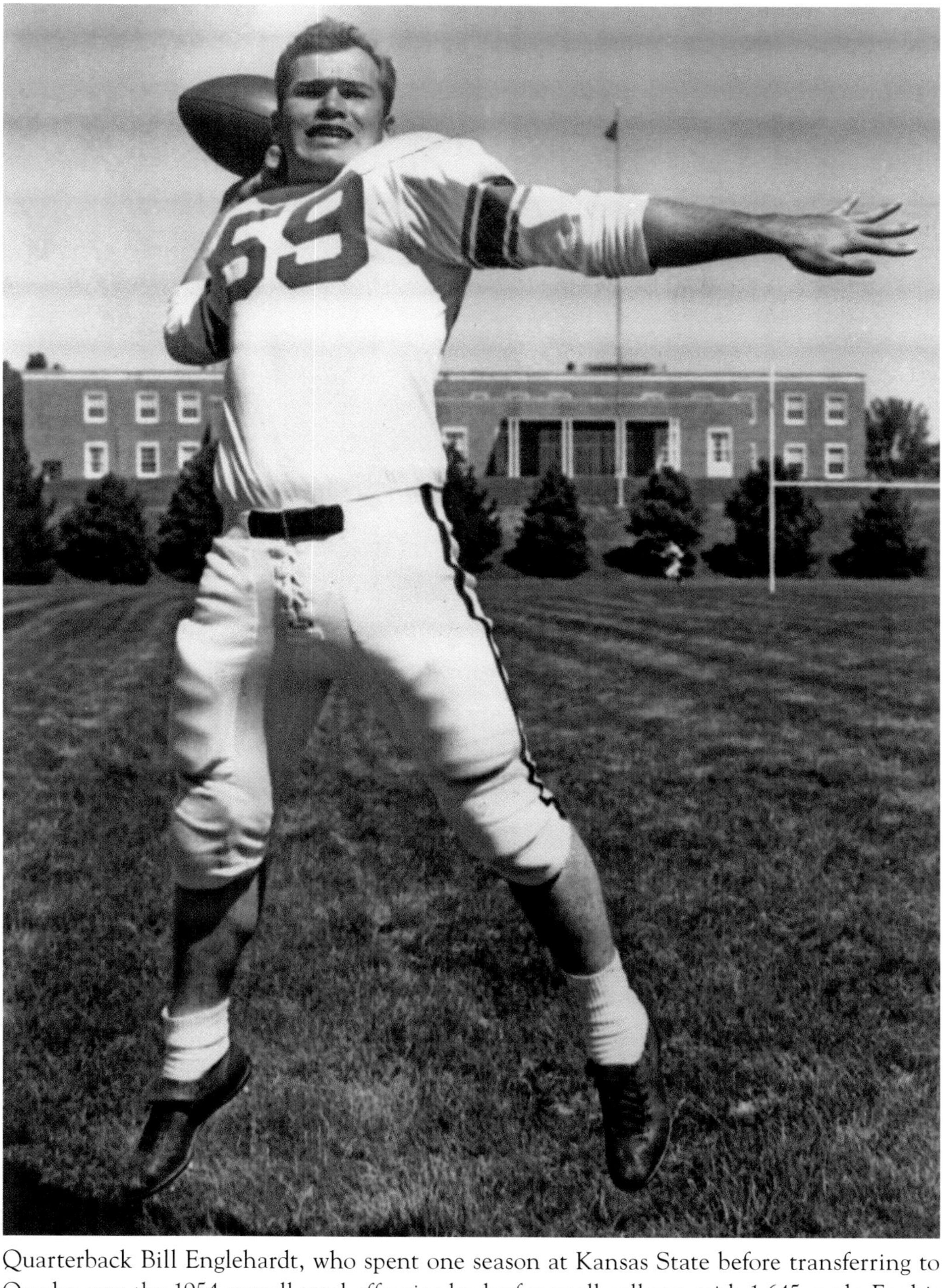

Quarterback Bill Englehardt, who spent one season at Kansas State before transferring to Omaha, was the 1954 overall total offensive leader for small colleges, with 1,645 yards. For his accomplishments, he was named a Little All-American in 1954. Using the single-wing offense, Englehardt would run the ball 25 times a game and also threw the ball, including the game-winner in the Tangerine Bowl.

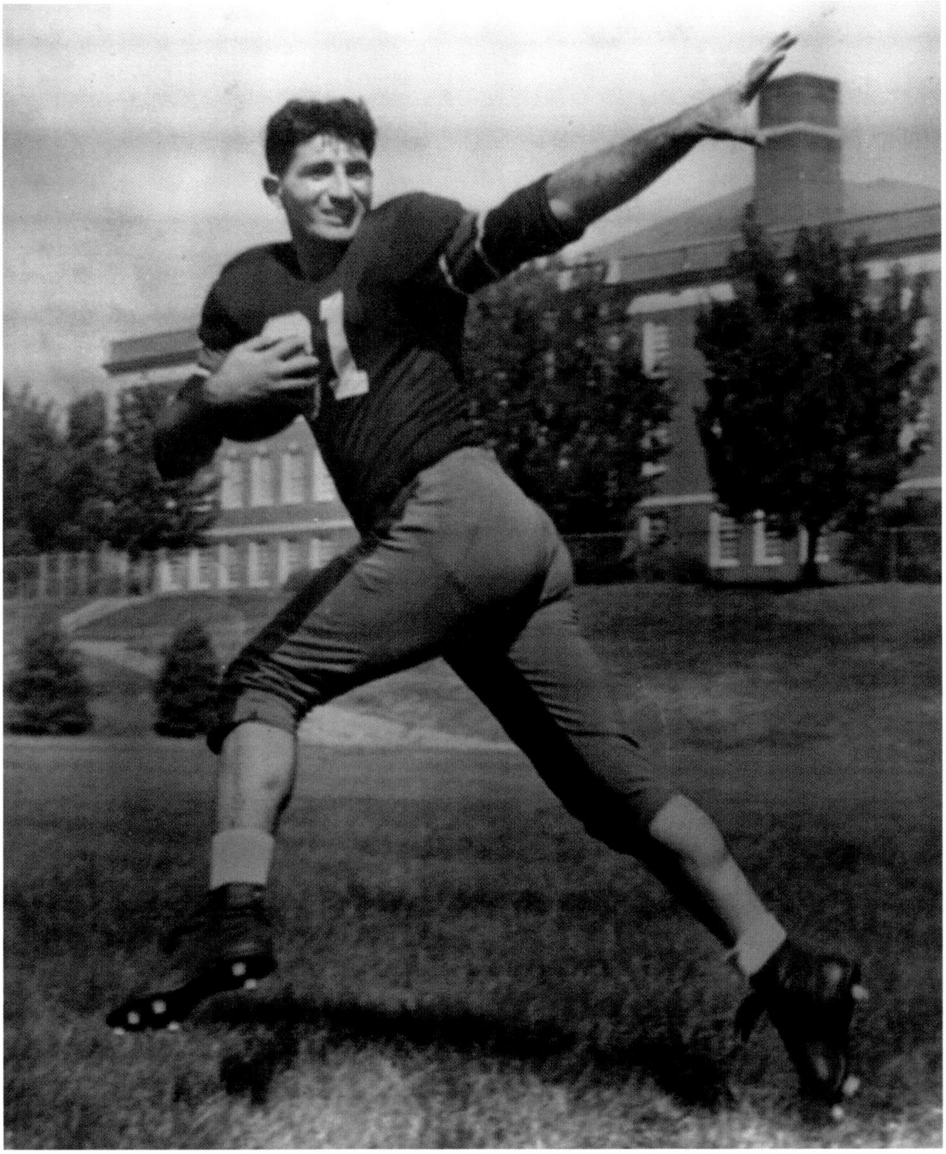

Rudy Rotella was one of the stars of the 1954 team, with his "fancy pass catching and hard tackling." Rotella had attended Omaha University in 1949 and earned a spot on the team, despite not playing football at Omaha North. He was a standout on the 1950 team, but he left school and served in the Air Force from 1950 to 1952. While in the service, he played football for three years. Rotella returned in 1953 to captain the squad and lead the team in receiving. In 1954, he had his best season, earning All-American honors after making 32 catches for 462 yards and five touchdowns. He was also voted the team's most valuable player by his teammates. Following college, Rotella was drafted in the 11th round by the San Francisco 49ers, who already had former Indian Joe Arenas on their squad. "I think the key ingredient is that we had a bunch of guys who didn't like losing, even a little bit," Engelhardt was quoted as saying. "And we had a very good leader in Rudy Rotella. He probably hated losing more than any of us."

Due to Marv Nevins's professional baseball experience, Omaha University got into trouble two years later with the NCAA. At the time, an athlete who played professionally in one sport was not allowed to play any other amateur sport.

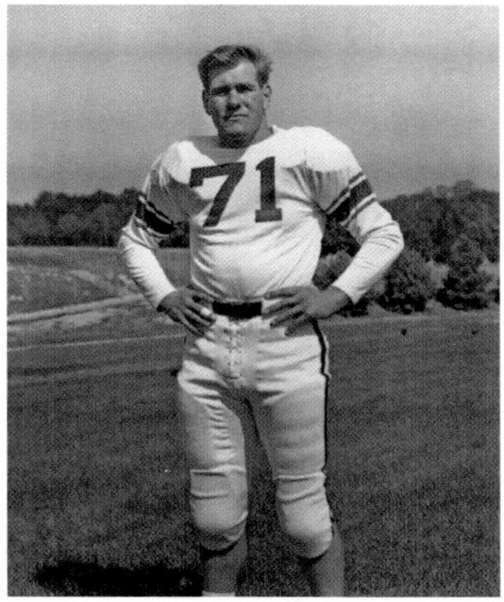

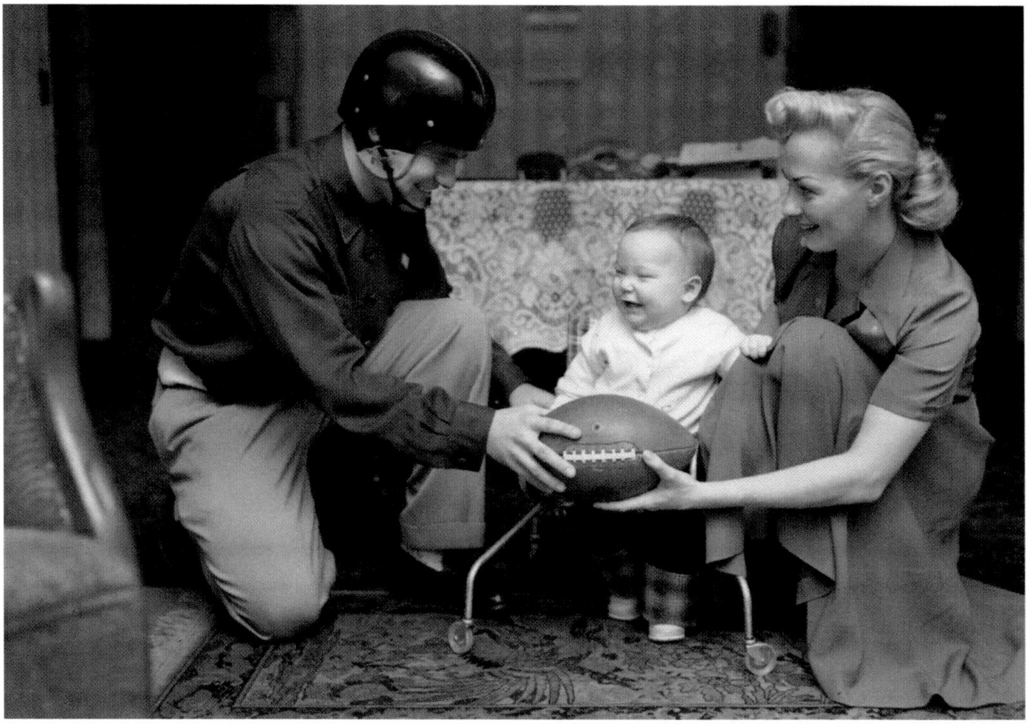

Marv Nevins and his sister Gladys Helen Nevins (aka Helen Hild of professional wrestling fame), who was living in Florida at the time, hand a football to a child during a visit to the Harry-Anna Crippled Children's Home in Umatilla, Florida, before the Tangerine Bowl, which raised money for this facility. Nevins was a starter on the 1954 football team. He also was a professional baseball player for the 1953 Omaha Cardinals, a Class-A team of the St. Louis Cardinals in the Western League. As a 19-year-old in 1953, he appeared in 47 games and had a .150 batting average in 100 at-bats. In 1954, he played for the Joplin Cardinals, a Class-C affiliate of the St. Louis Cardinals in the Western League. He batted .202 in 34 games. Nevins was a catcher according to several newspaper accounts. Marv and Gladys's parents, Edgar and Marie, later moved to Wilcox, Arizona, to run a café. Marv returned to Omaha University as a coach.

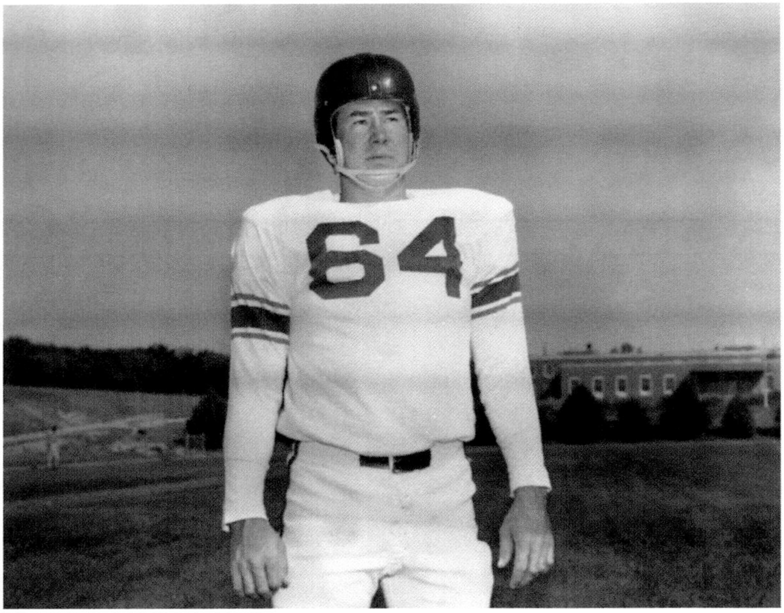

Frank Hahn was a stalwart of the offensive line, helping open large holes for the talented backfield.

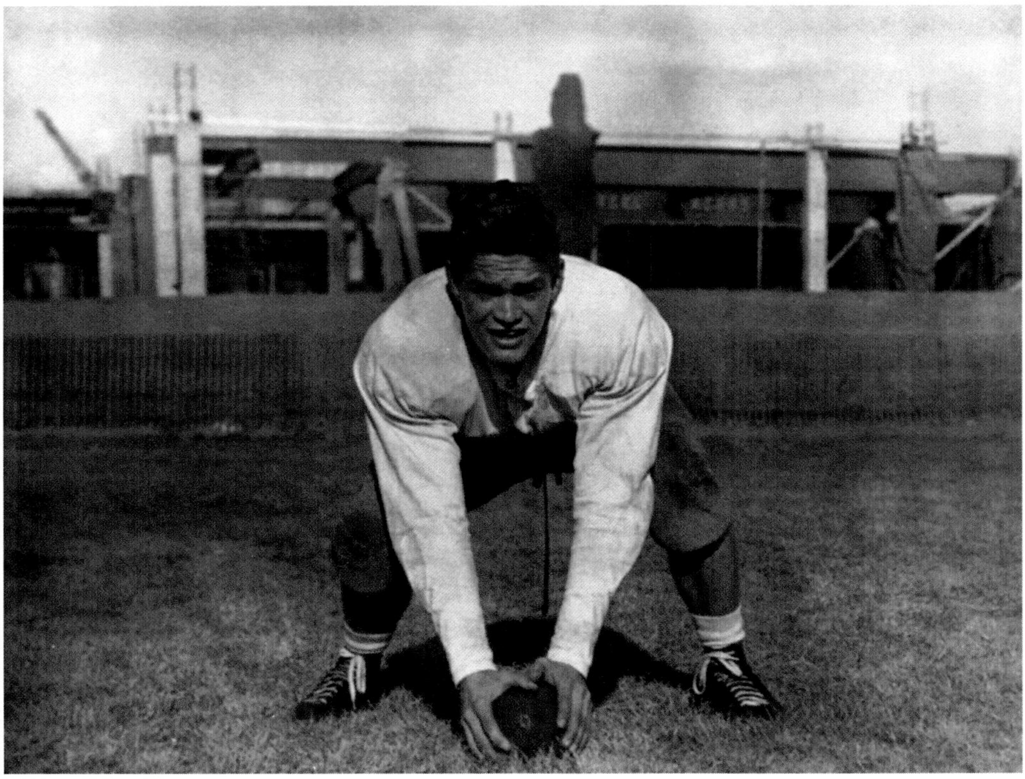

Center Harry Johnson was another key member of the line, which helped the Indians set a school-record 37 first downs in a game against Wayne State. It remained the most first downs ever in a game by a UNO team when the program ended.

Tackle Kenneth Leeper (75) was the biggest player on the 1954 team. Here, he holds Dick Tannahill (24) and Jerry Tannahill (22), the two smallest players.

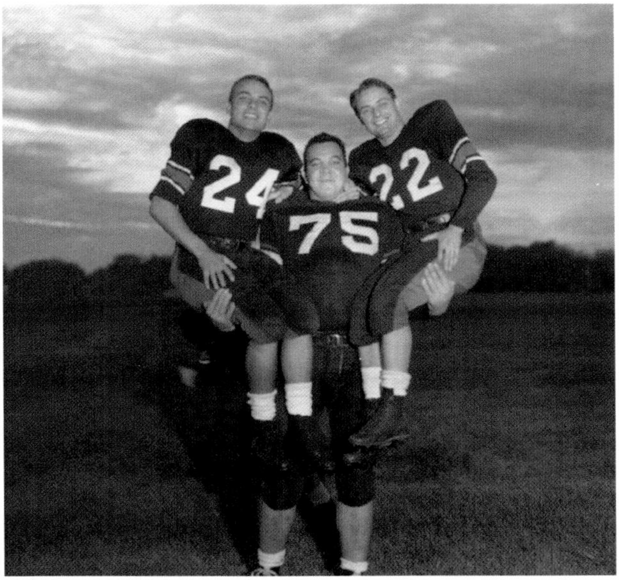

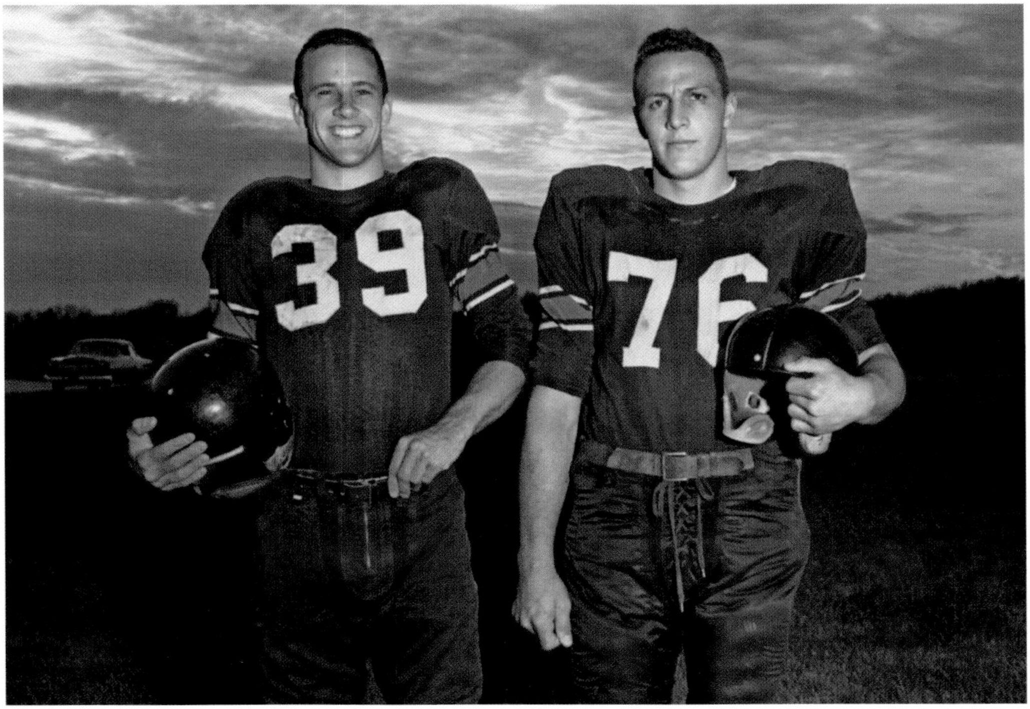

Brothers Ed Baker (39) and Howard Baker (76) pose for a photograph. Ed was an end, and Howard played tackle on the 1954 team. According to the *Gateway*, offensive and defensive tackle Ed came out of the service in 1953, where he played plenty of football with big-name players. The six-foot, 200-pound tackle was "one of the reasons that Omaha backs were running so freely last season." After his freshman season, he was drafted by the San Francisco 49ers, but he turned down the offer to concentrate on a degree. Prior to the service and attending Omaha University, Ed had attended Omaha North High School, where he lettered for two years in football and wrestling.

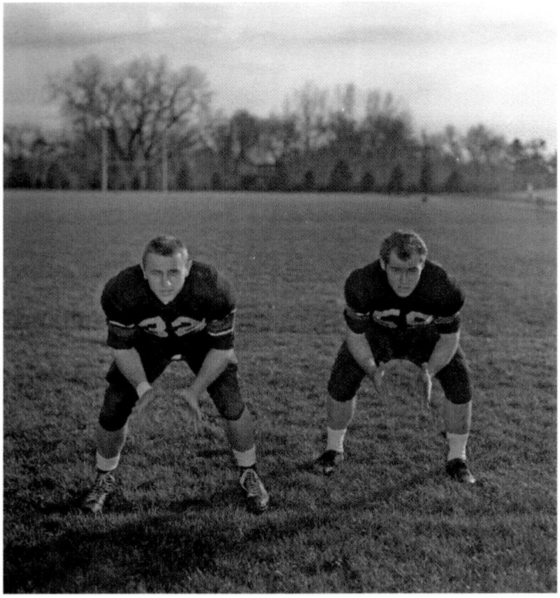

Senior Emil Radik (32) and sophomore Bill Englehardt (59) were stalwarts in the Omaha University backfield. Radik finished the regular season with 94 carries for 520 yards. He also completed 16 of 49 pass attempts for 468 yards and five touchdowns. Meanwhile, Englehardt finished the regular season as the total offensive yardage leader among small-college players, with 1,645 yards, including 584 rushing yards on 134 carries and 1,061 passing yards on 56 completions in 109 attempts.

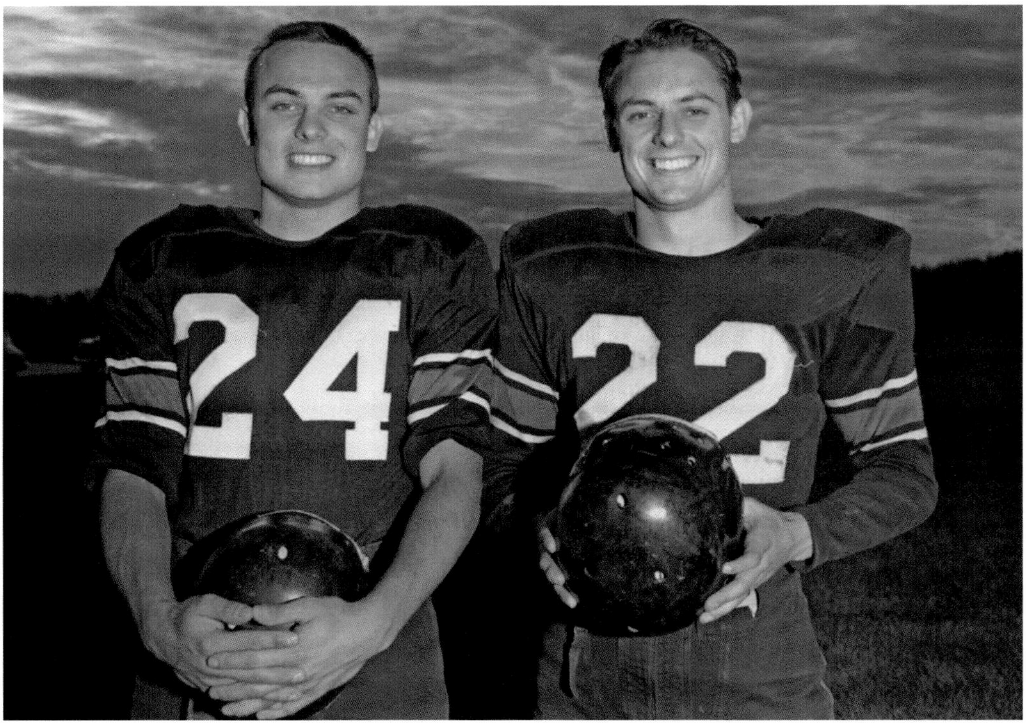

Jerry Tannahill (22), a senior on the 1954 squad, played varsity all four years. Despite being just five feet, six inches tall, he finished the 1954 regular season with 11 catches for 281 yards and two touchdowns. Brother Dick Tannahill, who also was a 1951 Omaha North High graduate, attended Kansas State for one year, gaining a baseball letter. Because of this, Dick was able to play football in 1955. He faced his brother in an exhibition game with the alumni. Dick went on to be a coach at Lewis Central High School in Council Bluffs.

Pete Rigatuso was a talented running back on the 1954 squad, carrying 41 times for 254 yards and five touchdowns. He was enjoying a successful season in 1955 when he suffered a knee injury in the eighth game of the season.

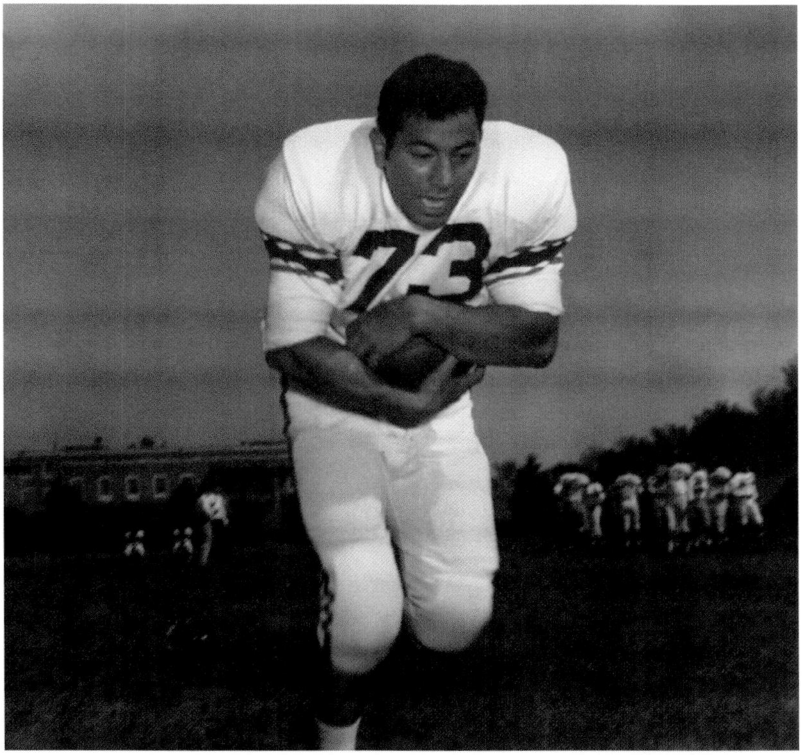

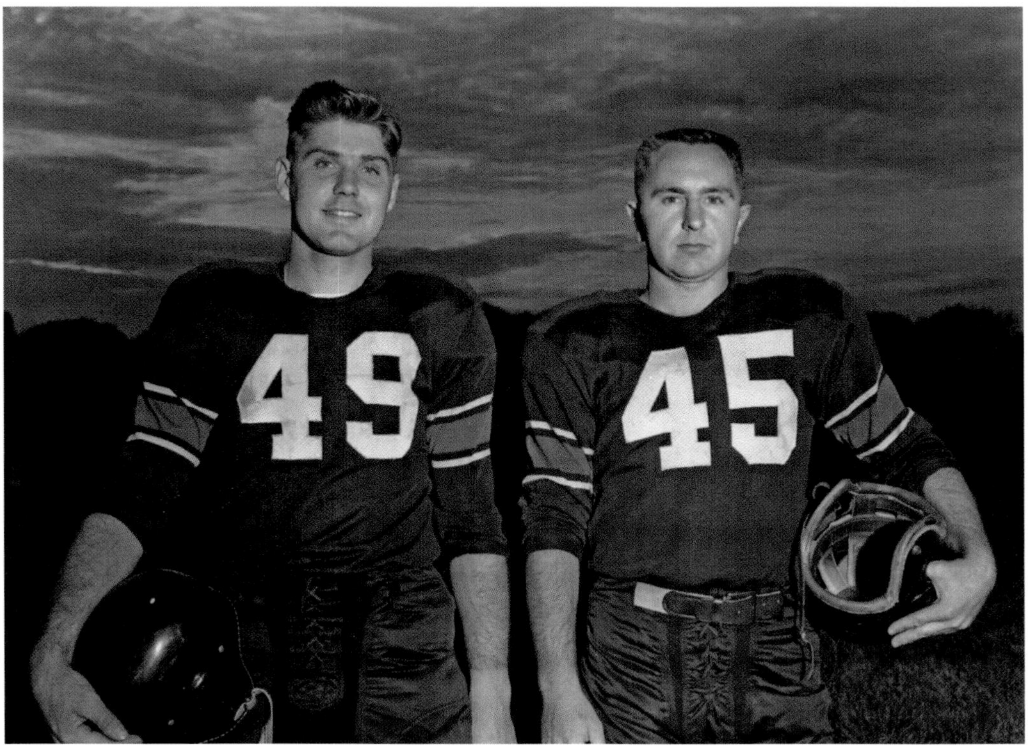

Running back Ken Conrad (left) and senior guard Fred Adams pose for a photograph.

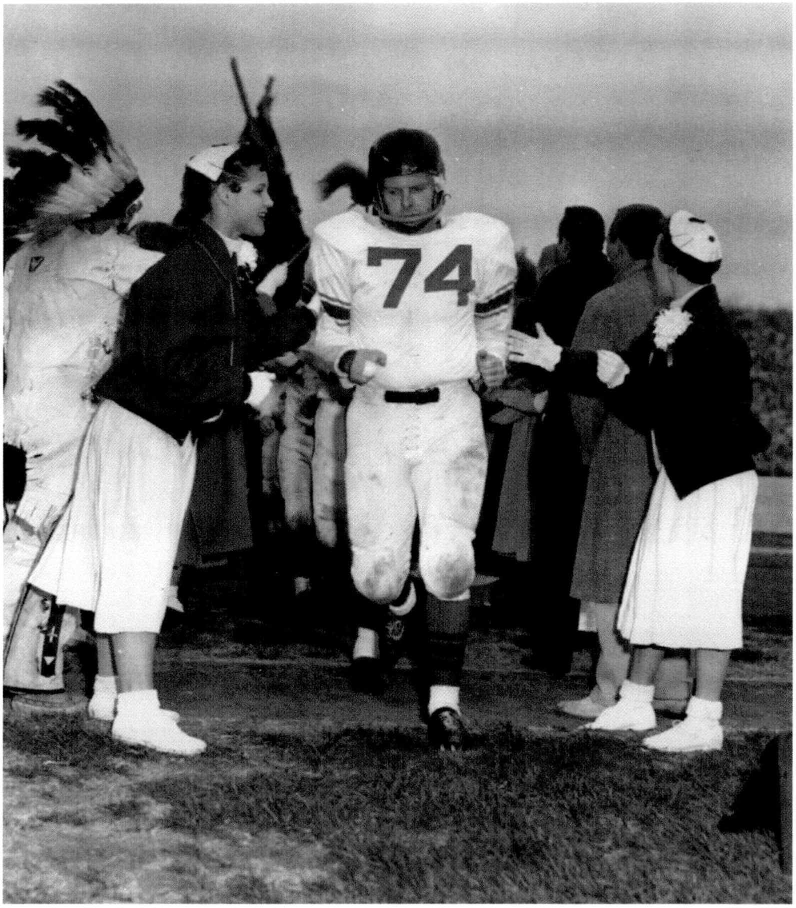

Center Tom Harper jogs onto the field during a game in 1954.

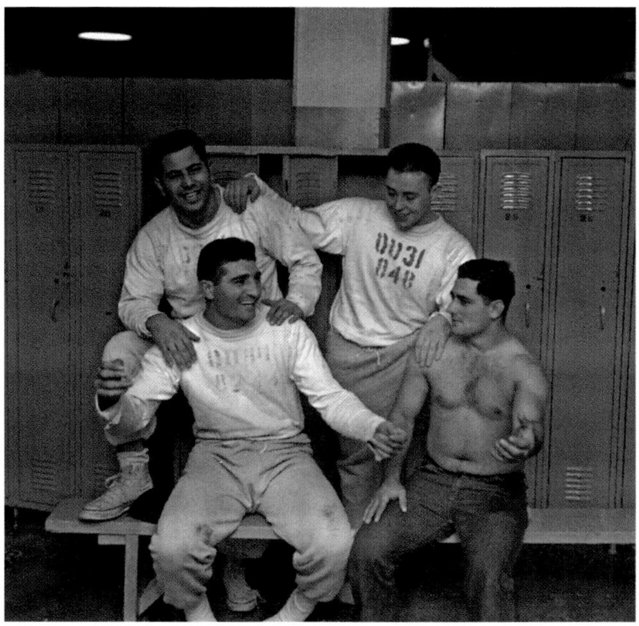

OU players sing in the locker room after the 7-6 victory over Eastern Kentucky. They are, clockwise from the top left, Pete Rigatuso, Fred Moyer, Arnold Smith, and Rudy Rotella. The *Gateway* called Rotella "Omaha University's answer to Dean Martin" and stated that he was as well known on campus for singing as he was for football. He supposedly received four curtain calls for his 1949 performance in the *Tom Tom Revue*. The newspaper stated that he was always entertaining players on trips with his singing.

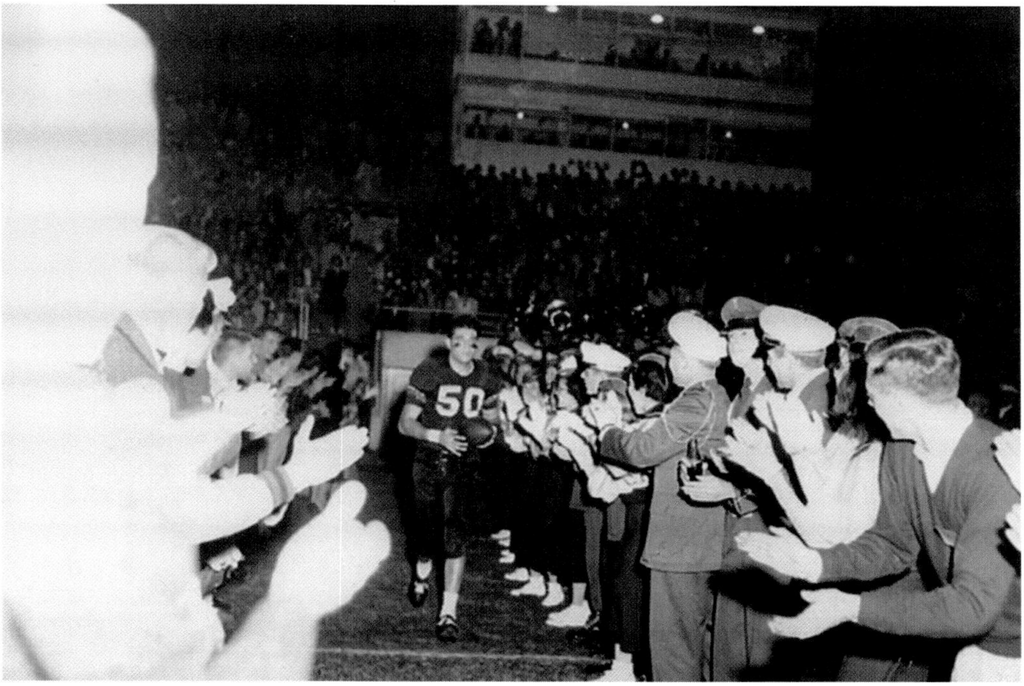

Captain Rudy Rotella enters the field before the bowl game. He caught the game-winning, 30-yard touchdown pass from Bill Englehardt in the 7-6 victory over Eastern Kentucky. Rotella was named an All-American in 1954.

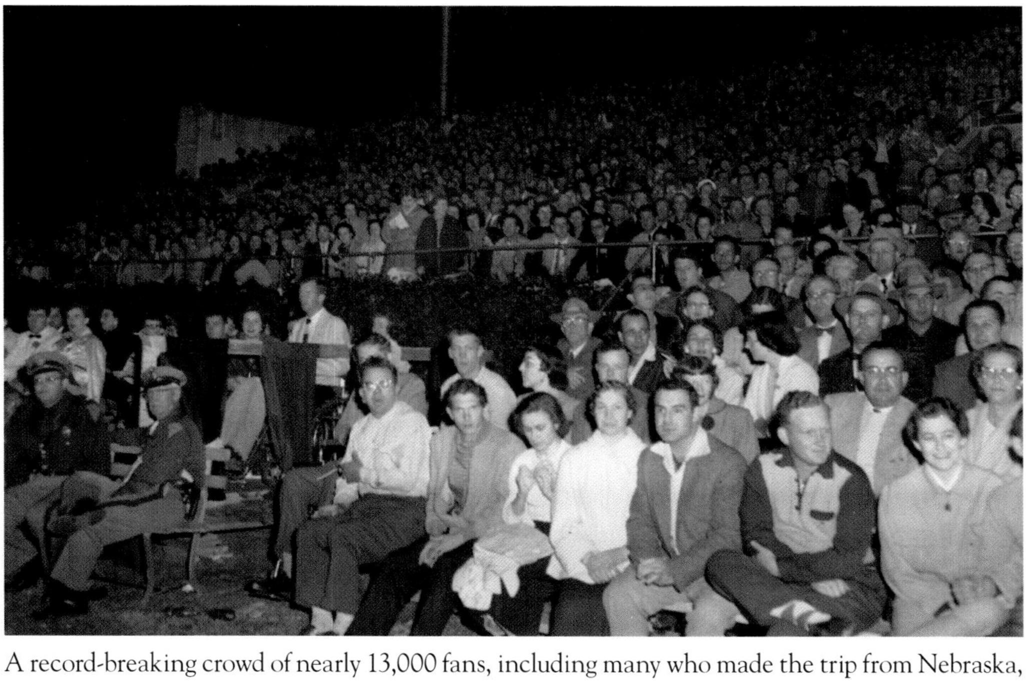

A record-breaking crowd of nearly 13,000 fans, including many who made the trip from Nebraska, was on hand at the ninth annual Tangerine Bowl (now Capital One Bowl) on January 1, 1955, in Orlando.

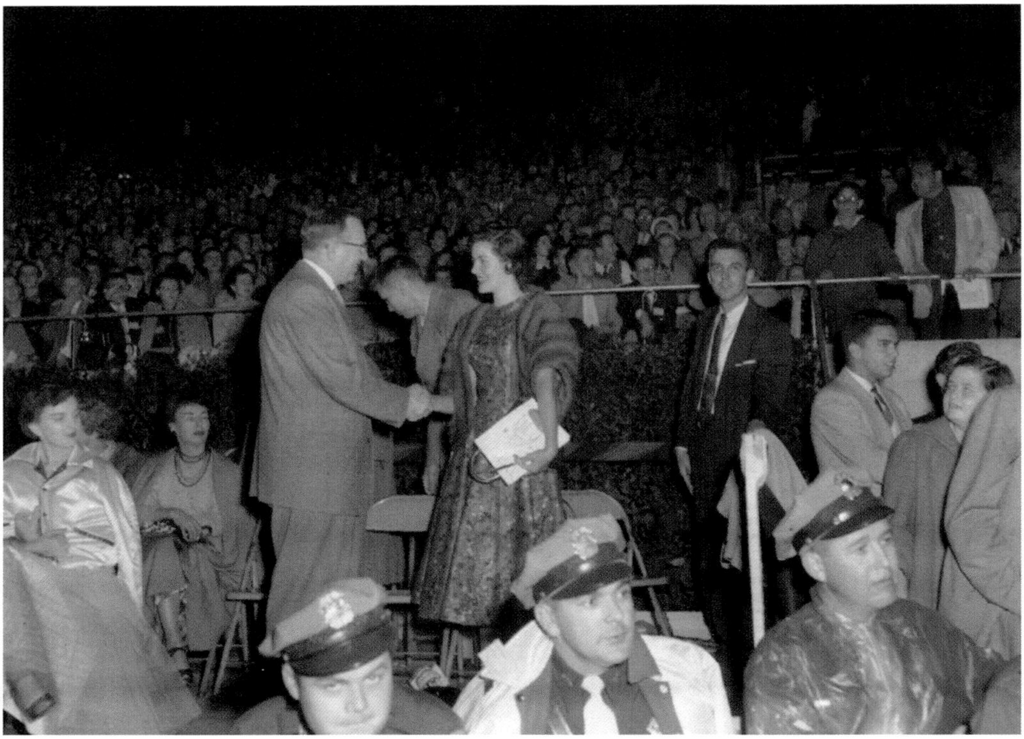

Omaha University president Milo Bail, who served as campus president from 1948 to 1965, meets 1955 Miss America Lee Ann Meriwether before the 1955 Tangerine Bowl. Meriwether later went on to play "Catwoman" in the 1966 movie *Batman* and had a successful acting career.

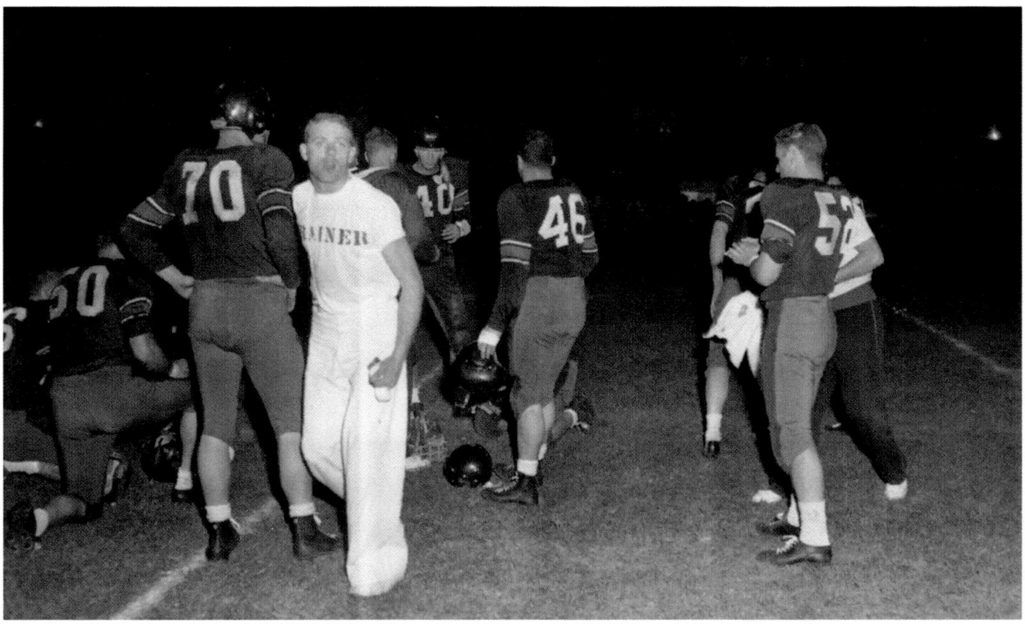

Bill Steck (52), Harry Johnson (70), Arnold Smith (46), Dick Cotton (40), and Rudy Rotella (50) warm up before the Tangerine Bowl.

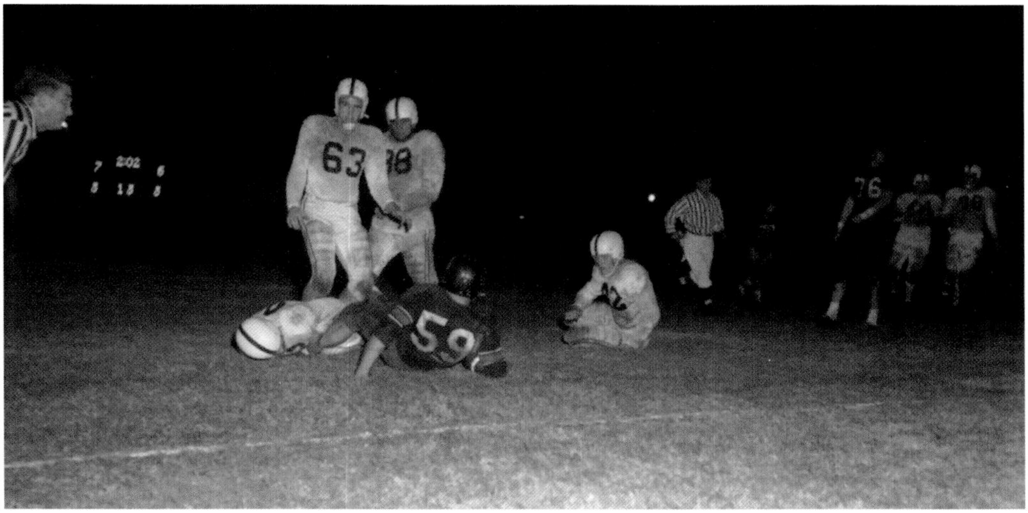

Bill Englehardt (59) gets tackled by several Eastern Kentucky defenders. Englehardt threw for 104 yards and ran 23 times for 47 yards in the Tangerine Bowl victory. He kicked the game-winning extra point after connecting on a 30-yard touchdown pass to Rudy Rotella in the first quarter.

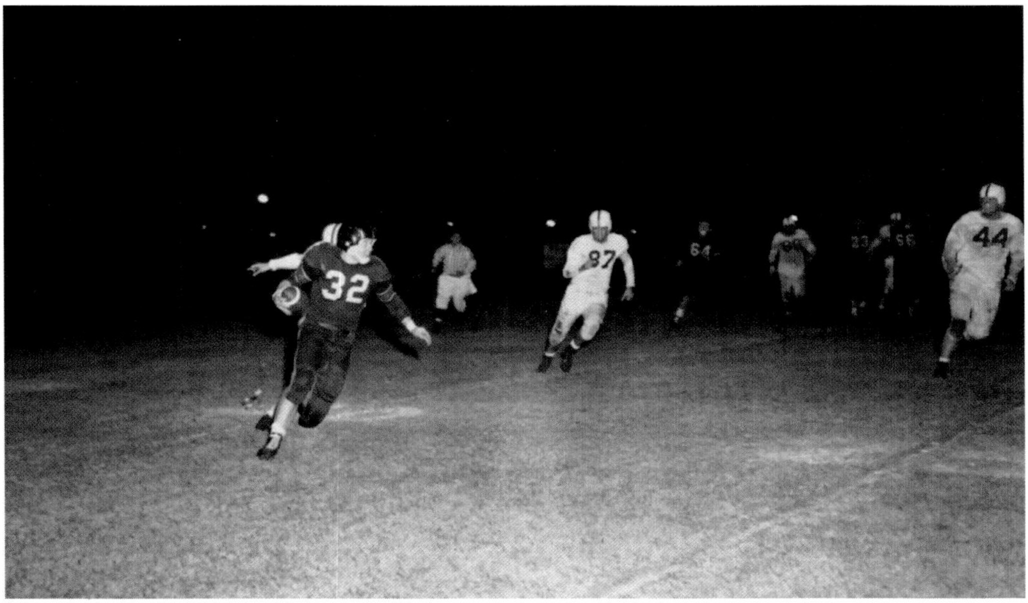

Emil Radik (32) carries the ball during the Tangerine Bowl. He ran nine times for 24 yards in the game. In 1955, he was drafted by the Baltimore Colts in the 11th round as a fullback. The *Gateway* described Radik as one "who believes in running over tacklers, not around them. Radik is a power runner and when the former South High grad comes into the Indian lineup, something has to give—it's usually the opposition." Radik earned 13 letters in high school for golf, track, basketball, and football. He started his career at the University of Nebraska but came to Omaha University at the end of his sophomore year. He competed in football, track, and golf at OU. According to the *Gateway*, Radik was "an outstanding passer and kicker, but his brilliant running is what grabs the eye of the fans."

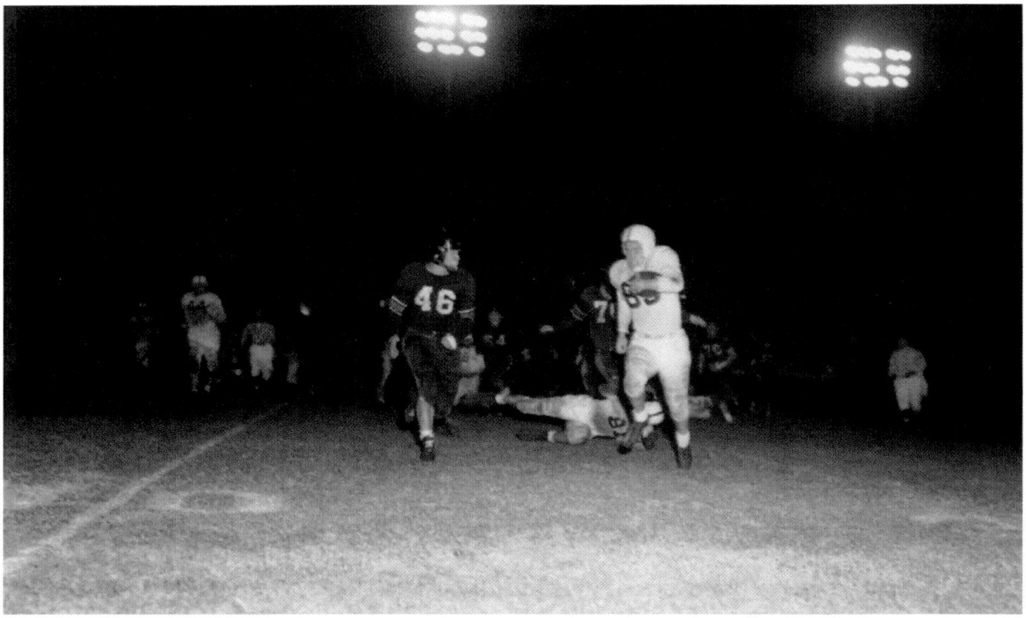

Arnold Smith attempts to make a tackle against Eastern Kentucky.

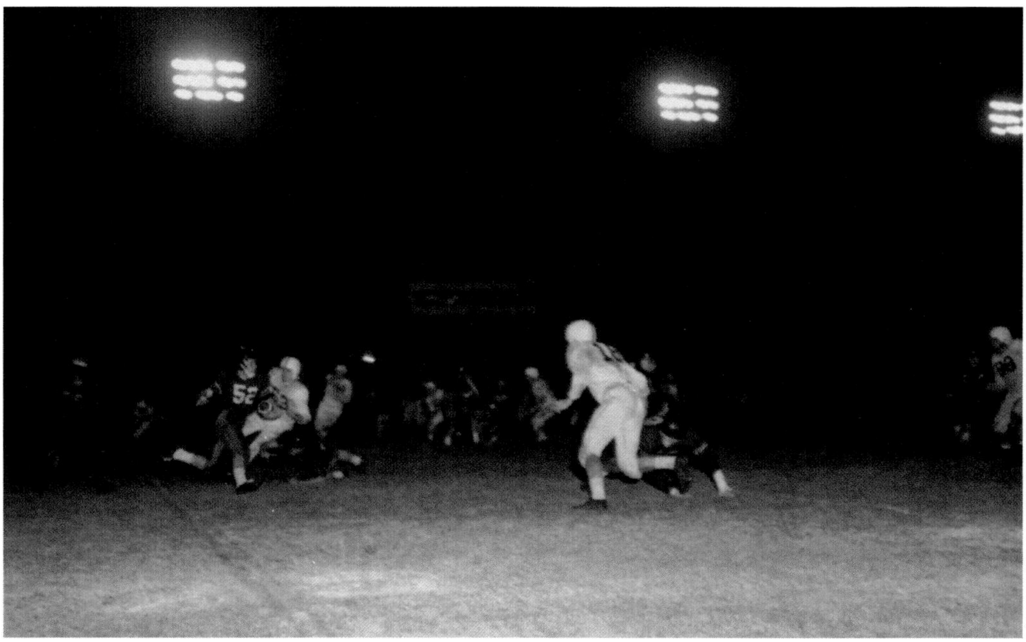

Bill Steck (52) carries the ball against Eastern Kentucky in the 1955 Tangerine Bowl.

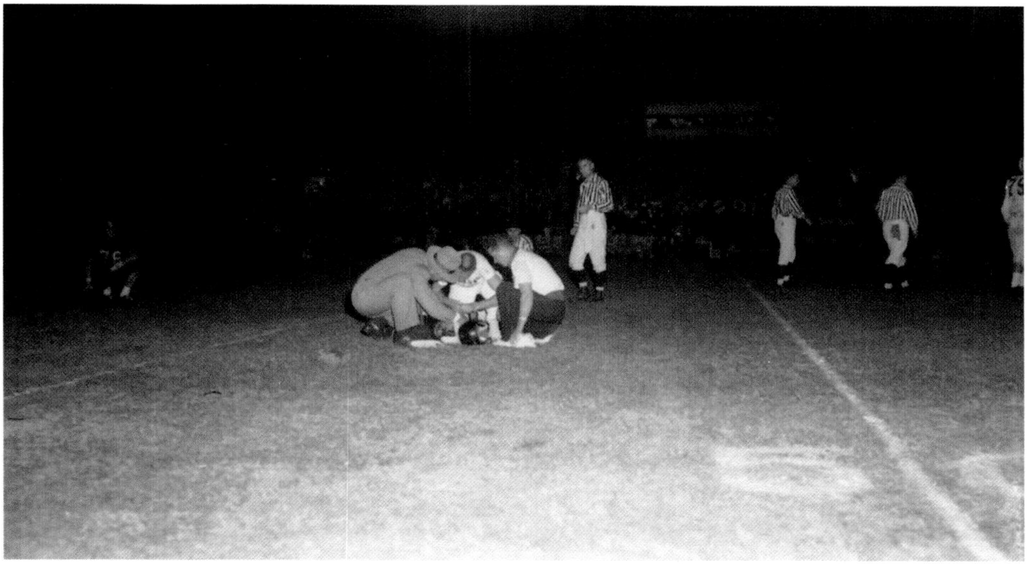

Trainers attend to an injured Omaha University player in the Tangerine Bowl. In those days, many players saw action on both sides of the ball, so playing for 50 to 60 minutes a game was not unusual. In the latter half of the season, an article in the *Gateway* mentioned that all 11 OU starters were nursing one injury or another. "They wouldn't let you know if they were hurt, they were afraid we wouldn't let them play," coach Lloyd Cardwell once said. "To them, that was the worst thing that could happen."

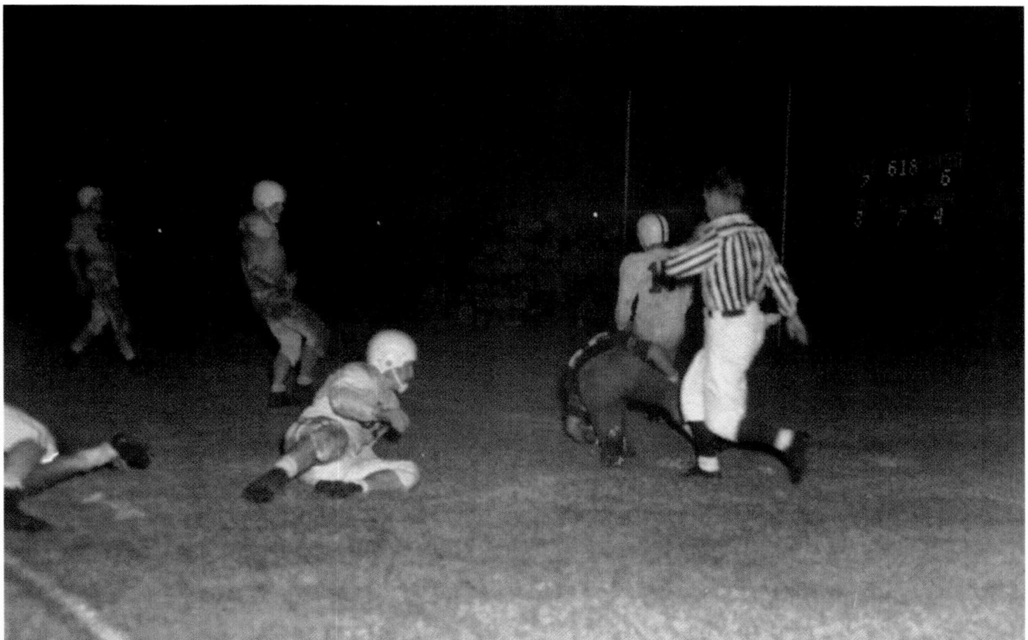

Bill Steck is stopped a little short of the goal line in the fourth quarter. Omaha University strung together a 17-minute drive in the second half. It did not result in points, but it kept Eastern Kentucky's offense on the sidelines.

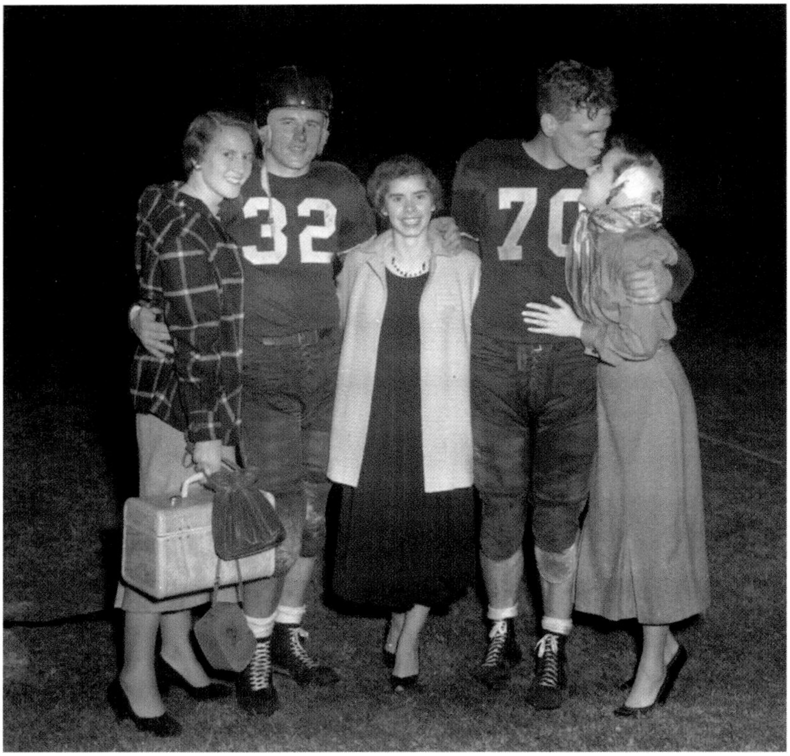

From left to right, Bonnie and Emil Radik, Joyce Tannahill, and Harry and Gloria Johnson celebrate after the hard-fought victory.

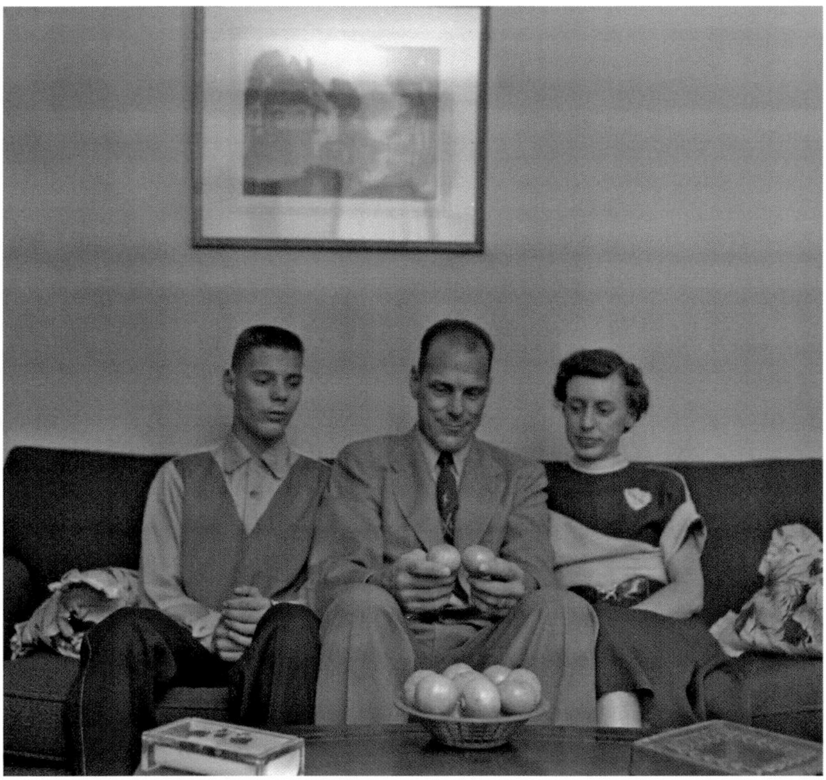

Coach Lloyd Cardwell, his wife, Beth, and their son Butch pose for a photograph in Florida.

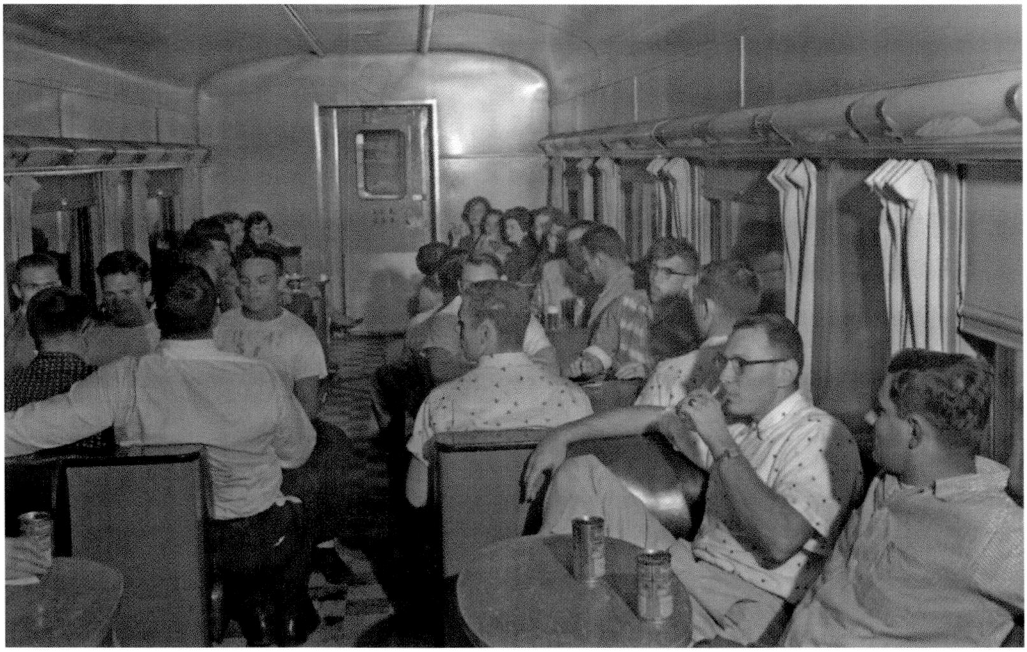

The team left Orlando by train on January 3 to head to Washington, DC. The Indians were guests of Nebraska senator and vice president of Omaha University's board of regents, Roman H. Hruska. The team also visited the White House.

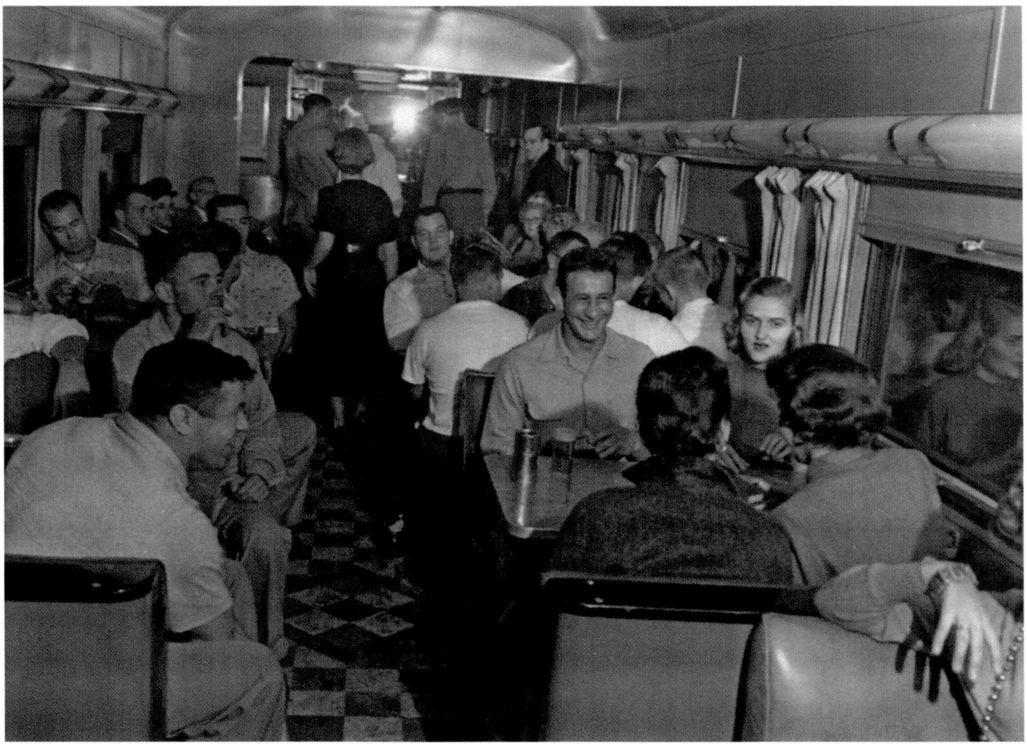

It was a happy train ride home for the football players, especially after some coeds joined the car.

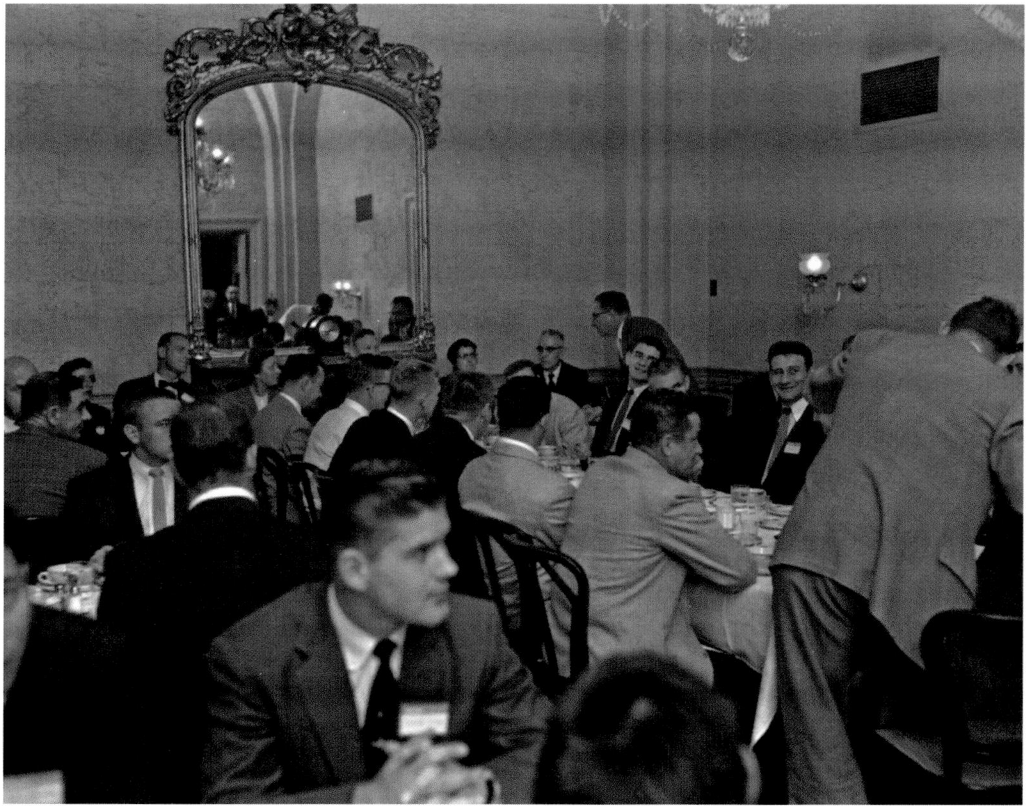

From Orlando, the Omaha University football team traveled by train to have breakfast and meet with Nebraska senator Roman L. Hruska. Pictured at the head table in the Senate dining room are, from left to right, Beth Cardwell, coach Lloyd Cardwell, Mrs. Roman Hruska, and Senator Hruska. The team then traveled by train from Washington, DC, back to Omaha.

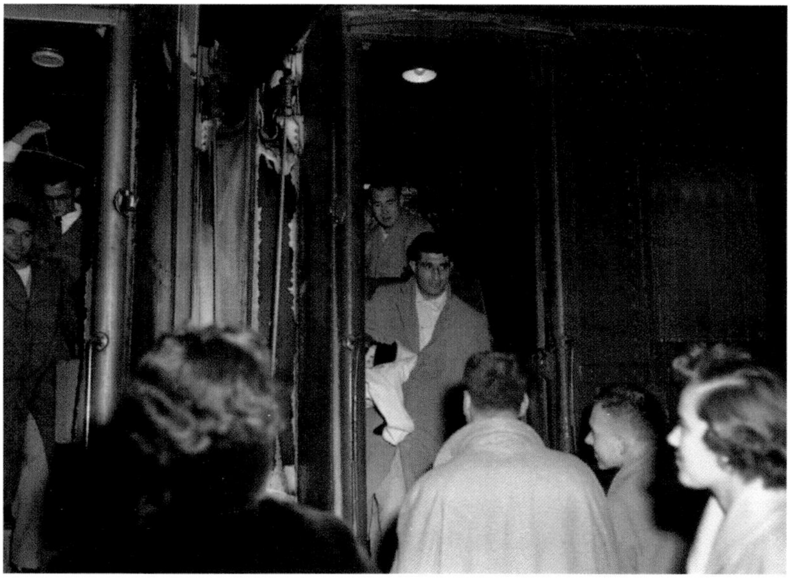

Omaha University players received a heroes' welcome when they finally returned to Omaha. Captain Rudy Rotella steps off the train in Omaha, where more than 500 people showed up to welcome the team home.

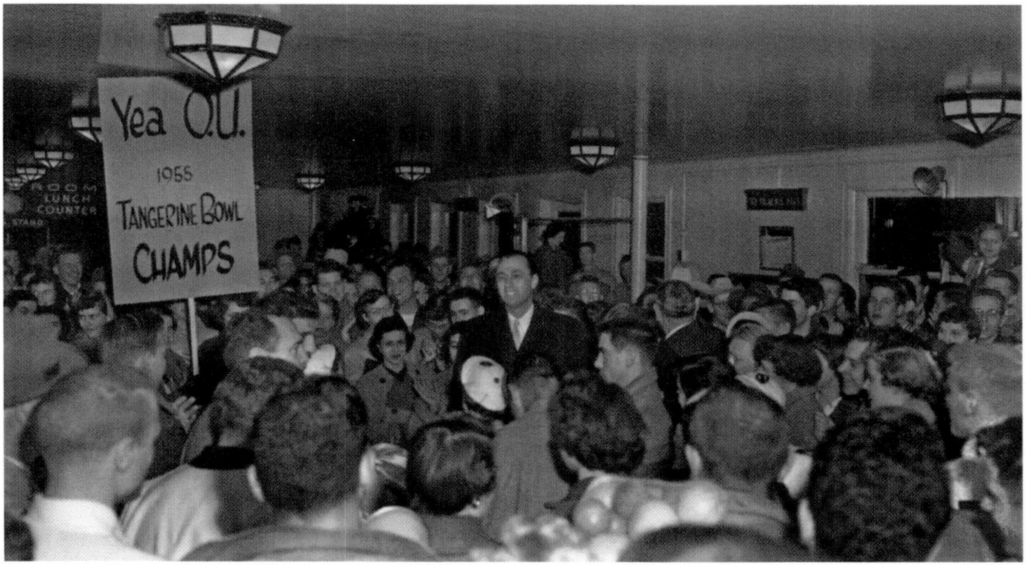

Omaha mayor John Rosenblatt, towering above the rest, smiles at the "1955 Tangerine Bowl Champs" sign as football players interact with family and fans in the train station upon their arrival in Omaha.

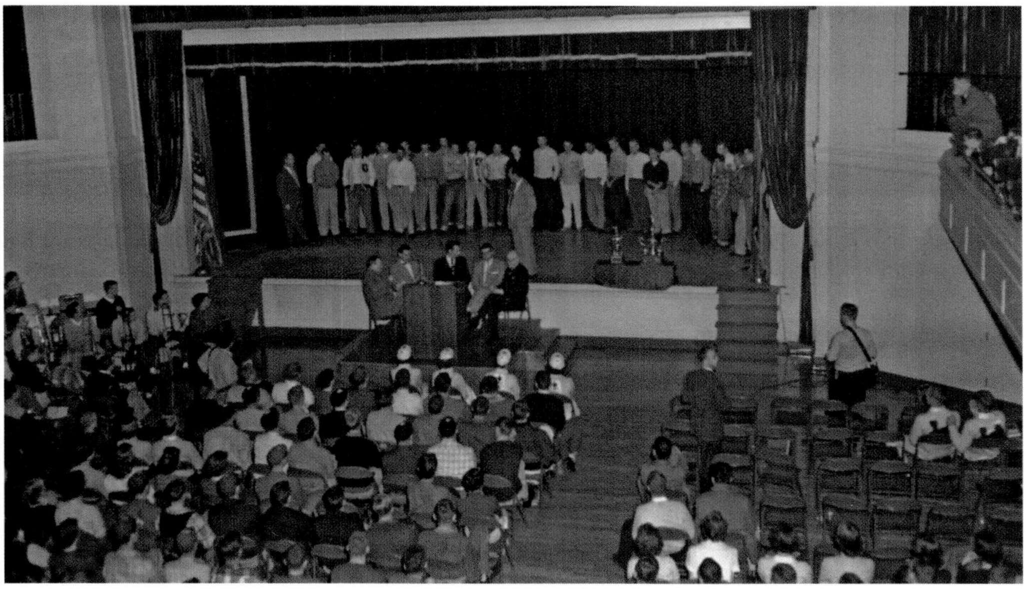

On January 15, 1955, Omaha University hosted a thank-you party for the football team and all the "Bowl Backers" in the school auditorium. More than 450 people attended. Films taken by Bruce Linton, as well as the bowl game victory itself, were shown. The event was also an opportunity to thank the Rotary, Omaha Association of Retailers, Omaha Banks, Eppley Foundation, the chamber of commerce, and KMTV. When the Omaha gridders were honored at a special pep rally in the school auditorium, line coach Tom Brock summed up the factors that enabled the team to go undefeated. He said, "Every game we played was a team victory. The boys had excellent spirit and a strong desire to win. They never wanted to be second best."

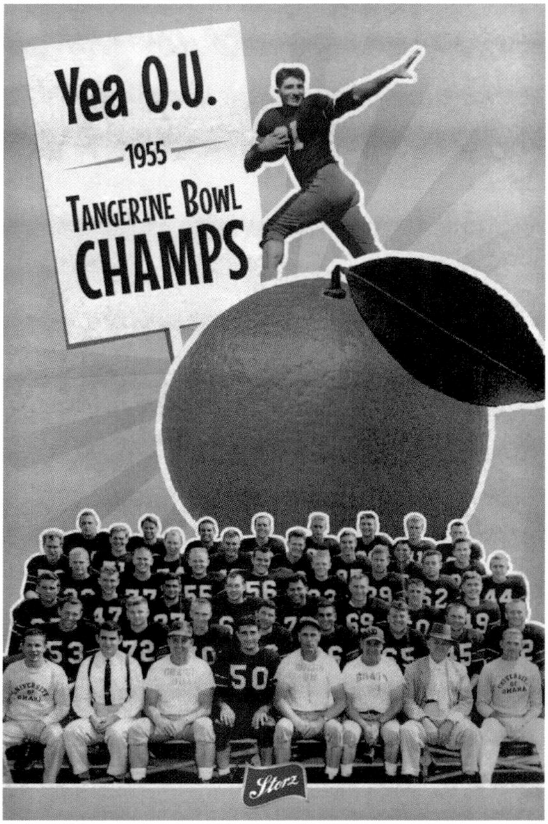

In 2014, UNO archivist Les Valentine organized a reunion for many of the surviving members of the 1954 football team and put together this program, featuring the team picture, Rudy Rotella, and the sign that awaited the team when it came home. They watched game film from the Tangerine Bowl and listened to Jack Payne's broadcast of the contest, which Valentine had synced with the video footage.

Members of the 1954 team who came back for the reunion in 2014 include, from left to right, (first row) Emil Radik, Tom Harper, Jerry Tannahill, Marv Nevins, Mike Watanabe, Fred Adams, Pete Rigatuso, and Dennis Brewster; (second row) John Welch, Bob Wheeler, Melvin Decker, Howard Baker, and Gene Sage.

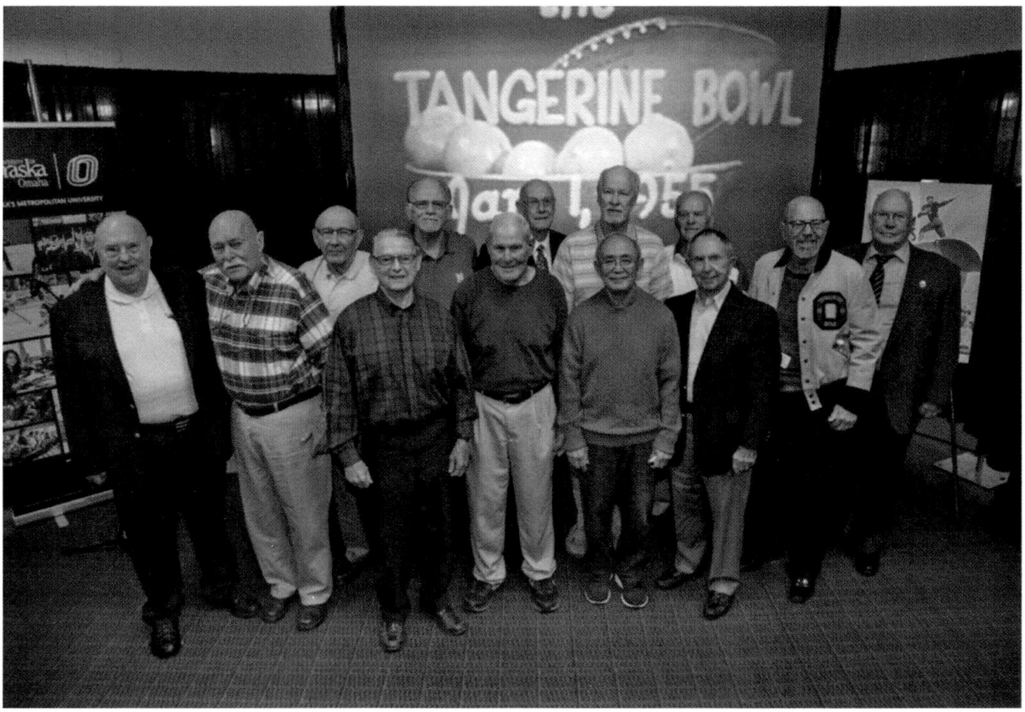

5

Coach Caniglia's Teams

Assistant coach Al Caniglia took the reigns of the Omaha University football program in 1960 after serving two years under Lloyd Cardwell, who went 2-22 in his final three seasons at the helm before resigning on December 21, 1959.

Following a successful high school career at Omaha Central and a college football career as a lineman for Creighton University from 1940 to 1942, Caniglia attended Iowa. While there, he joined the Green Bay Packers for one season (1945) before coaching a team in Norfolk, Virginia, and a development team for the Detroit Lions in Patterson, New Jersey. He then spent two years as the freshman coach at St. Louis University before that school dropped its football program. Caniglia served as a student assistant at Omaha University under Cardwell in 1950 until he finished up his bachelor's degree in 1951. He left to become athletic director and head football coach at Hillsboro High School in Illinois. Returning to Omaha University in 1958 as an assistant coach under Cardwell, Caniglia was promoted to head coach in 1960.

Caniglia's first Indians team was comprised of mostly freshmen and sophomores, and it struggled to a 1-7-1 record as he implemented the wing-T offense. By year two, and with the help of a grant aid for student-athletes that was set up in 1960 to help with recruiting, Caniglia had Omaha at 6-3. His 1962 team was arguably his best, as it finished 8-1-1 and beat East Central Oklahoma in the All-Sports Bowl. The Indians were No. 12 in the final National Association of Intercollegiate Athletics (NAIA) poll and No. 16 in the Little America poll.

During this time, Omaha was a member of the NAIA and NCAA, but it played in the two-year-old bowl that, while sanctioned by the NAIA, was not by the NCAA. The Indians found themselves on probation from the NCAA.

Caniglia's squads at Omaha University won five of seven CIC titles. He later switched to a more pro-style offensive attack and is credited with developing quarterback Marlin Briscoe, who went on to become the first African American quarterback to start in the NFL. Other All-Americans included Paul Blazevich, Charles McWhorter, and Dom Polifrone.

Caniglia finished with a 74-55-5 record. He died suddenly from a heart attack on February 19, 1973, at the age of 52.

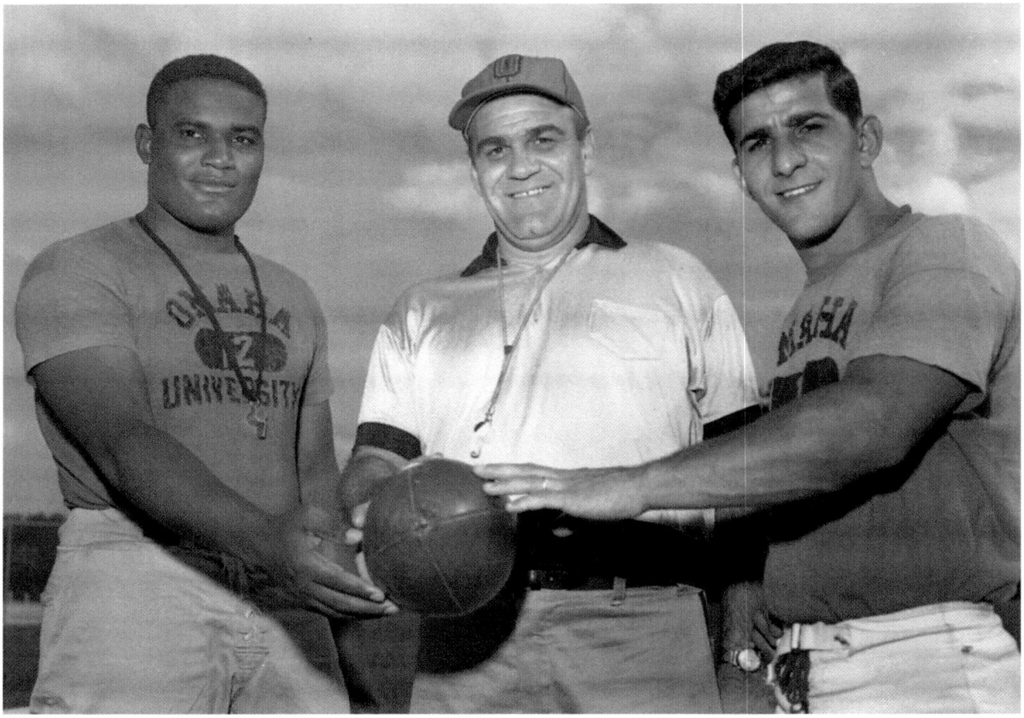

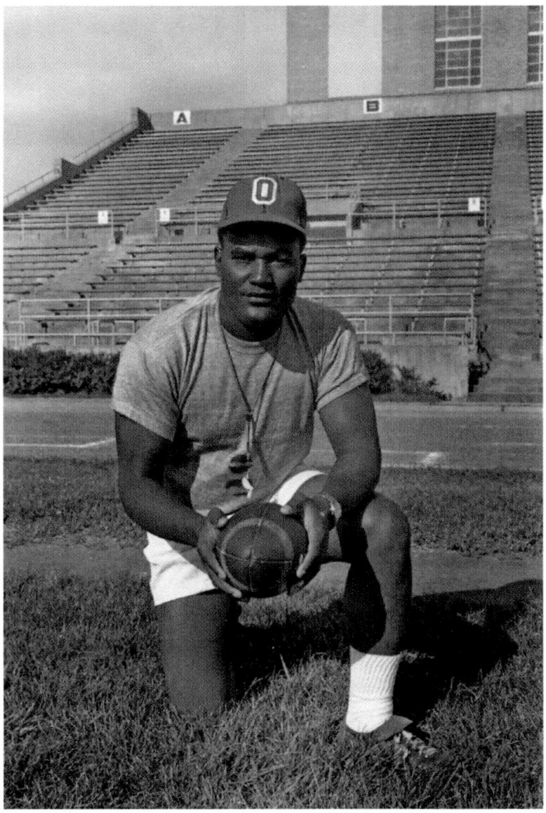

Assistant coaches Don Benning (left) and Louie Miloni (right) joined head coach Al Caniglia in 1963. Benning and Miloni were both former Omaha University running backs. Not pictured is assistant Ken Fischer.

Don Benning played football and wrestled at Omaha University in the 1950s. He assisted with football for several years and also was the head wrestling coach at OU.

Al Caniglia had served as an assistant coach for Lloyd Cardwell in 1958 and 1959 before being promoted to head coach in 1960.

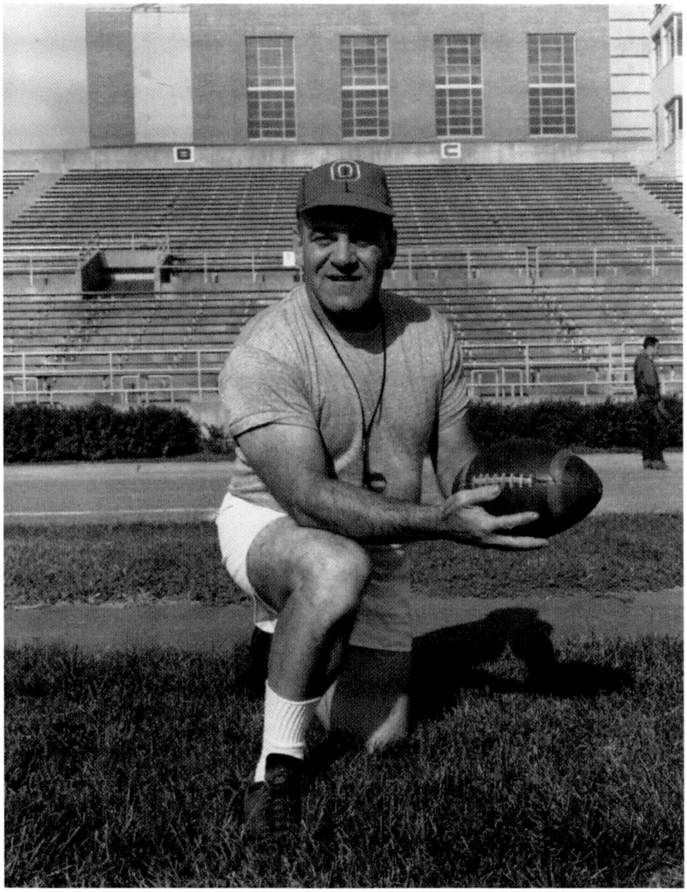

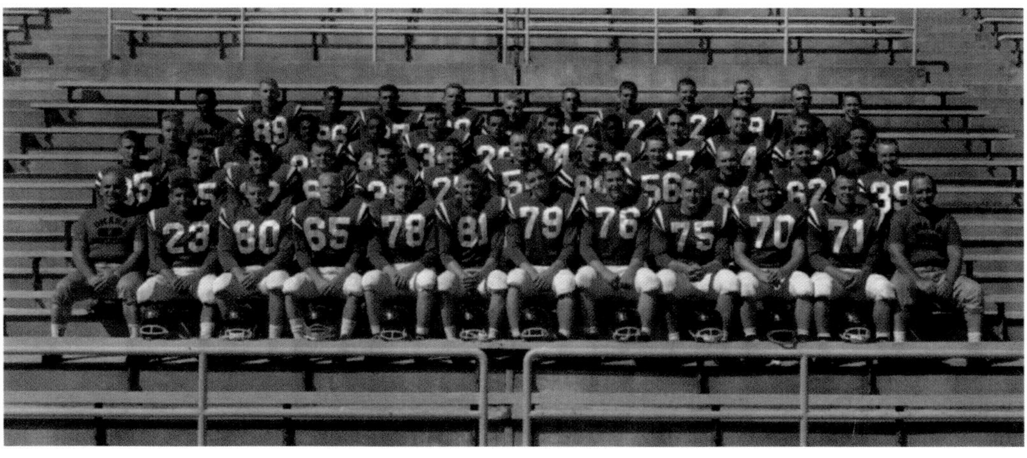

The 1960 OU football team struggled to a 1-7-1 record under first-year head coach Al Caniglia and assistant Don Watchorn. The lone victory was a 7-0 win over Emporia State. But, there were many bright spots, including speedy running back Roger Sayers, older brother of Pro Football Hall of Fame inductee Gale Sayers.

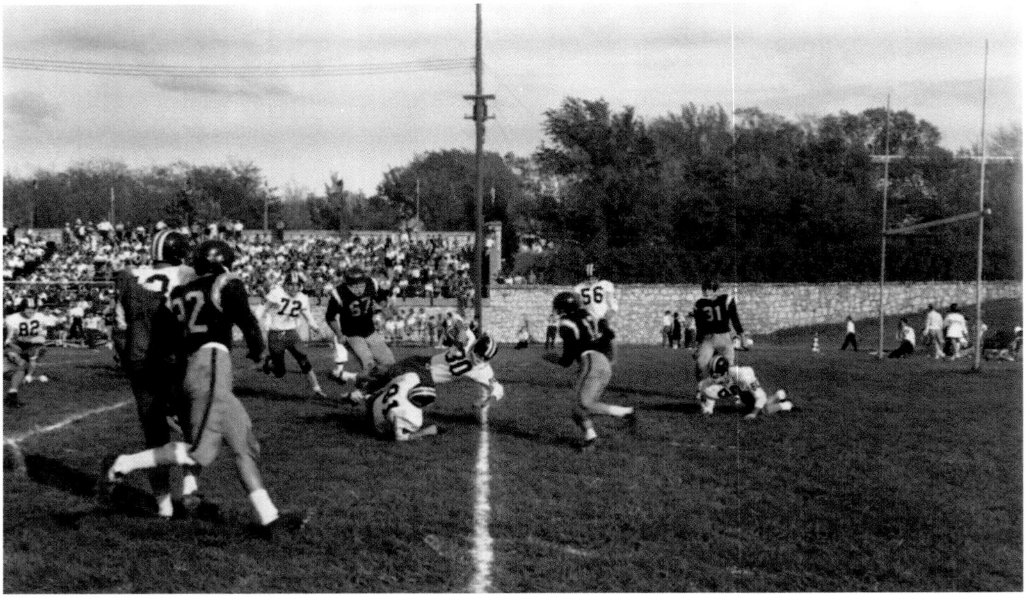

By 1961, Caniglia had recruited talented players, and the Indians posted a 6-3 season, which included a 6-1 start. Carl Meyers, seen here diving in for a touchdown, had established himself as the starting quarterback in 1961, while Roger Sayers and Louis Miloni were talented backs. End Paul Blazevich was a favorite target of Meyers on the outside.

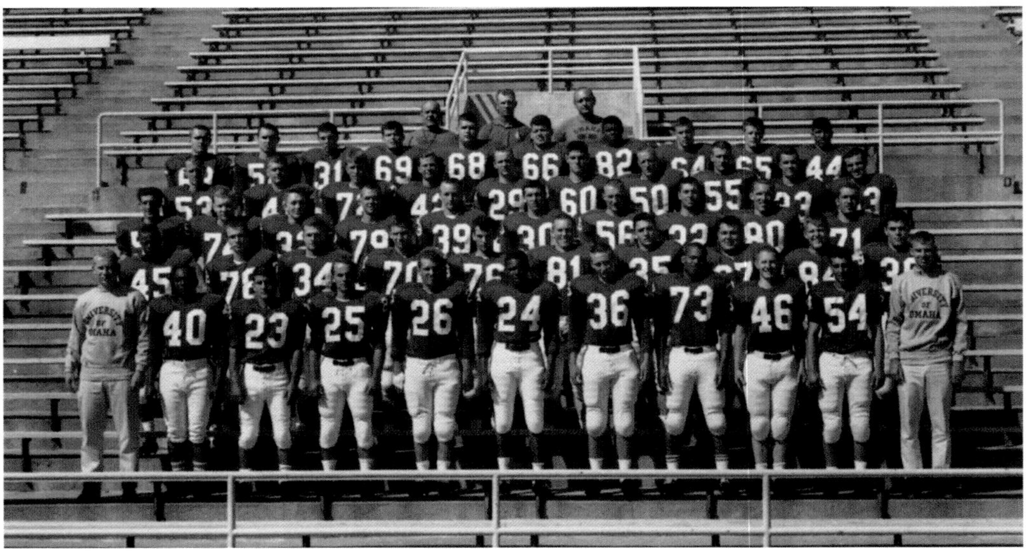

The 1962 team was arguably one of Caniglia's best squads, and he earned national coach-of-the-year honors. The Indians went 8-1-1 and won the Central Intercollegiate Conference title and earned a bid to the All-American Bowl in Topeka, Kansas, where they met East Central Oklahoma. The bowl game was the final contest for Louie Miloni, a co-captain of the squad. A three-time all-conference performer at running back, Miloni's best season was his senior year, when he gained 758 yards on 120 carries, including 72 yards on 17 attempts and one touchdown in the All-Sports Bowl win.

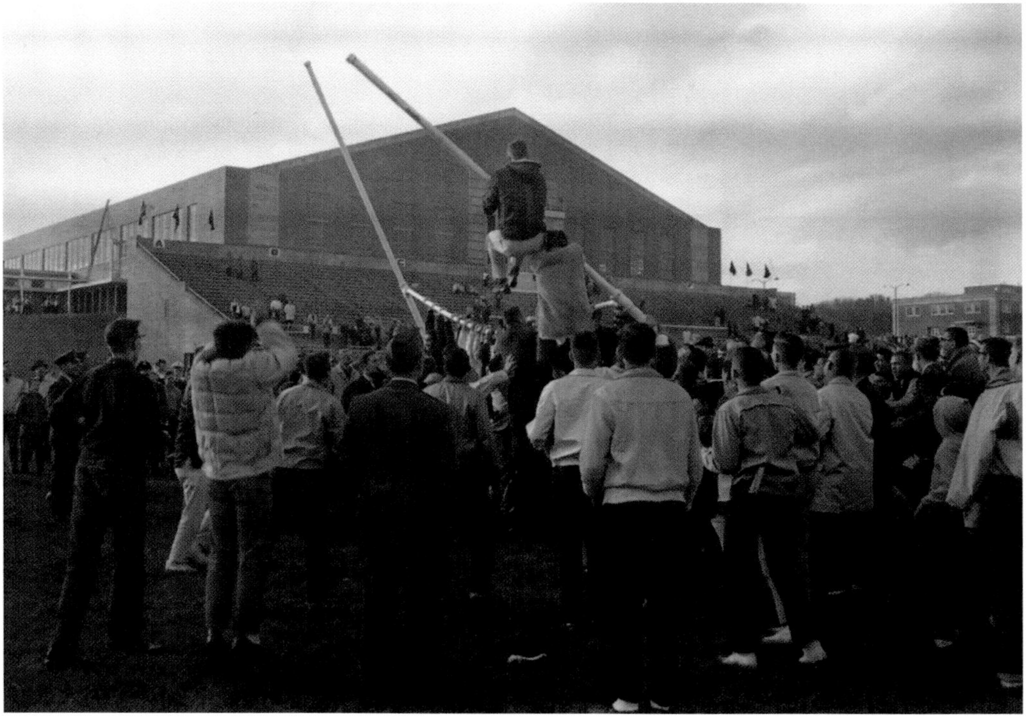

Fans tear down the goalposts after Omaha University defeated Pittsburg State 35-0 to win its first CIC title in 1962. According to a *Gateway* article: "The four unique ingredients of the OU football squad are pointed to with pride: OU is content to play in its own class—there are no visions of big-time football; the players are true amateurs, for financial aid to them is minimal; like the student body, most of the players are home-town boys; and they have the complete backing of the students, faculty, Alumni and Regents."

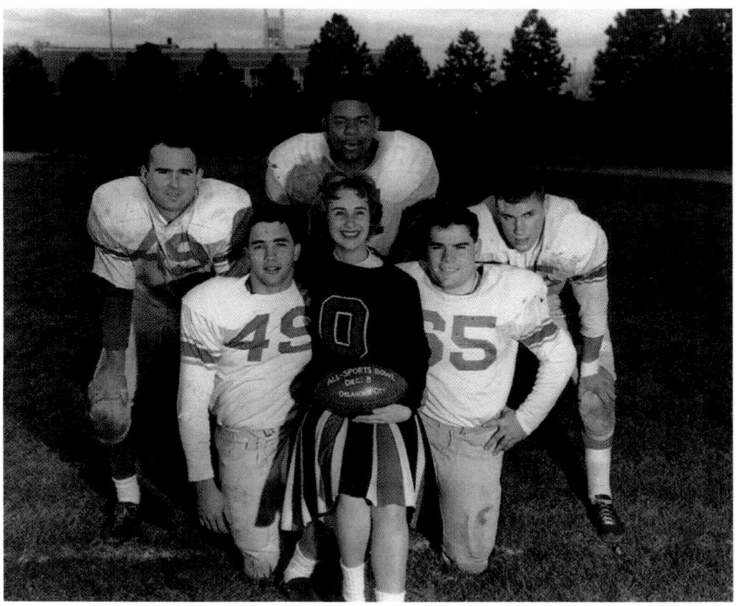

Members of the OU team pose with the All-Sports Bowl Queen Sandra Hancock before the December 8, 1962, All-Sports Bowl at Taft Stadium in Oklahoma City. Pictured behind the queen is Roger Sayers, older brother of Gale Sayers.

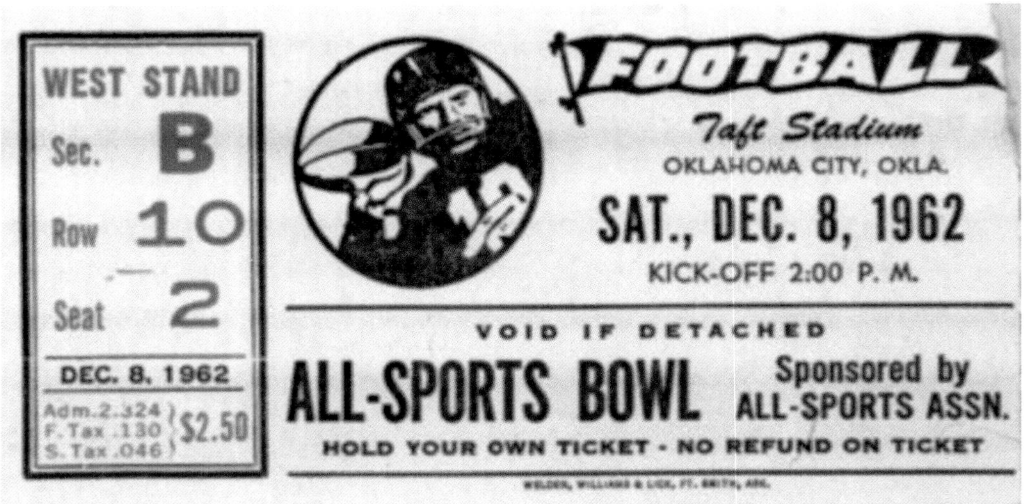

OU originally wanted a bid to the NAIA Camelia Bowl, but that did not happen. However, attending the two-year-old All-Sports Bowl in Oklahoma City was the "icing on the cake for the rejuvenation of Omaha U football," Caniglia said at the time. For playing in this non-NCAA-sanctioned bowl game, Omaha University faced a NCAA one-year probation. The school played in the NAIA from 1962 to 1972.

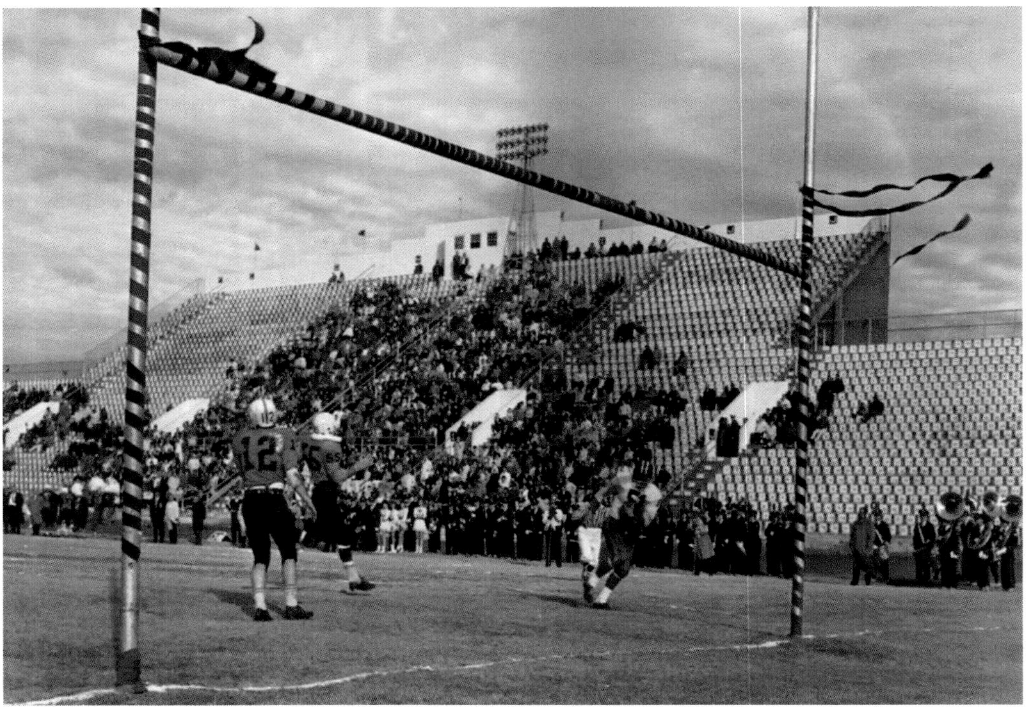

Paul Blazevich hauls in a six-yard touchdown pass from Carl Meyers in the 34-21 victory over East Central Oklahoma in the All-Sports Bowl. Blazevich's second touchdown catch gave OU a 27-14 halftime lead. He also hauled in an 80-yard touchdown pass from Meyers on OU's first offensive play of the game.

Quarterback Carl Meyers was a standout athlete at Omaha Creighton Prep High School before coming to Omaha University in 1960. He earned the starting spot in his sophomore season and maintained it throughout his OU career. In the All-Sports Bowl, Meyers threw for 238 yards and two touchdowns and kicked four extra points. He earned the award for Most Outstanding Back in the game.

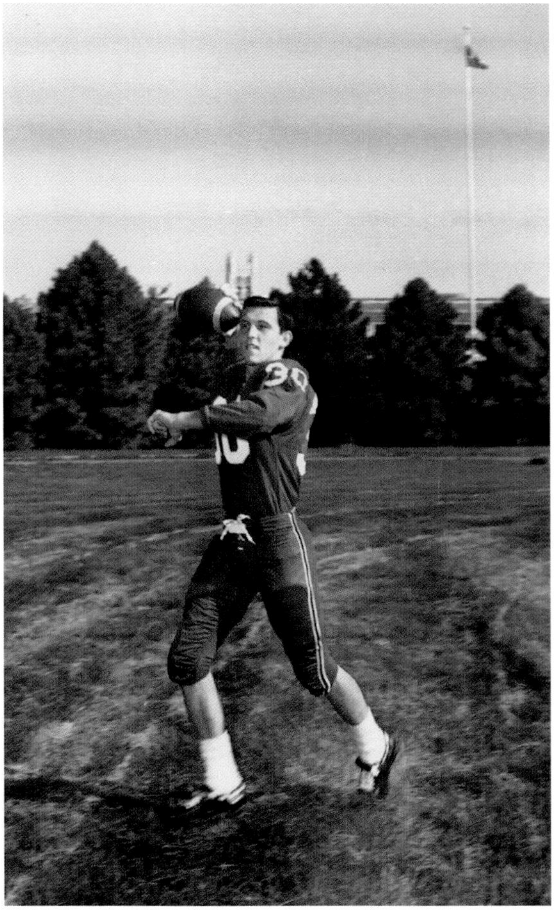

Carl Meyers, five feet, eleven inches tall and weighing in at 175 pounds, went out in style in his final game at Omaha University. Trailing Drake 29-27 late in the fourth quarter, Meyers and his Indian teammates took over on their own 1-yard line. On the very first play, he and Roger Sayers connected on a 99-yard touchdown completion that gave OU the 34-29 victory and Meyers and Sayers the NAIA record for longest passing touchdown. When he graduated, Meyers held the single-season school passing yardage record with 1,125 yards.

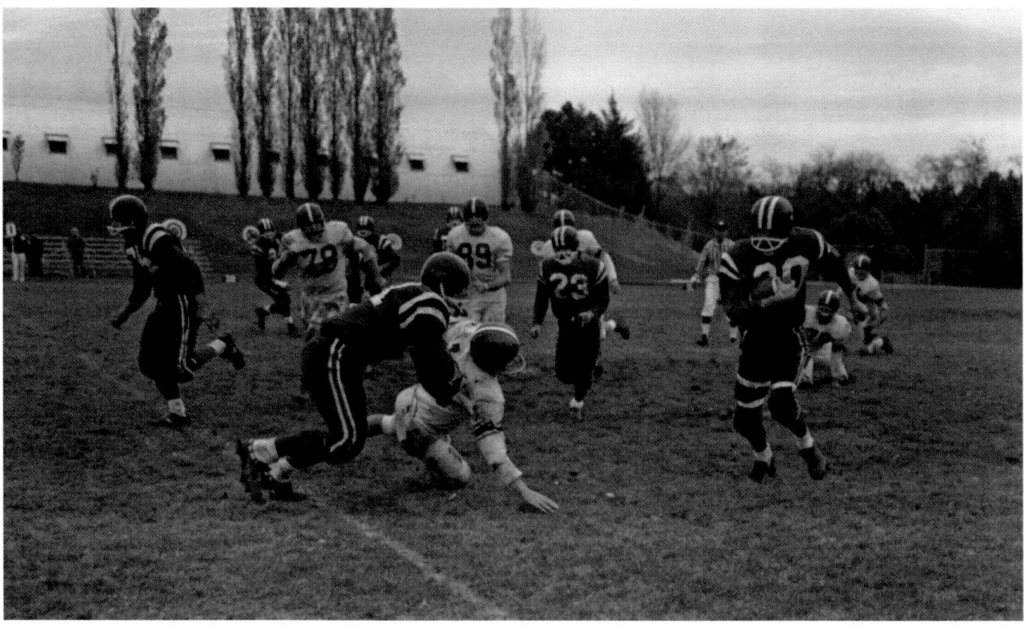

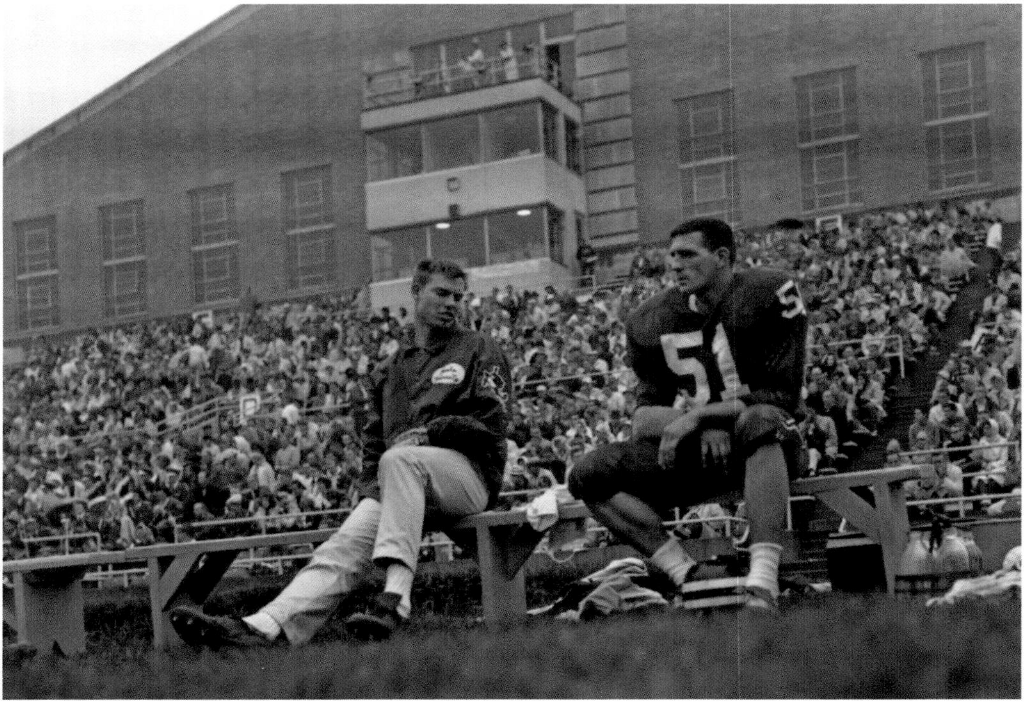

Paul Blazevich of Wall, Pennsylvania, was an AP All-American end for Omaha University in 1961 after catching 30 passes for 446 yards and five touchdowns. The El Dorado Junior College transfer is shown sitting on the bench at a home OU game in 1962. Omaha students raised enough money to pay for his mother and two siblings to come to his final home game in 1962 against Pittsburg State. It was his first college game that they had been able to see. Following graduation in 1962, he played professionally with the Omaha Mustangs and later coached at Omaha South High.

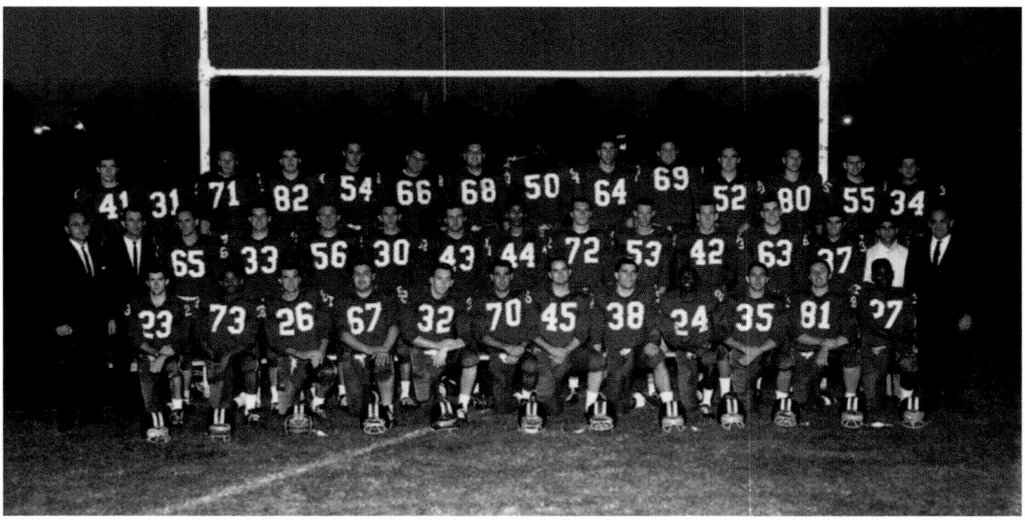

The 1963 Omaha University football team dropped two of its first three games, to Morningside (33-26) and Northern Illinois (18-7), before ending with six consecutive victories and winning the CIC title for the second straight season.

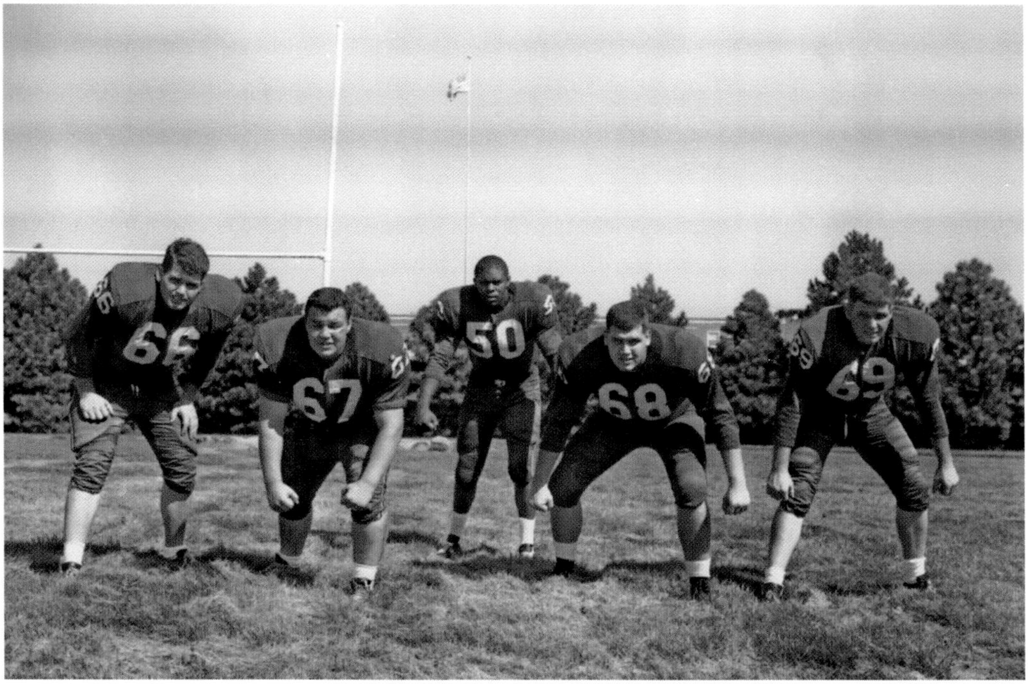

The 1963 defensive line was quite large for that era. Seen here are, from left to right, 280-pound Brian Kadow, Paul Limas, Jim Jones (50), 300-pounder Jack Peterson, and 280-pound Kevin Kadow.

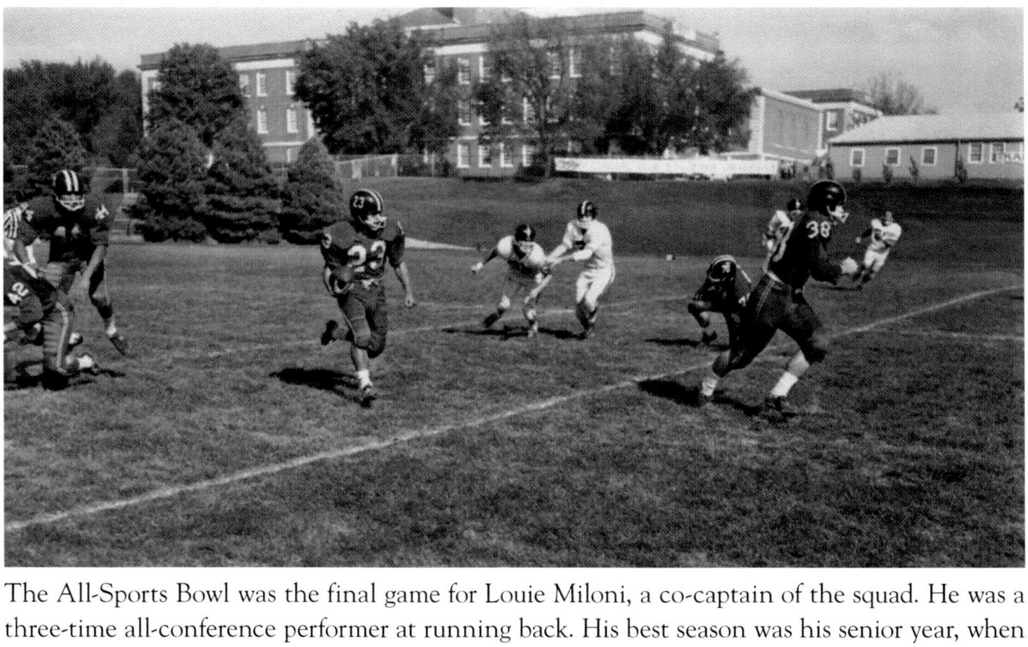

The All-Sports Bowl was the final game for Louie Miloni, a co-captain of the squad. He was a three-time all-conference performer at running back. His best season was his senior year, when he gained 758 yards on 120 carries, including 72 yards on 17 attempts and one touchdown in the All-Sports Bowl win.

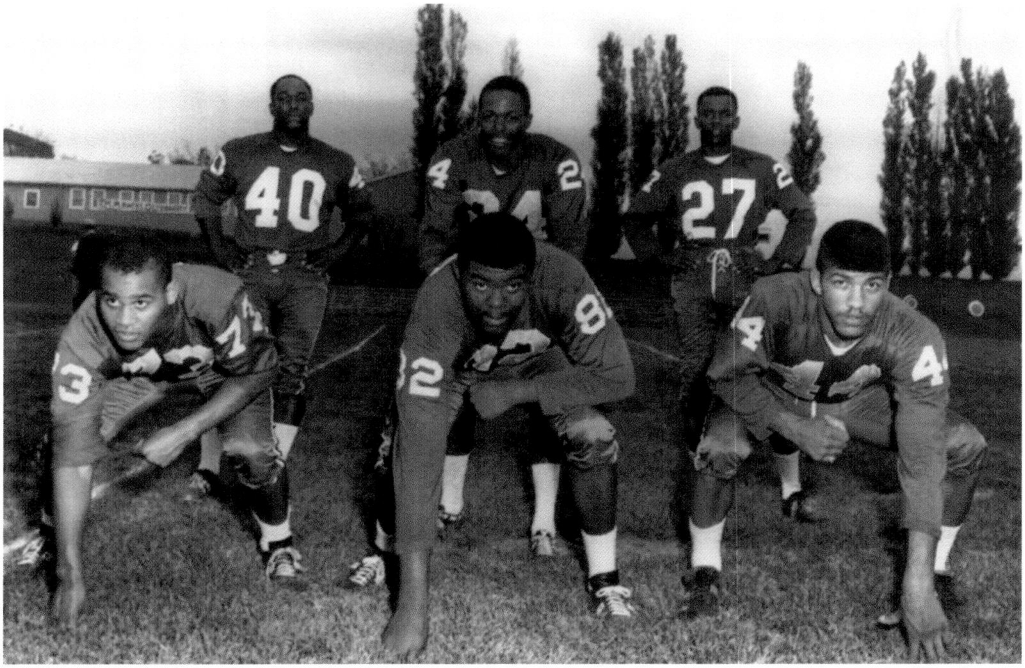

As a freshman in 1963, quarterback Marlin Briscoe (27) was among a group of several African American players, including Artie Reynolds (40), Roger Sayers (24), Willard Shepard (73), Jim Jones (82), and Gerald Allen (44). Sayers, the older brother of Gale Sayers, was a standout sprinter and football player for Omaha University. Allen, a Massillon, Ohio, native, went on to play professional ball for the Baltimore Colts and Washington Redskins from 1966 to 1969. Briscoe, Sayers, Jones, and Allen all are members of the Nebraska Football Hall of Fame.

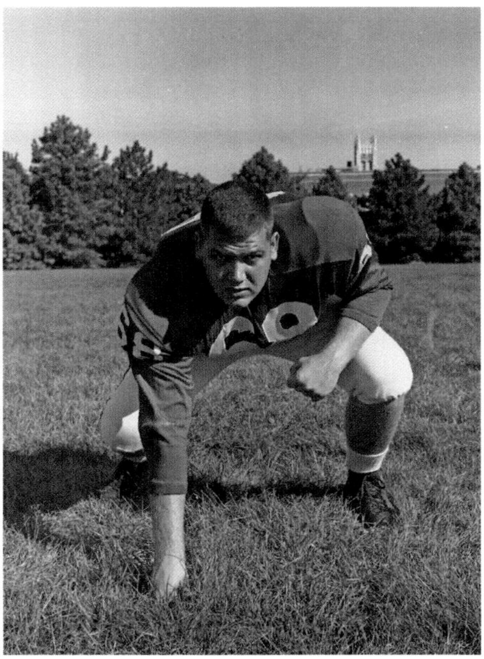

Tackle Jack Peterson was drafted by the Green Bay Packers and Kansas City Chiefs in the 1964 NFL and AFL drafts, respectively. He was the first Omaha University draft pick since Emil Radik in 1955.

Defensive end Jim Jones was drafted in the 18th round by the Green Bay Packers (NFL) and in the ninth round by the New York Jets (AFL) in 1966.

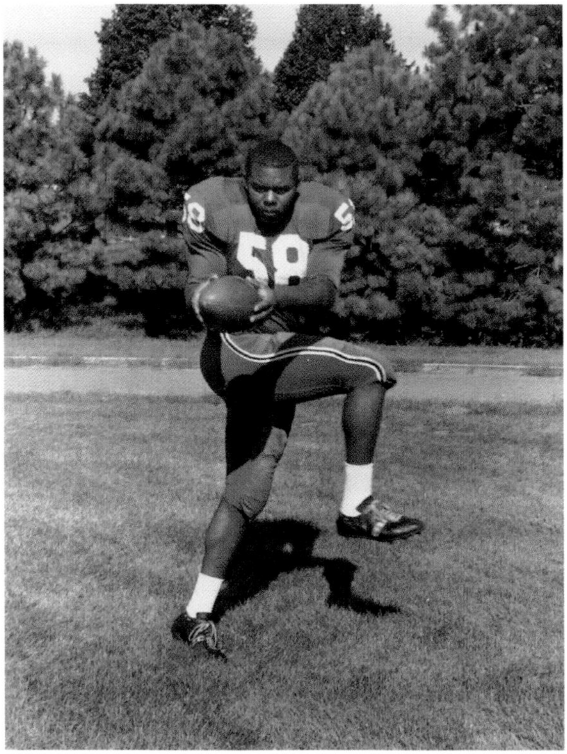

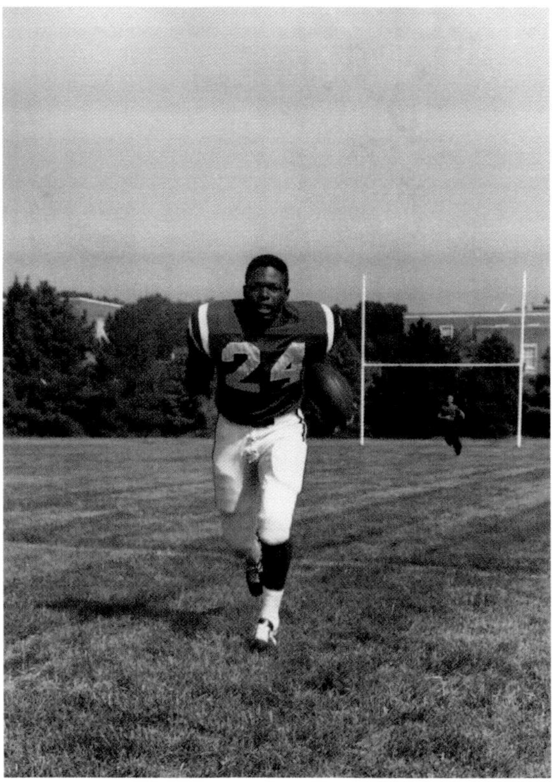

Omaha Central High graduate Roger Sayers was one of the prized recruits for Al Caniglia. Sayers decided to play at Omaha University following high school in 1960. Sayers was small (five feet, nine inches and 155 pounds) but very speedy, and he remained the all-time leader at 8.3 yards per carry, even 47 years after graduating. When the program folded, he ranked ninth all-time in career scoring, with 180 points.

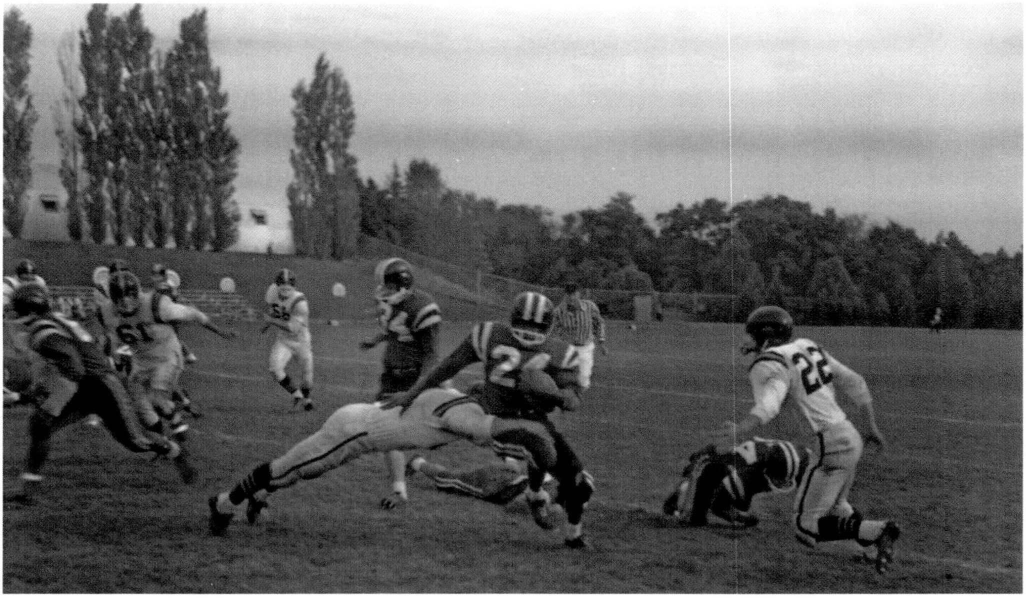

Roger Sayers (24) breaks a tackle during a game. He finished with 2,033 rushing yards. In his final game against Drake, he caught a game-winning, 99-yard touchdown pass from Carl Meyers that was an NAIA and school record for longest touchdown catch. In his final three games of his career, he carried 13 times and scored seven touchdowns. "He made defenses look like they were standing still," said Paul Borge in a 1981 interview with the *Gateway*. While he was successful in football, Sayers was even more dynamic in track and field. He won the 100-meter dash at the NAIA championships in 1962 and 1963, running it in 9.5 seconds and defeating world-record holder "Bullet" Bob Hayes. Sayers pulled a thigh muscle in 1964 and was unable to try out for the Olympics.

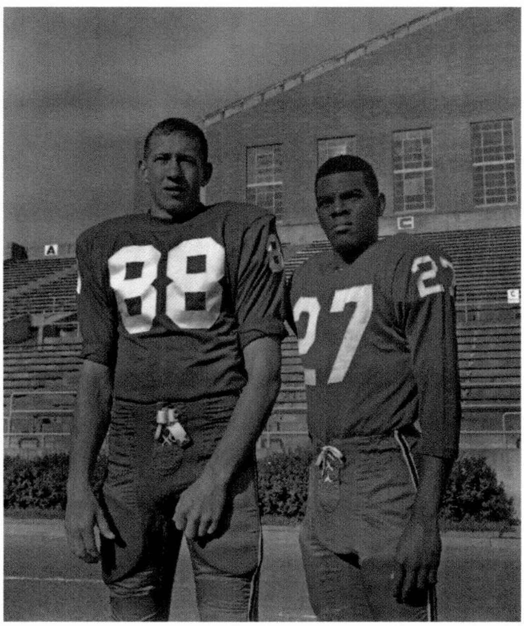

End Bill Haas (left) and quarterback Marlin Briscoe were drafted in 1968, with Haas going in the 11th round to Minnesota, and Briscoe going in the 14th round to Denver. Ironically, Haas filled in at quarterback in 1966 when Briscoe reinjured a broken vertebra in his neck in the first game of the season. Haas led the team in 1966 with 711 passing yards, completing 76 of 163 attempts.

Bill Haas earned all-conference honors in both football and basketball while playing for Omaha University from 1964 to 1968. The Ralston native caught 79 passes for 1,207 yards as a split end during his football career. He was also a placekicker and a quarterback. Haas led the Indians in scoring in 1967, scoring nine touchdowns and kicking 19 of 28 PAT attempts. As a receiver, he led the team with 55 receptions for 850 yards and nine touchdowns.

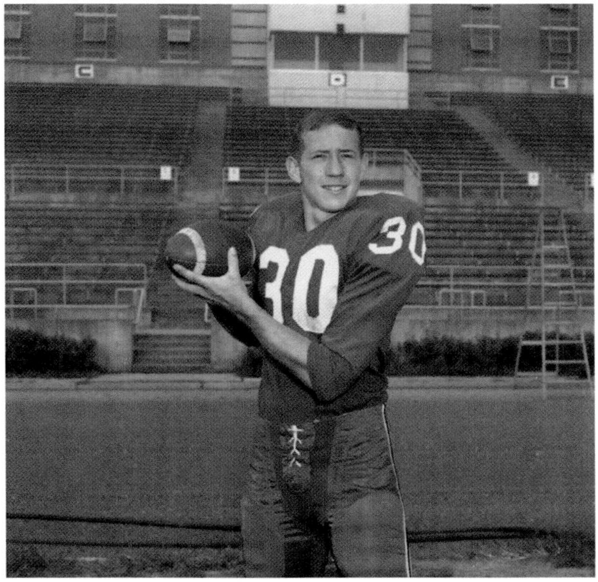

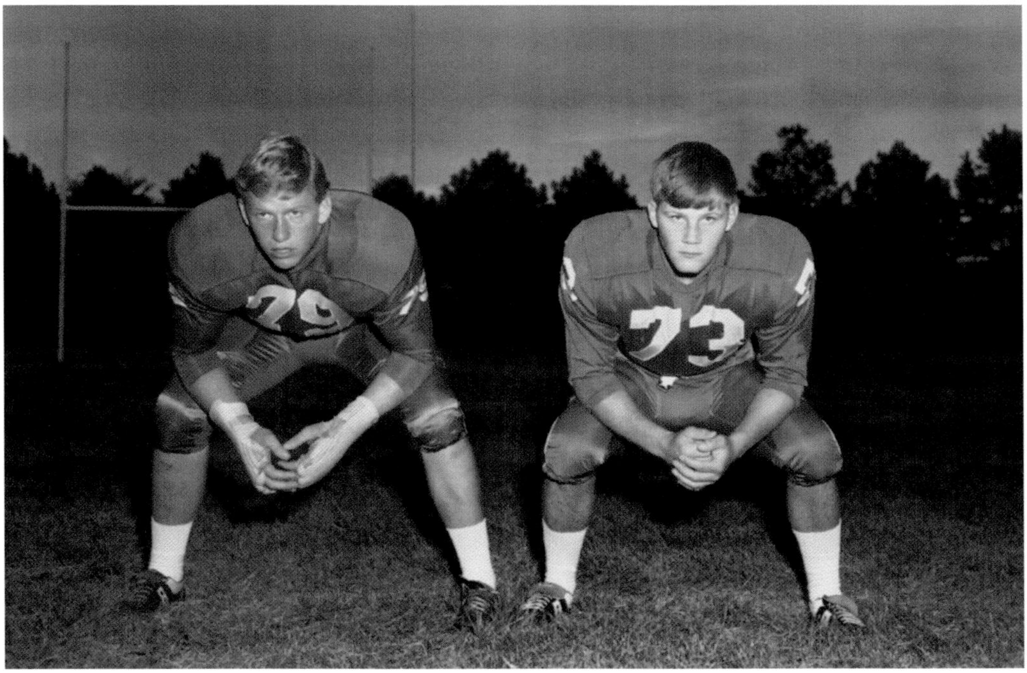

Offensive lineman Dan Klepper (79) and freshman offensive guard Tim McGill (73) pose for a photograph in 1967. Klepper, an Omaha South High graduate, was a four-year letter winner and a two-time all-conference offensive guard during his 1965–1968 football career under Al Caniglia. In 1967, he was an NAIA honorable mention on the All-American team. In 1968, he was named an AP Little All-American. Klepper was drafted by the Kansas City Chiefs because of his speed, agility, and blocking skills. McGill, a Creighton Prep High School graduate, moved to middle linebacker from 1968 to 1970 and led the linebackers with 64 tackles in 1969. Members of the 1970 defense that McGill helped lead were called the "Hatchet Men."

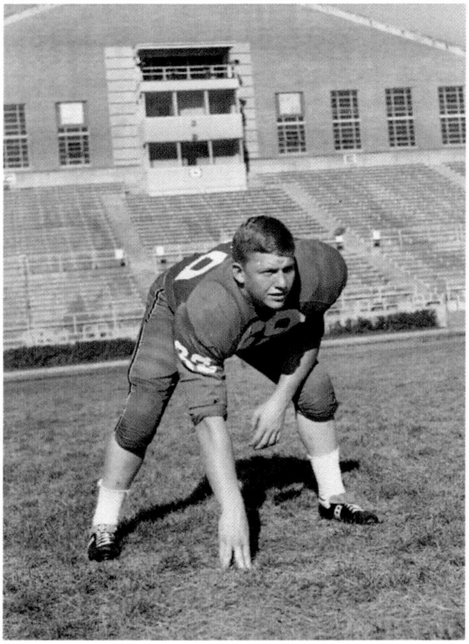

Dan Klepper was described as a six-foot, three-inch, 245-pound offensive lineman. According to a 1971 *Gateway* article, Klepper requested a contingency provision in his contract in which he would receive a bonus if he made the Kansas City Chiefs. But Chiefs coach Hank Stram and Klepper could not reach an agreement, so he missed out on an opportunity to play for the Super Bowl champs. "We couldn't come to terms so I asked that he trade me or release me and he wouldn't do either," said Klepper, who returned and helped coach linemen at Omaha Westside and then taught physical education at UNO. He was offered a contract with Regina in the Canadian Football League but turned it down and instead played for the semiprofessional Omaha Mustangs in 1970. He tried out for the Kansas City Chiefs again in 1971.

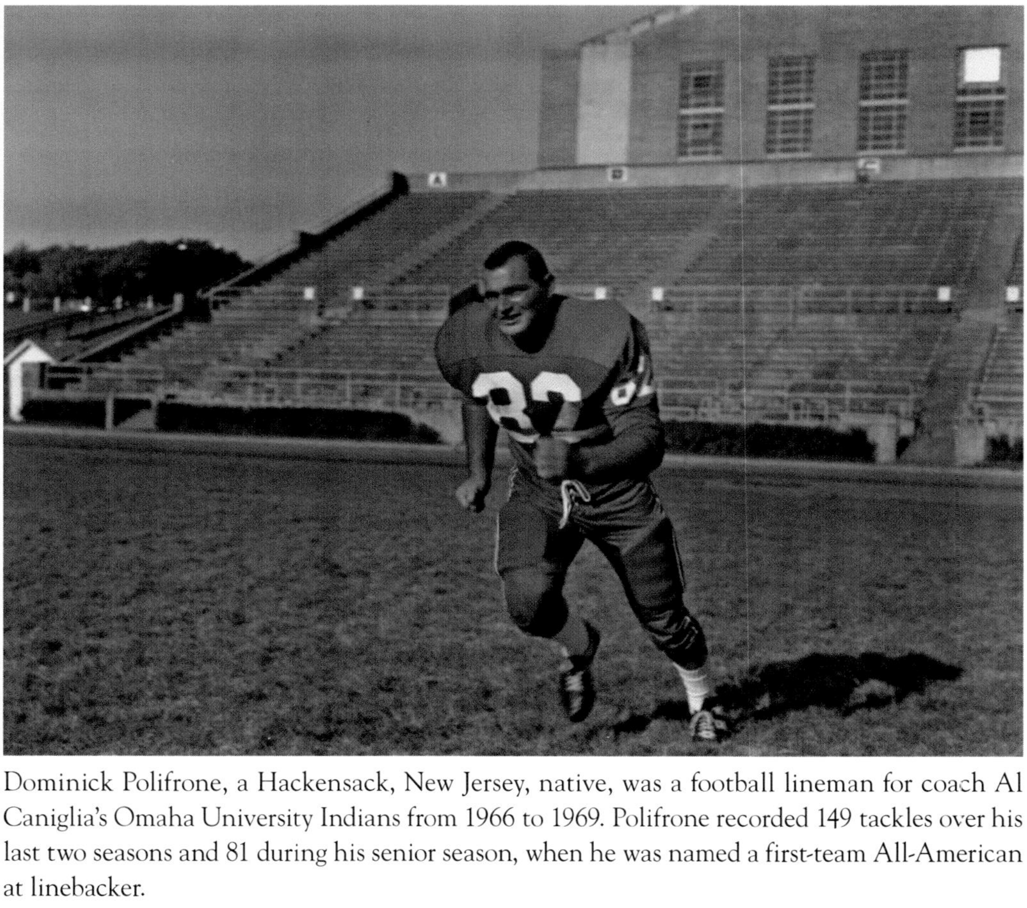

Dominick Polifrone, a Hackensack, New Jersey, native, was a football lineman for coach Al Caniglia's Omaha University Indians from 1966 to 1969. Polifrone recorded 149 tackles over his last two seasons and 81 during his senior season, when he was named a first-team All-American at linebacker.

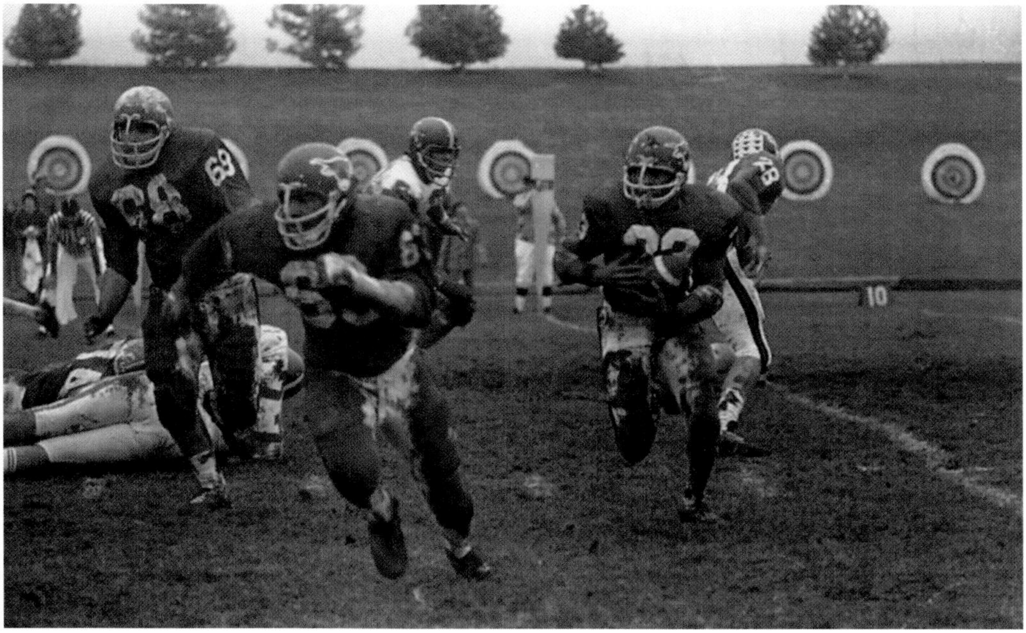

Charlie McWhorter's speed and agility helped him pile up 2,161 yards during his 1969–1972 career as a running back for the Mavericks under coach Al Caniglia. He earned first-team All-American honors in 1972, when he set school records with five touchdowns in a game and a 43.2-yard average on kickoff returns. He also set the career kickoff-return mark, with a 28.3-yard average. The Omaha North High School graduate was just the second UNO player to go over 1,000 yards in a season, when he ran for 1,018 in 1971. He led the Mavericks in rushing again in 1972, with 984 yards and 12 touchdowns.

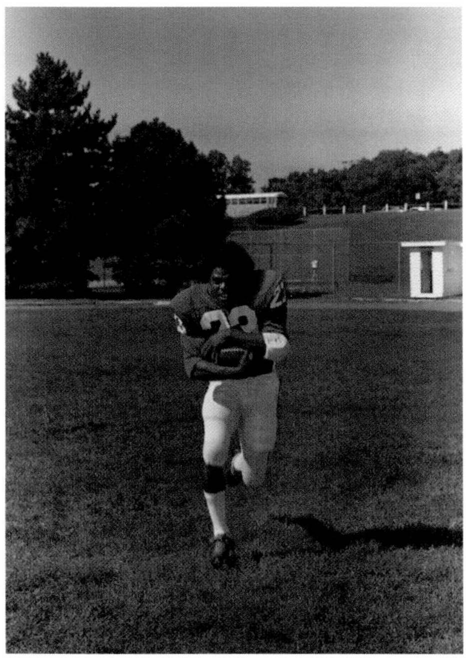

McWhorter, who wore no. 23 during his UNO playing days, is tied for the all-time school record of five touchdowns in a game. It occurred in a 1972 contest against Northwest Missouri State. He also is tied for most points scored in a single game, with 30, in that same game.

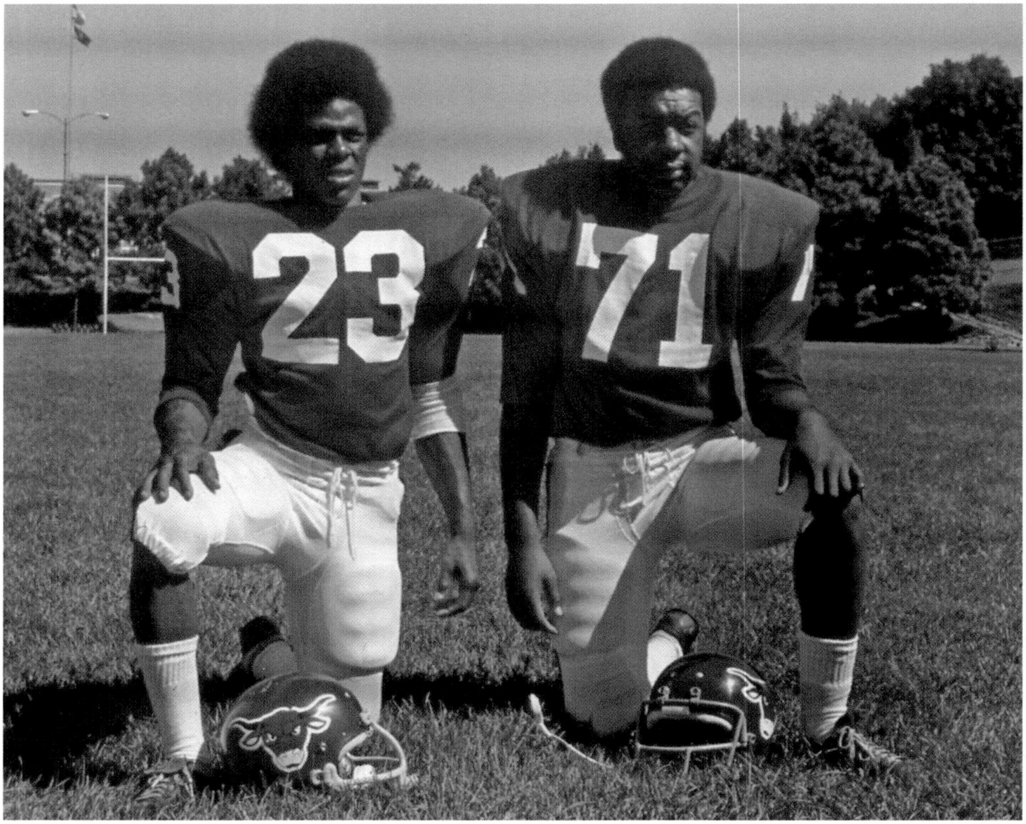

Running back Charlie McWhorter and linebacker Lou King were co-captains of the 1972 UNO football team. The 1972 squad finished 8-2. Its losses were a 6-0 defeat at the hands of Northern Colorado, and a 3-0 loss to Pittsburg State.

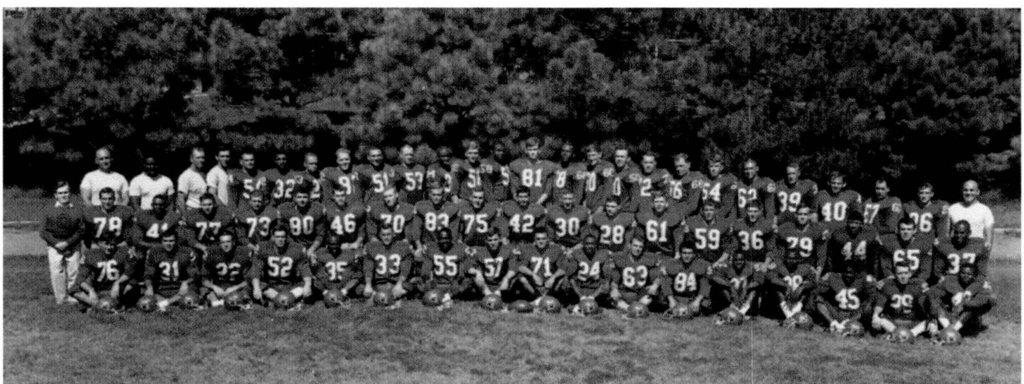

The 1965 Omaha University football team finished 8-2, with losses to Northern Illinois (27-13) and Drake (36-30). Despite those two losses, Omaha University was the CIC champions that season.

Harlan Aden, a Scottsbluff native, was named a second-team Little All-American in 1965. The 215-pound guard was a three-time All-CIC selection. He was able to gain an extra year of eligibility at Omaha University due to an injury suffered at Scottsbluff Junior College.

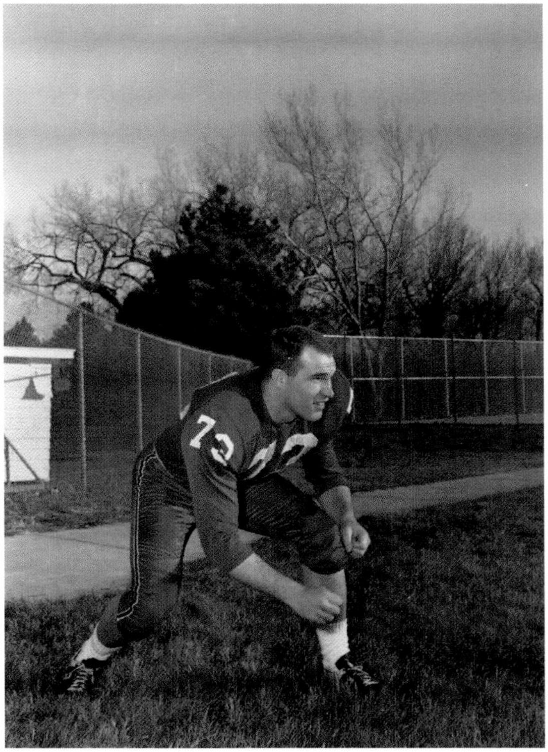

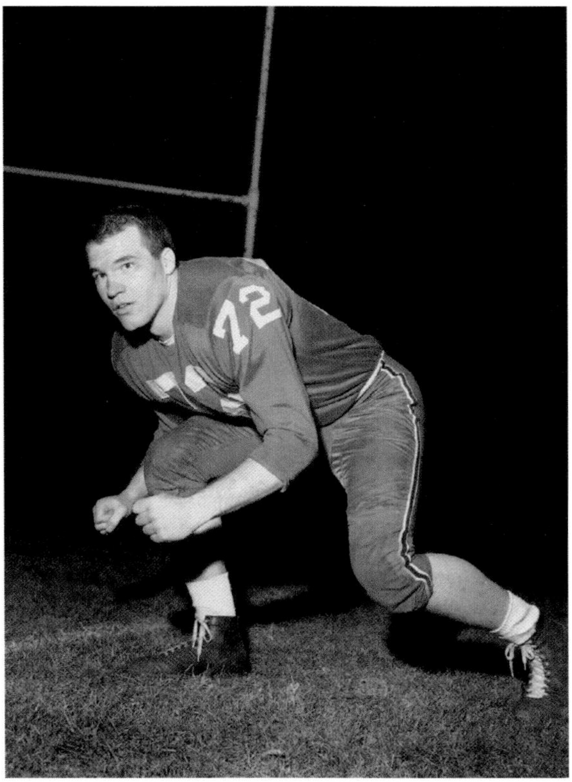

Harlan Aden played football from 1962 to 1965 under Al Caniglia. He led the OU Indians to a 20-8 record during his career, including Central Intercollegiate titles in 1963 and 1965. He served as one of the team captains from 1964 to 1965. In 1965, Aden was named to the AP Small College All-American team as a guard.

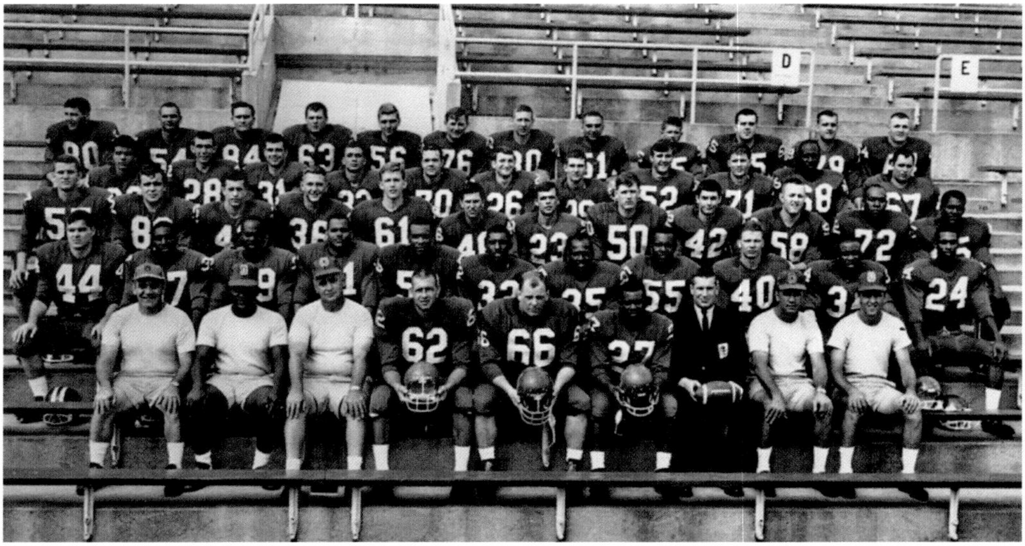

The 1966 team, missing quarterback Marlin Briscoe due to a neck injury, struggled to a 1-9 record. The only victory that year was a 13-0 win over Emporia State. Bill Dodd led the scoring for the year, with 24 points.

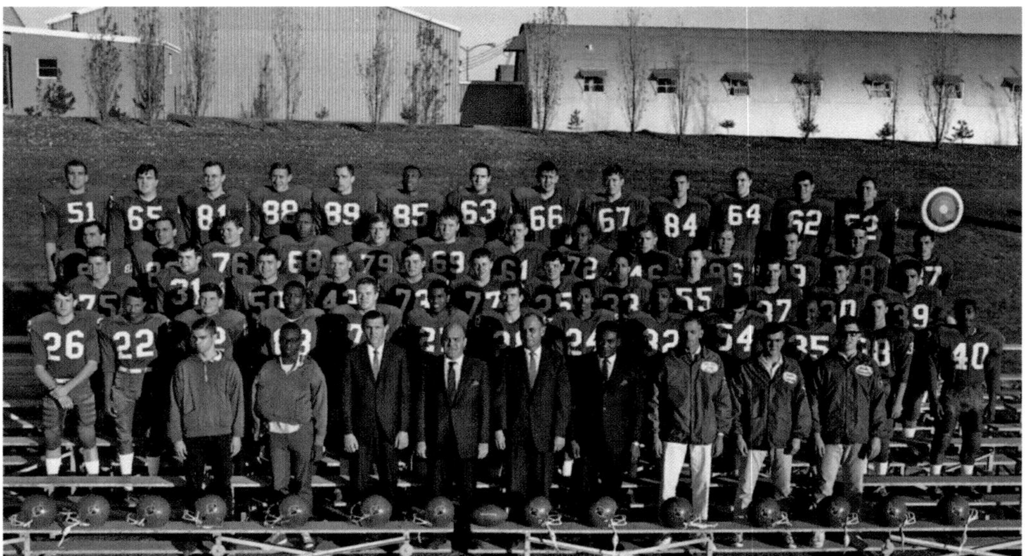

The 1967 season marked the return of quarterback Marlin Briscoe from an injury and resulted in a 7-3 campaign, highlighted by a CIC championship. The Indians won their final five games after dropping contests to Northern Arizona (41-13), Drake (23-15), and North Dakota State (41-33).

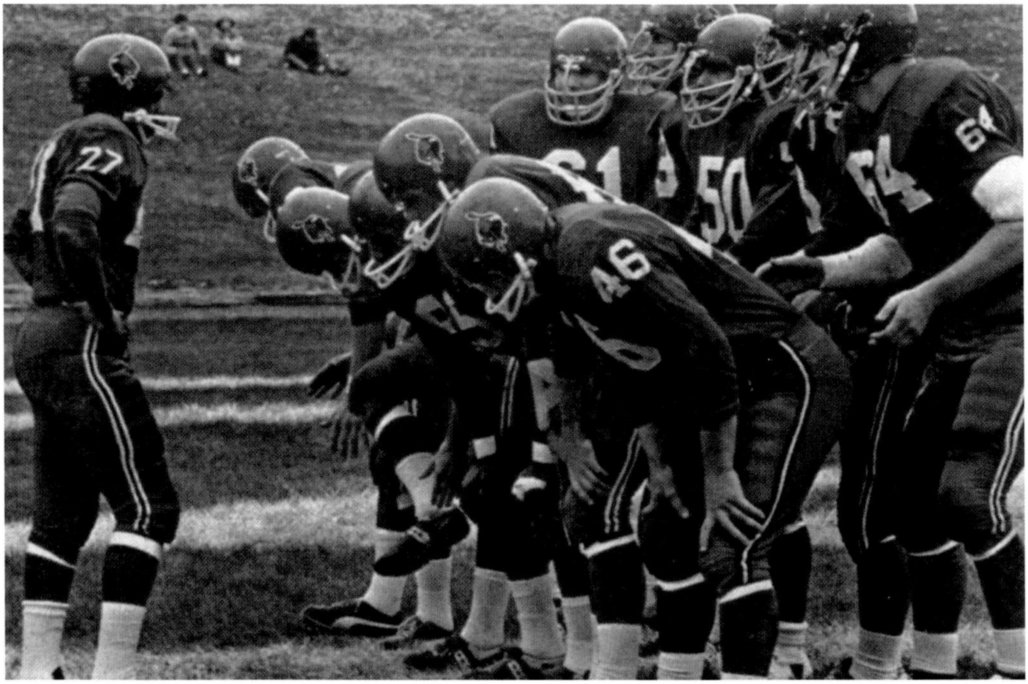

Marlin Briscoe returned to the quarterback spot in 1967 after sitting out the final nine games of 1966. He had suffered a neck injury in the opener at Idaho State. In 1965, Briscoe set Omaha University records for single-season total offense, single-season passing, and touchdown passes in a season. In 1967, he led the Indians to a 7-3 record and the CIC championship.

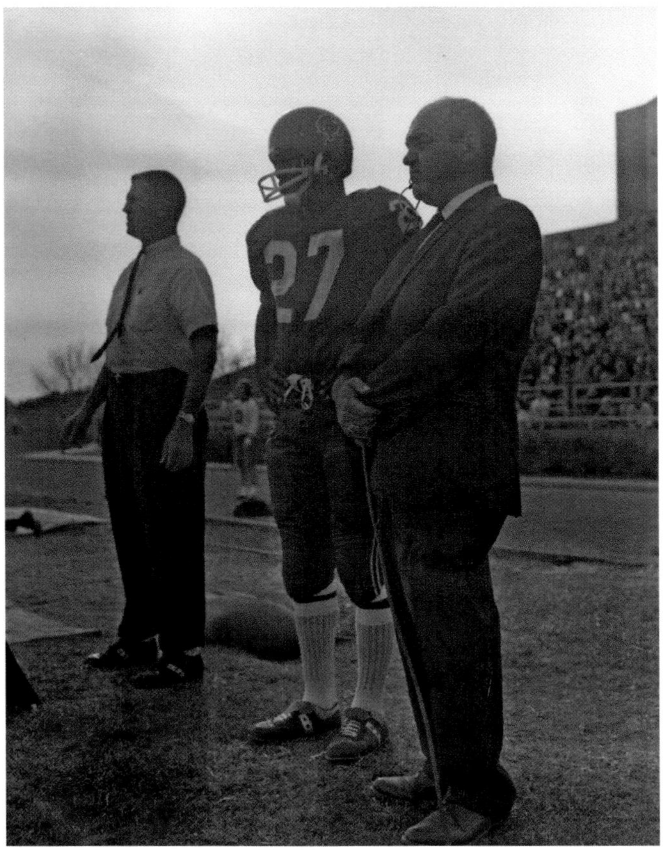

Marlin "The Magician" Briscoe stands with head coach Al Caniglia in 1966. Briscoe was drafted by the Denver Broncos and went on to become the first African American starting quarterback in the NFL.

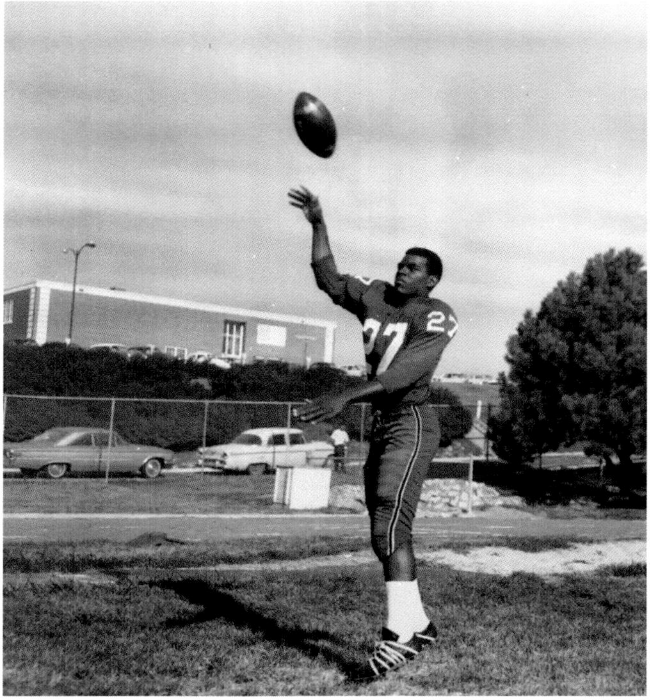

Prior to the 1966 season, Briscoe was a highly touted quarterback for UNO. He broke Carl Meyer's single-season passing record against Emporia State in 1965. Throughout his career, he set more than 20 school records for game, season, and career offensive production.

In his final game—also the final contest for Omaha University before becoming University of Nebraska–Omaha in 1968—Marlin Briscoe threw for 275 yards in a 27-20 win over South Dakota. Briscoe had thrown for 356 yards against North Dakota State in 1967.

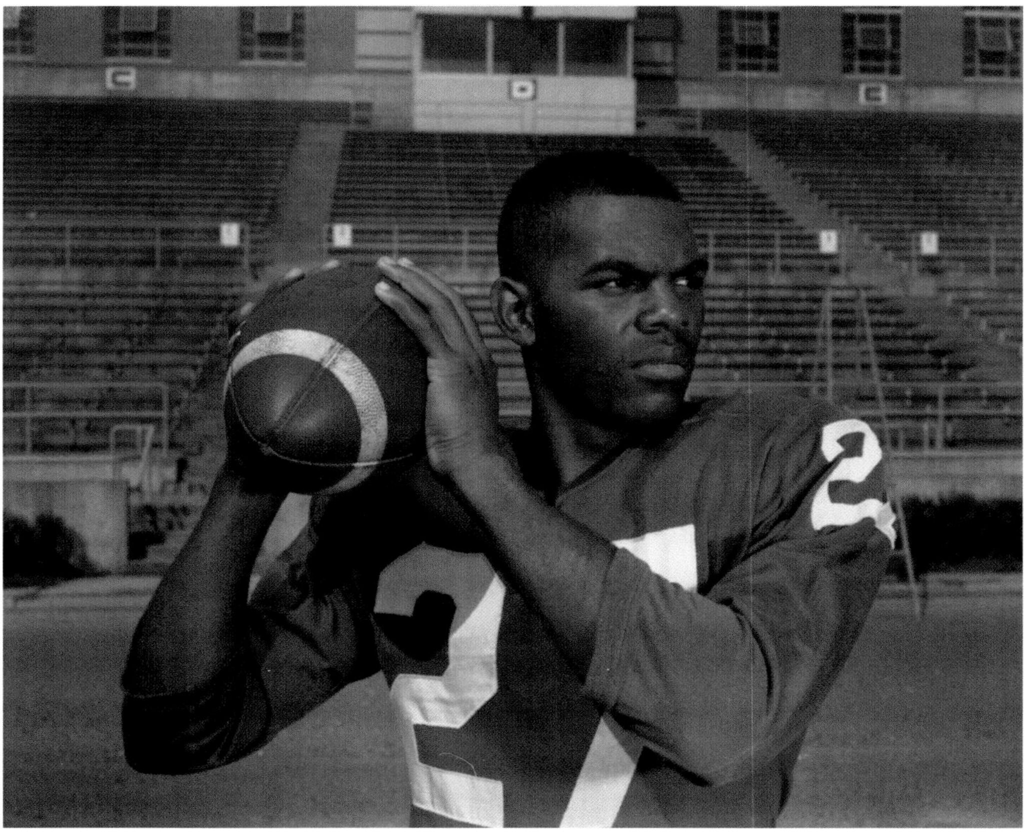

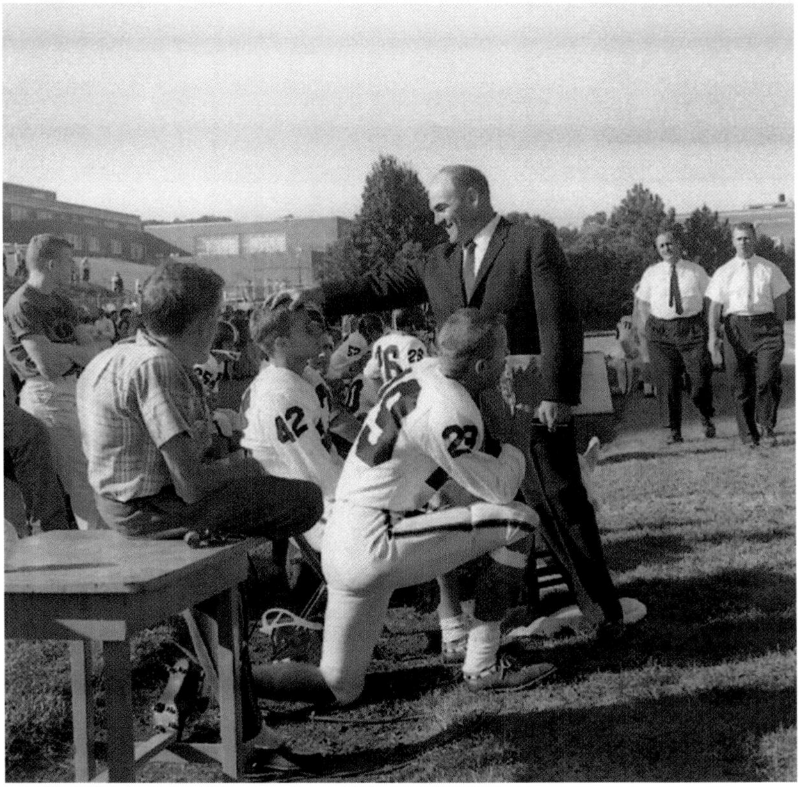

As seen here, head coach Al Caniglia interacted with players during his tenure on the sidelines from 1960 to 1973. At the time of his death in 1973, Caniglia was the all-time winningest UNO coach, with 74 victories. Sandy Buda and Pat Behrns later passed him, but he still ranks third on the all-time chart for victories.

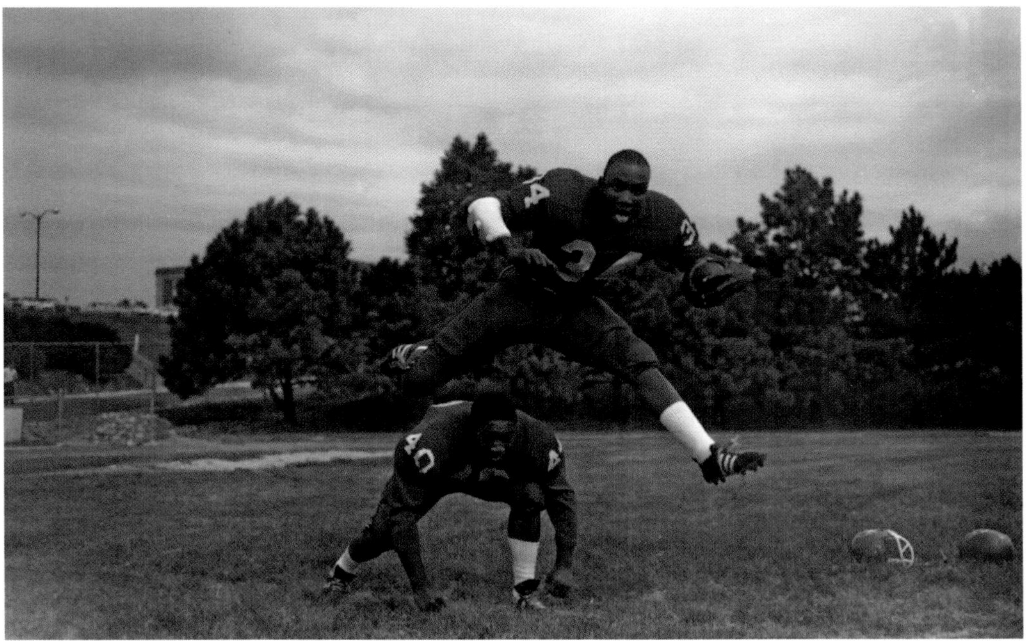

Ron Sayers, the younger brother of UNO alum Roger Sayers and Gale Sayers, was a standout for the Indians. He set the single-season school record with 171 carries, but it was quickly broken by Phil Wise in 1969.

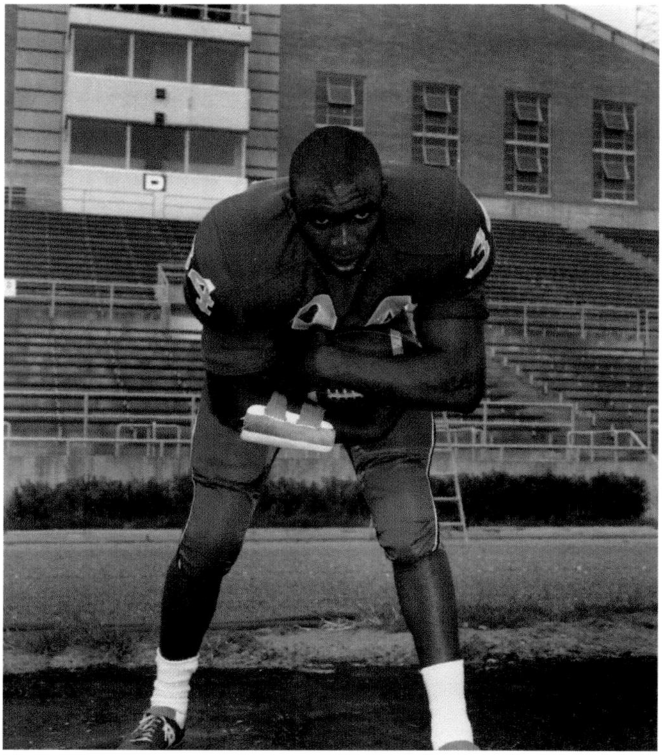

Ron Sayers was the leading rusher for UNO in 1967, with 464 yards and four touchdowns in 10 games, and in 1968 he had 691 yards and six touchdowns. Sayers became the highest-drafted played in UNO history, going in the second round in 1969 to the San Diego Chargers.

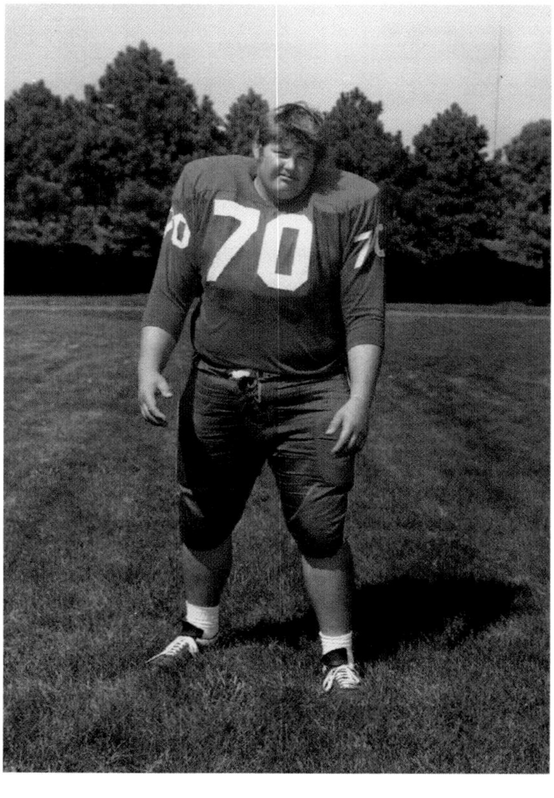

Center Gary Kipfmiller, six-feet, four-inches tall and 340 pounds, was taken in the 16th round of the 1972 NFL draft by the New York Jets. He was also a national wrestling champion for the Mavericks.

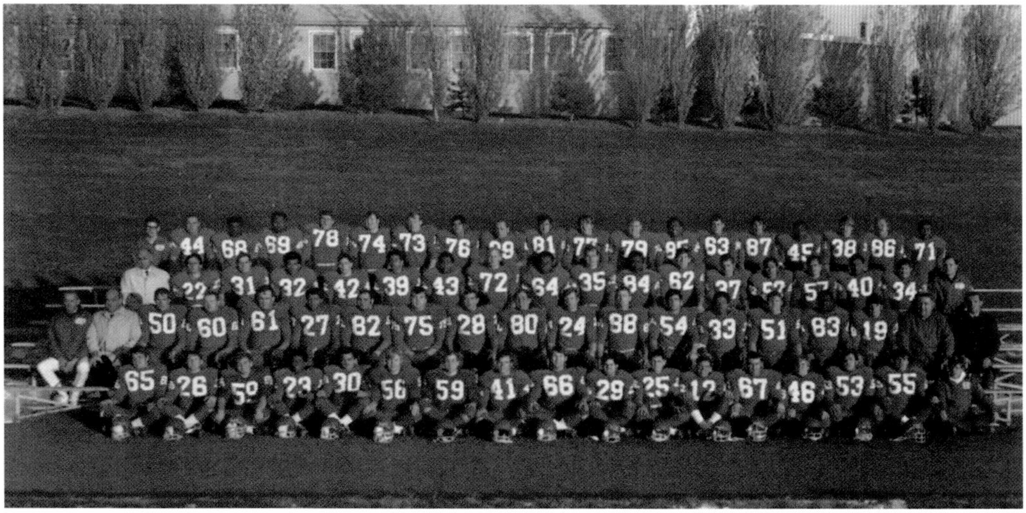

The 1969 Mavericks, in their second season as UNO, finished 3-6. The Mavs defeated Pittsburg State 25-14, Fort Hays State 28-20, and South Dakota 26-16.

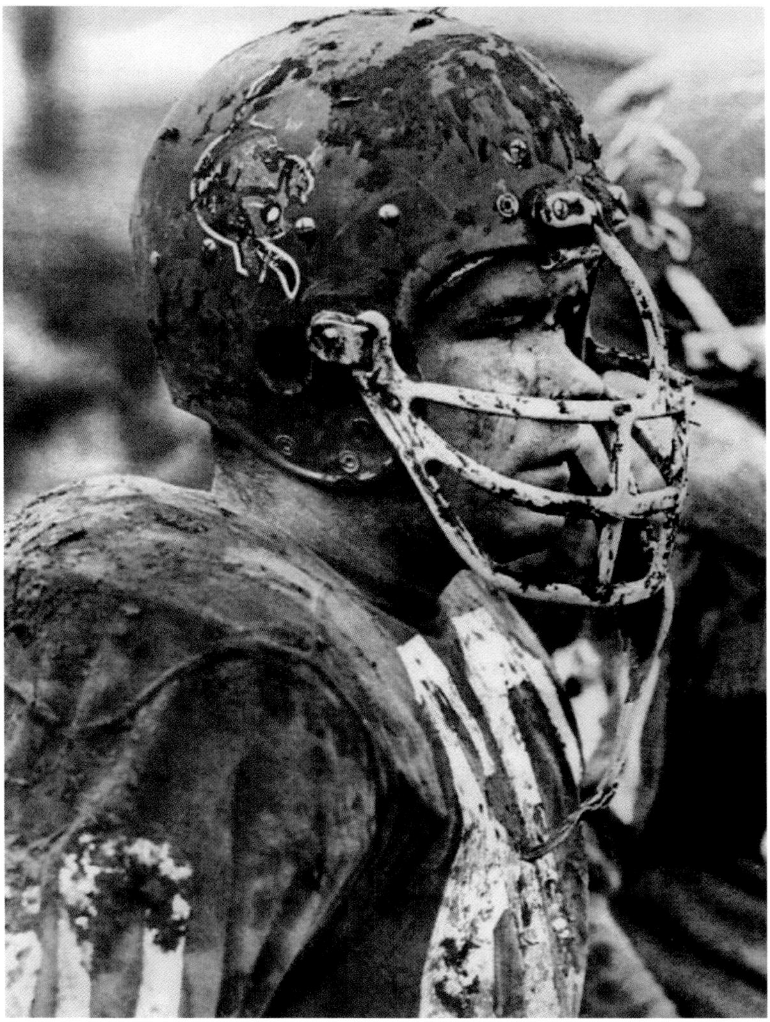

Tom McGinn was a junior linebacker in 1968. The Omaha Cathedral standout played all four seasons for the Mavericks.

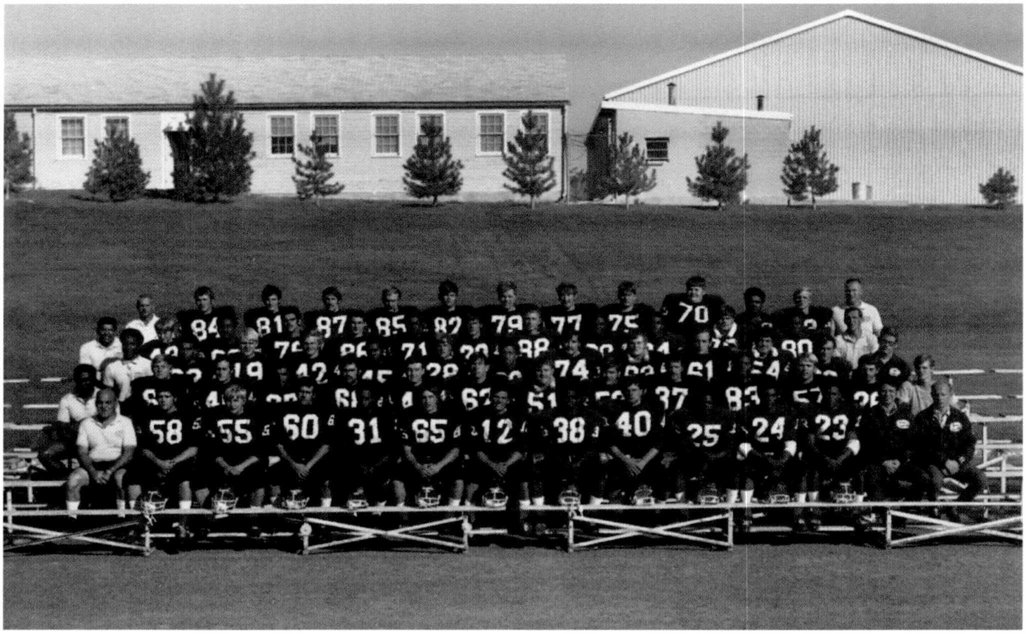

The 1970 UNO football team struggled to a 4-5-1 record. The Mavericks improved throughout the season, however, going 3-1-1 down the stretch.

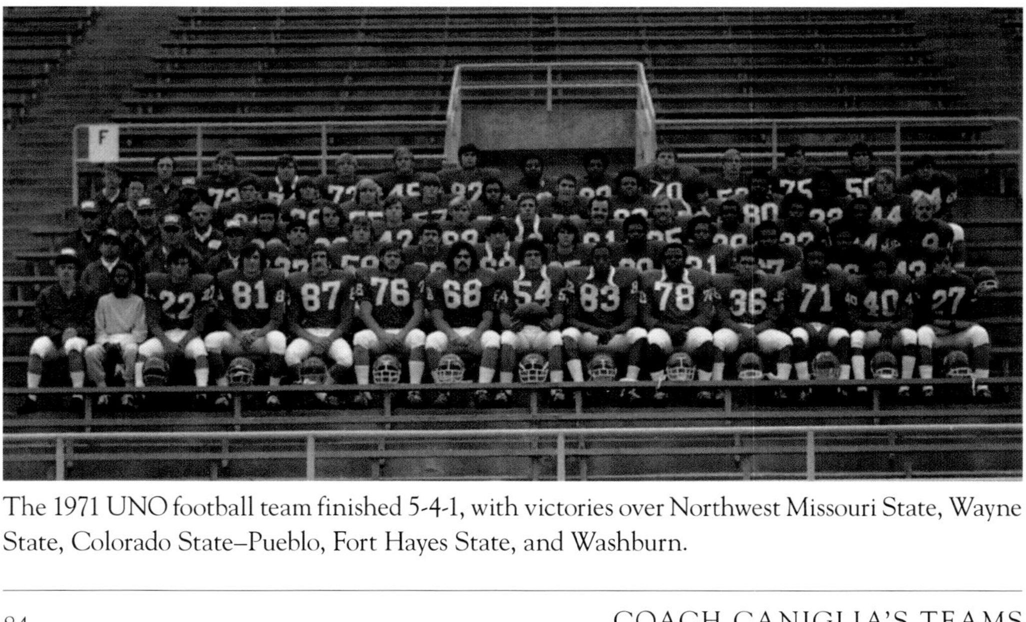

The 1971 UNO football team finished 5-4-1, with victories over Northwest Missouri State, Wayne State, Colorado State–Pueblo, Fort Hayes State, and Washburn.

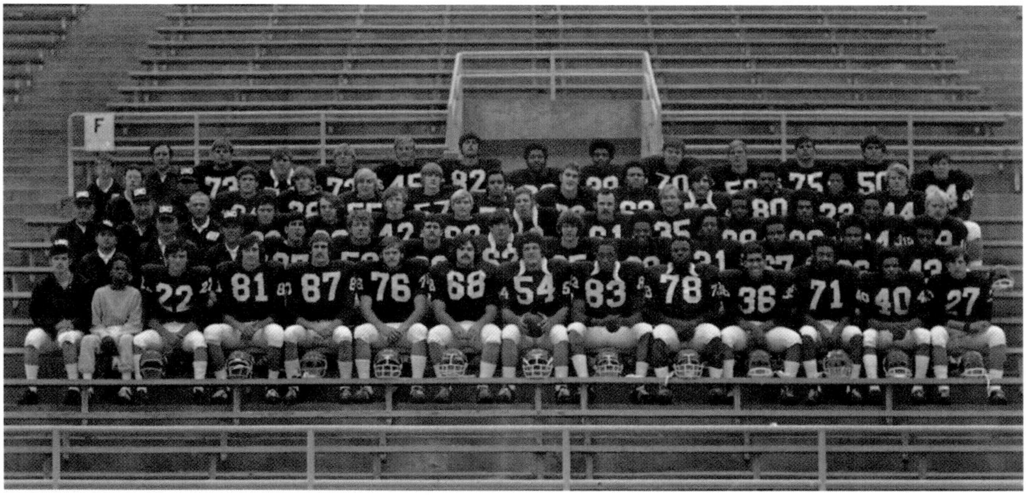

The 1972 UNO football squad was coach Al Caniglia's final team. The Mavericks finished 8-2, with losses to Northern Colorado (6-0) and Emporia State (17-7).

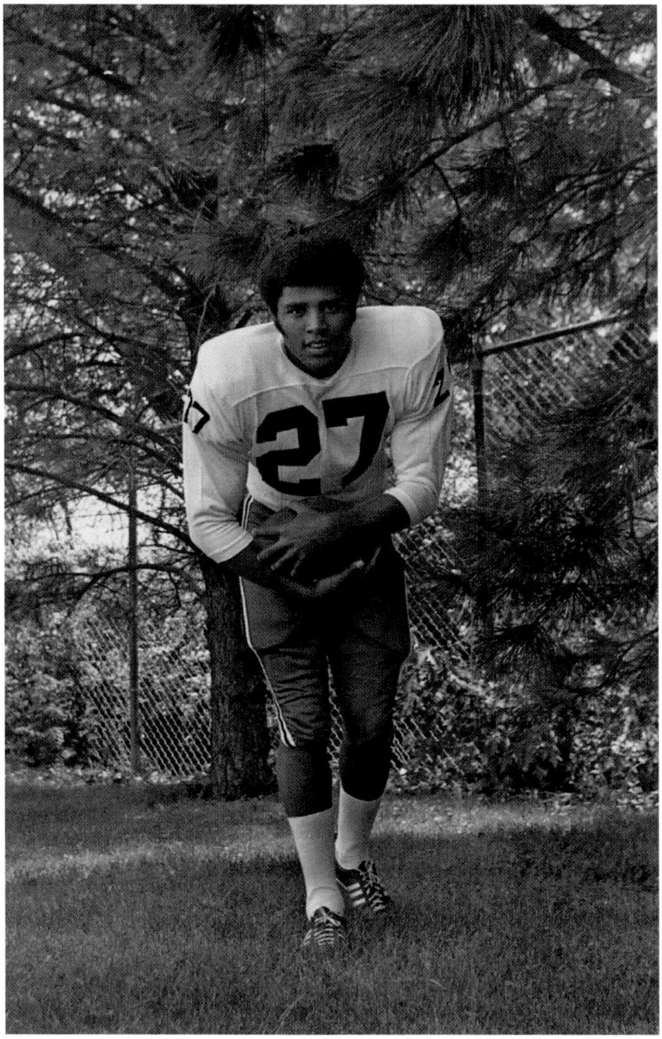

Phil Wise played behind Ron Sayers in 1967 and 1968, but after Sayers graduated, Wise took over as the leading rusher and scorer for the Mavericks in 1969 and 1970. He amassed 1,146 yards and 15 total touchdowns as a junior and 983 yards and 13 touchdowns as a senior. Wise remains in the top-10 career and single-season charts in several rushing and scoring categories. He was drafted in the sixth round of the 1971 NFL draft by the New York Jets.

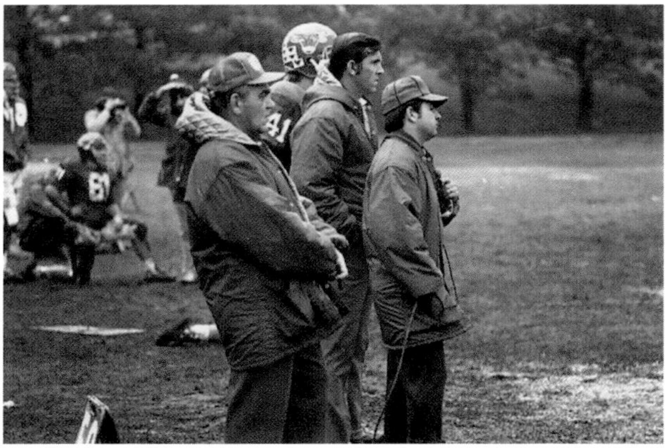

Al Caniglia (front) watches from the sidelines in 1972 as the Mavericks finished 8-2. Their only losses were to Northern Colorado and Emporia State. Caniglia finished with a .571 winning percentage. At the time of his death, he was the winningest football coach in school history. UNO decided to honor Caniglia by naming its football field after him.

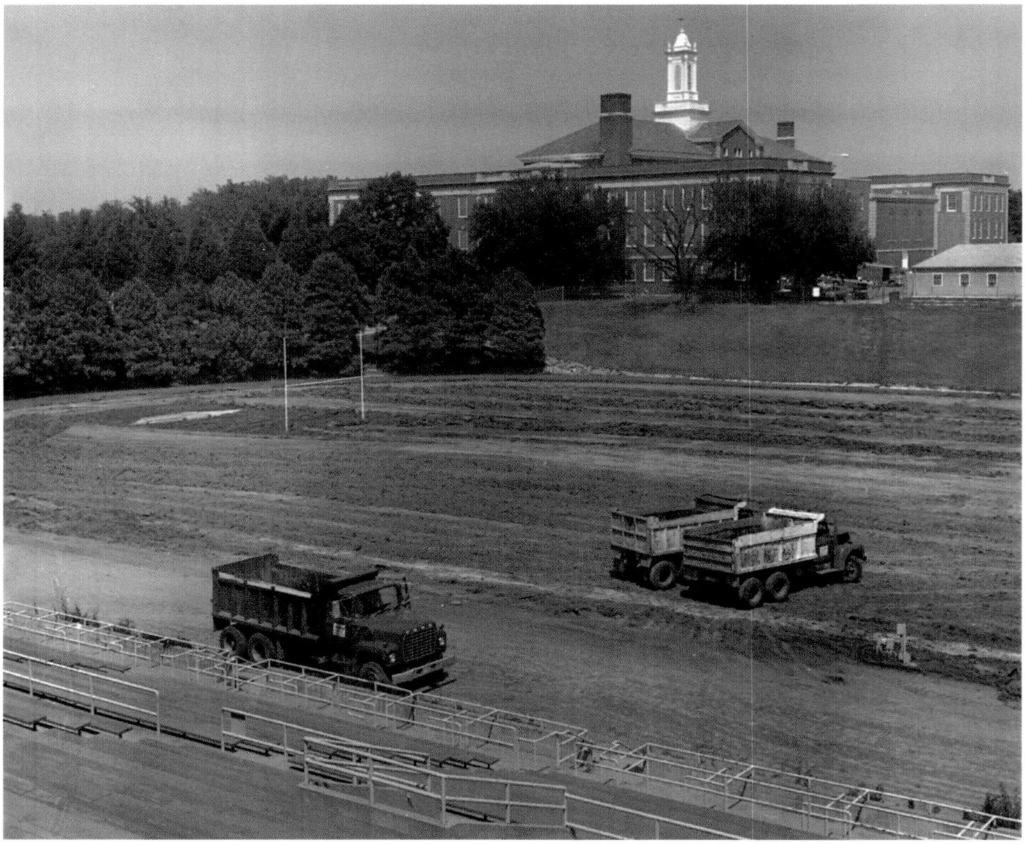

UNO made a major step in upgrading its facilities in 1973, with the switch from natural grass to artificial turf, installation of a new track around the football field, and the addition of lights. The changes coincided with UNO leaving the Great Plains Athletic Conference and returning to NCAA Division II status. Regarding the construction at the stadium, "The new turf and lighting will play a helpful role in the recruiting of athletics for all sports," coach Al Caniglia told the *Gateway* as he began his 14th and final season as the head coach of the Mavericks. During the construction, UNO's first games of the 1973 season with Jackson State and Angelo State were played at Rosenblatt Stadium.

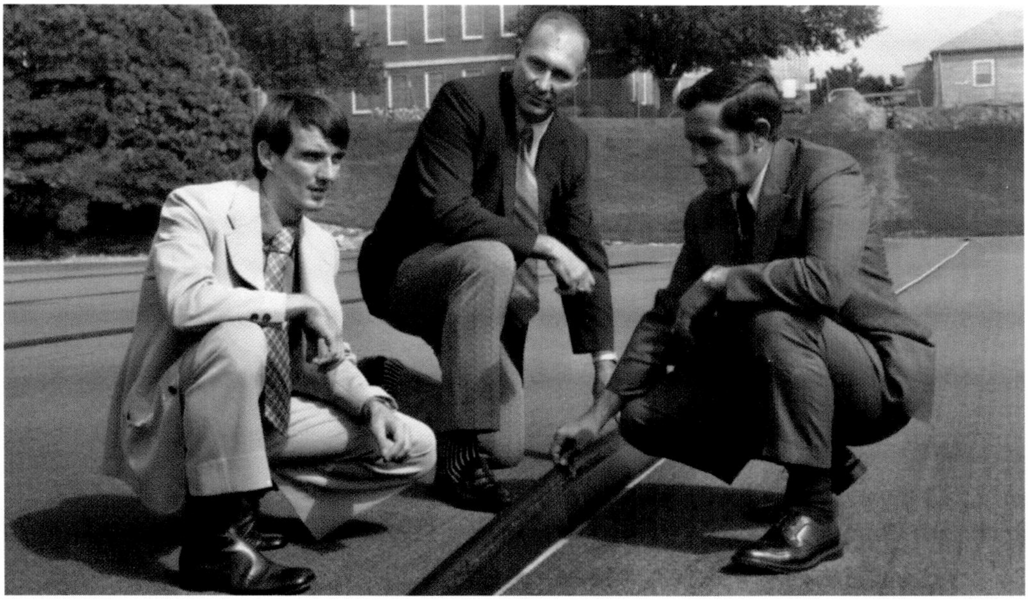

Seen here inspecting the AstroTurf project are, from left to right, Dr. Richard Flynn, director of the School of Health, Physical Education, and Recreation; athletic director Clyde Biggers; and Dr. Rex Engebretson, assistant to the chancellor for planning. "It will be a facility in which the University community can take great pride," Engebretson told the *Gateway*.

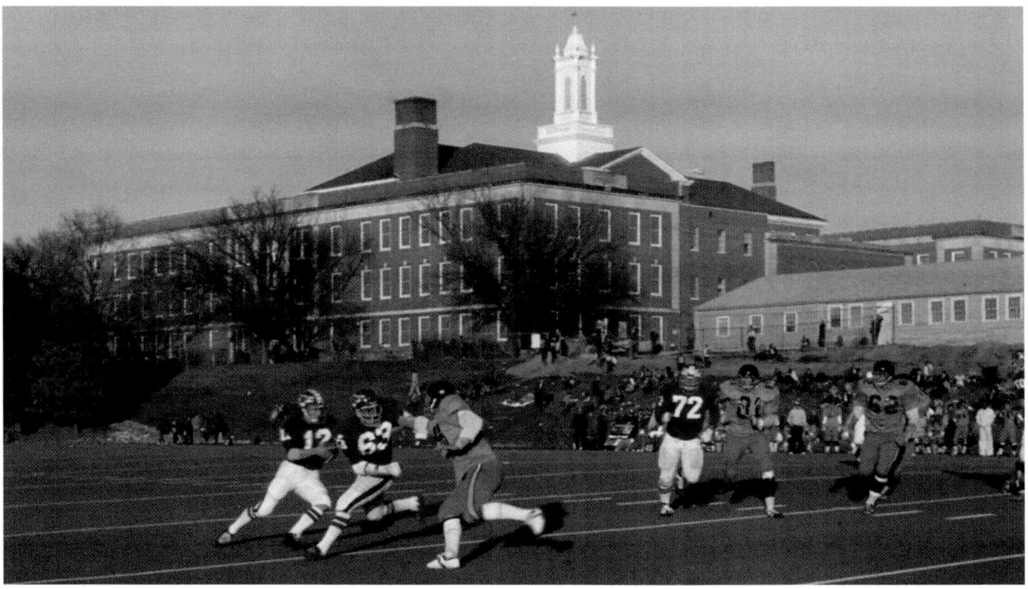

The stadium improvements were supposed to be done in time for the homecoming game against Northern Colorado in October, but delays occurred. The only game in 1973 played at the UNO stadium was the contest against University of Wisconsin–Milwaukee on November 17. Quarterback Bob Bangston (12) carries the ball against UW-Milwaukee. For the season finale and the debut of the AstroTurf field, 6,121 fans overflowed the 4,200-capacity stadium. The Mavericks defeated the Panthers 28-13 and finished the season 7-2-1.

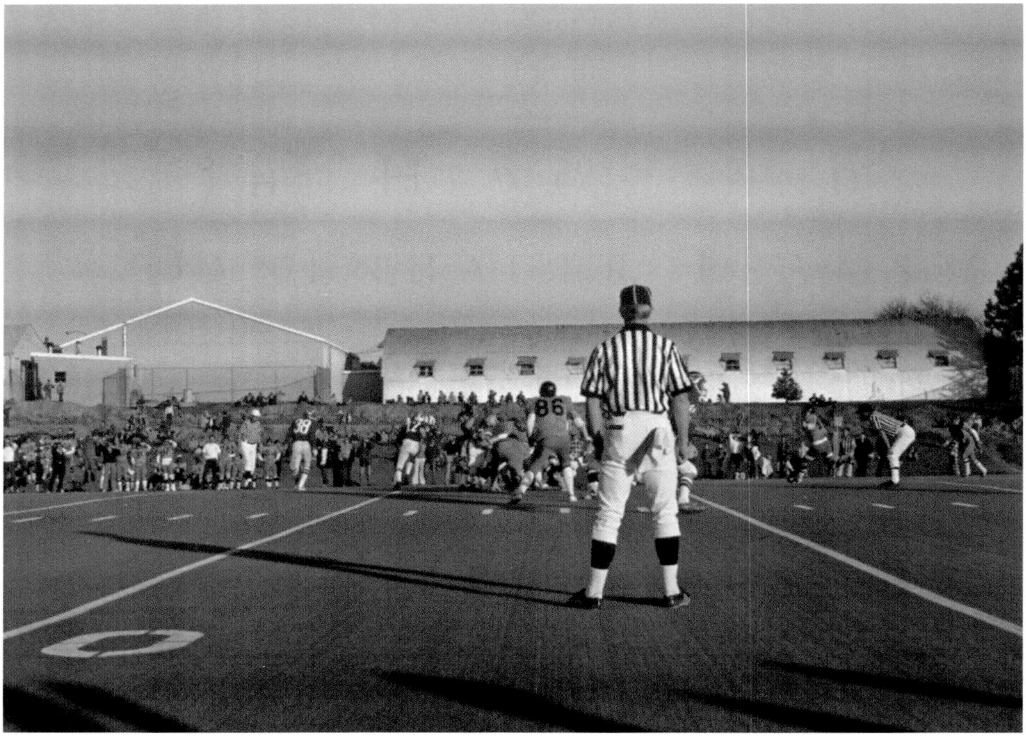

The Mavericks run a sweep play against UW-Milwaukee with Syracuse, New York, native Saul Ravenell (38) acting as a decoy. He stole the show for the Mavericks, rushing 33 times for 211 yards. It was his third straight game of more than 200 yards. He broke Phil Wise's single-season rushing record. Ravenell also broke the school's single-season scoring record, with 92 points. His 15 total touchdowns tied a single-season school mark. The next season, Ravenell became the school's all-time career rushing leader, with 2,346 yards; he ranks eighth all-time.

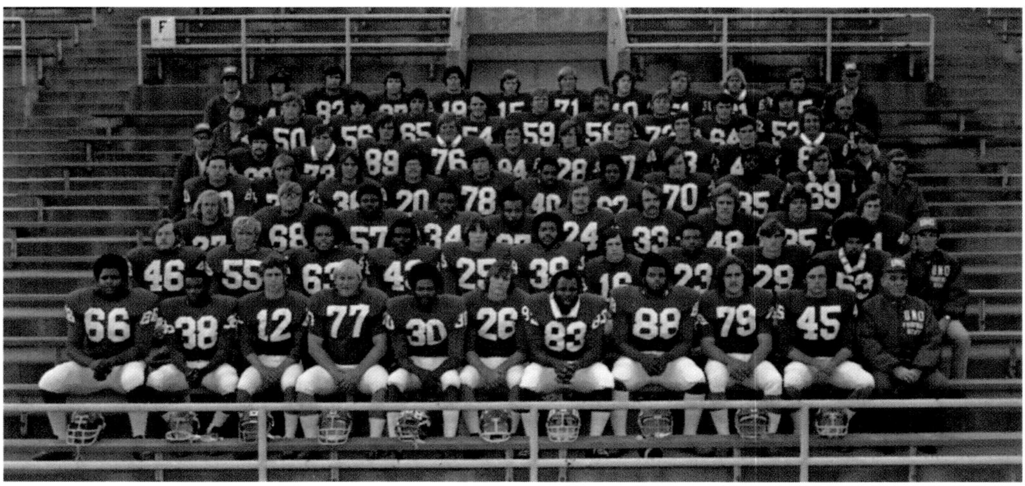

The 1973 football team turned out to be Al Caniglia's final squad. He suddenly died of a heart attack on February 19, 1974, at the age of 52. The Mavericks finished 7-2-1 in their first season in NCAA Division II after a period in the NAIA.

6

The Hewgly and Danenhauer Teams

Following the death of longtime head coach Al Caniglia in February 1974, UNO athletic director Clyde Biggers chose to go outside the program, hiring as the next coach C.T. Hewgley.

Hewgley grew up in Nashville, Tennessee, and enlisted in the Army in time to drive a tank during World War II. He was a second-team All-American at Wyoming his final year and graduated in 1950. Hewgley left the Army in 1967 after 25 years of active and reserve duty. He went to the University of Miami, where he served as the head coach of the freshman team. From 1971 to 1973, he was the offensive line coach at Wyoming. His wife had been transferred to Omaha for her job, so he decided to apply for the position. "It really was a perfect situation," Hewgley told the Gateway in 1974. "My wife already was here."

Hewgley tried to implement a veer offense and then switched back to an I offense, but the Mavericks scored more than 10 points only once all season. "After only the third game of the season, Hewgley had demoralized most of the team," the *Gateway* wrote. "The players did not know Hewgley when he arrived and they were in a precarious position of trying to impress him and get to know him," offensive coordinator Noel Martin told the *Gateway*. "Being a newcomer definitely was a handicap, particularly in communication."

Hewgley lasted just one season in Omaha before he was fired by Don Leahy following a 3-7 season. "We played below par for much of the season and that 75-0 loss to Jackson State was a real blow to everyone involved with the football program here," said Bill Danenhauer, who went on to be the next coach. "It's too bad to see him go, but there's nothing I can do about it. He was in the wrong place at the wrong time."

Most of the UNO players signed a petition expressing their support of Danenhauer being promoted to head coach. Don Leahy honored their wishes in naming the five-year defensive coordinator the new head coach for 1975. Despite the players' support, he failed to achieve a winning season in any of his three years at the helm, going 2-8 in 1975, 3-8 in 1976, and 3-6-2 in 1977.

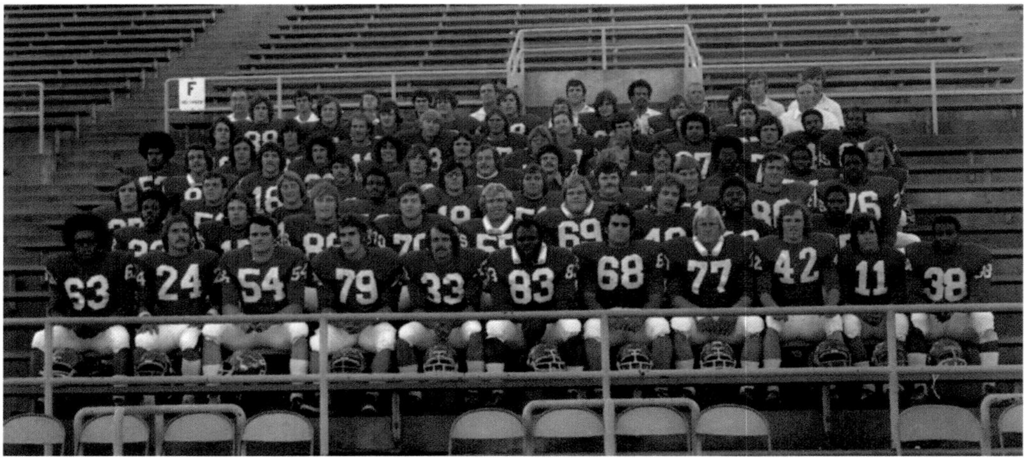

The 1974 UNO football team returned 36 letter winners from the 7-2-1 squad of 1973, but the new coaching staff and players did not click, and the team struggled to a 3-7 mark.

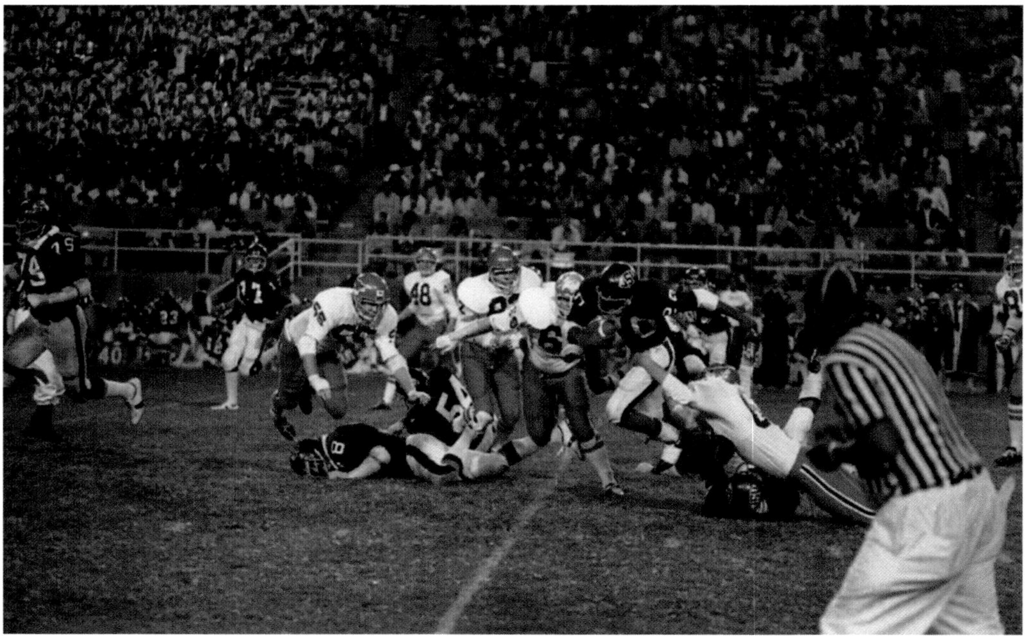

UNO was no match for Jackson State, suffering a 75-0 loss to Walter Payton and company. The Mavericks hurt themselves with nine turnovers, and Payton rushed for 188 yards and six touchdowns in this particular game. His running-back teammates, including Joe Lowery and Rickey Young, also went on to the NFL. It was the second time UNO had faced Payton, who ran for 115 yards and caught four passes for 72 yards in a 17-0 win at Rosenblatt Stadium in 1973. The 1973 Jackson squad was the first predominantly African American team UNO played.

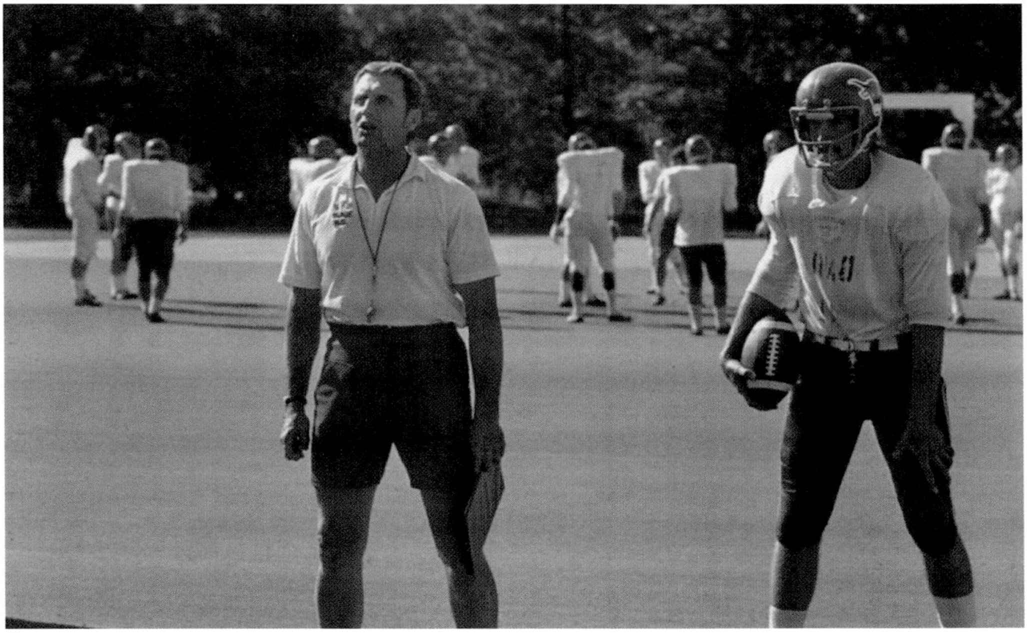

C.T. Hewgley conducts practice before the 1974 season. After being fired by UNO, he was the recruiting coordinator for Michigan State (1976–1979) and offensive line coach at Arizona State (1980–1982). He was then the defensive line coach with the Kansas City Chiefs (1983–1988).

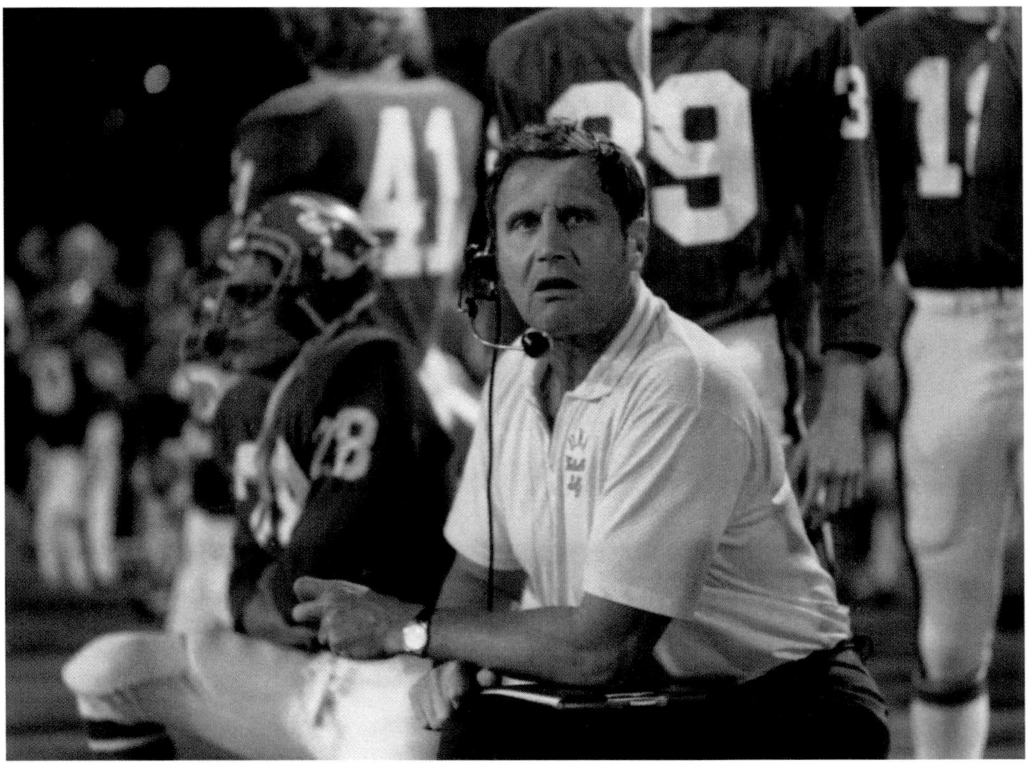

Coach Hewgley watches from the sidelines as the Mavericks struggle to move the ball offensively.

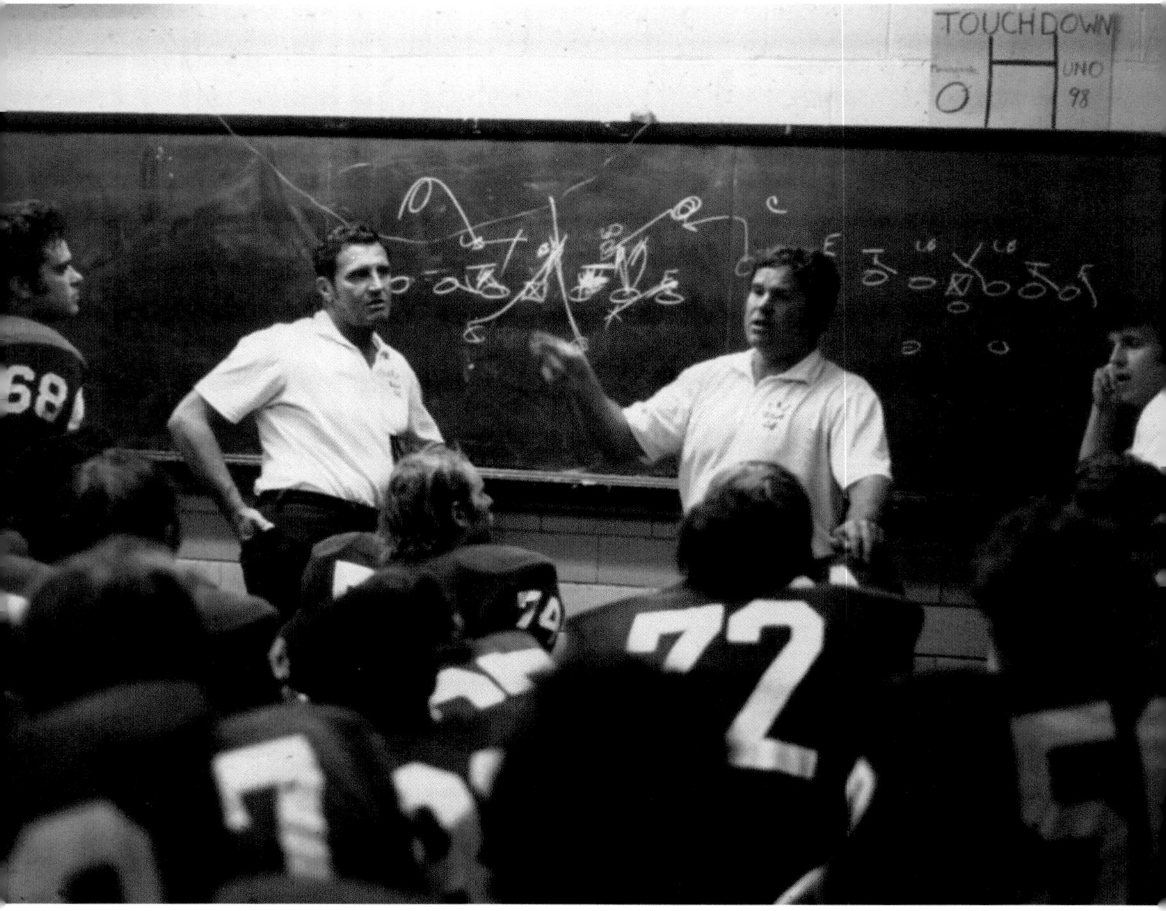

C.T. Hewgley (left) listens as one of his assistant coaches addresses the team at halftime of the Morningside game, which UNO won 31-21.

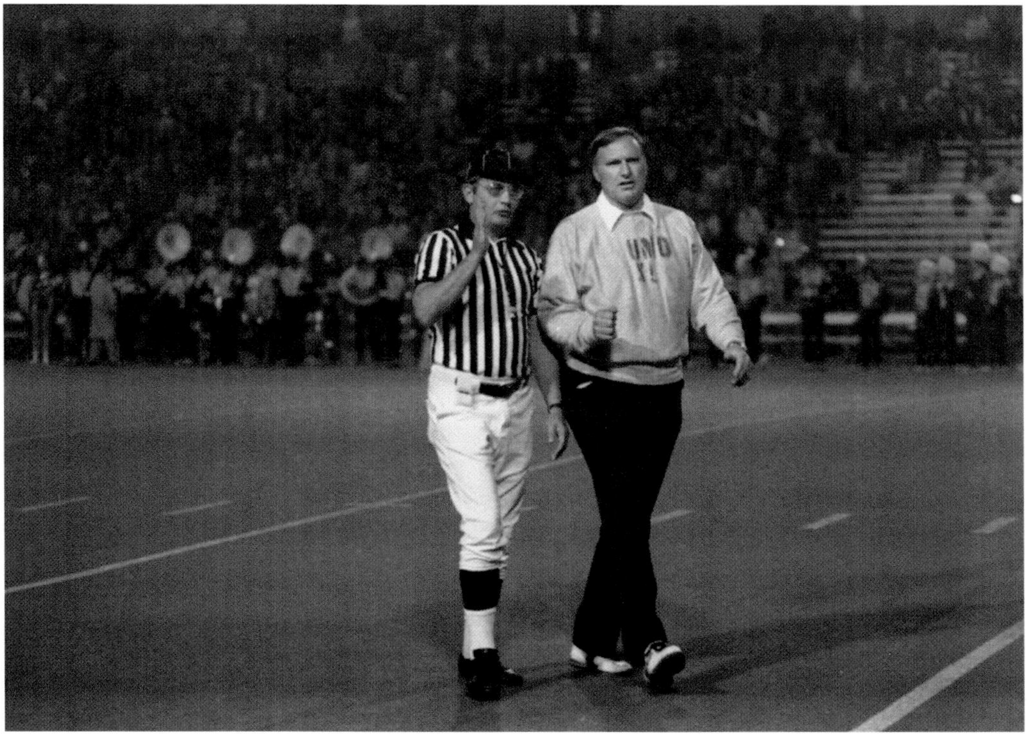

Bill Danenhauer, who had served for five years as a defensive coordinator under Al Caniglia and Hewgley, was elevated to head coach for the 1975 season.

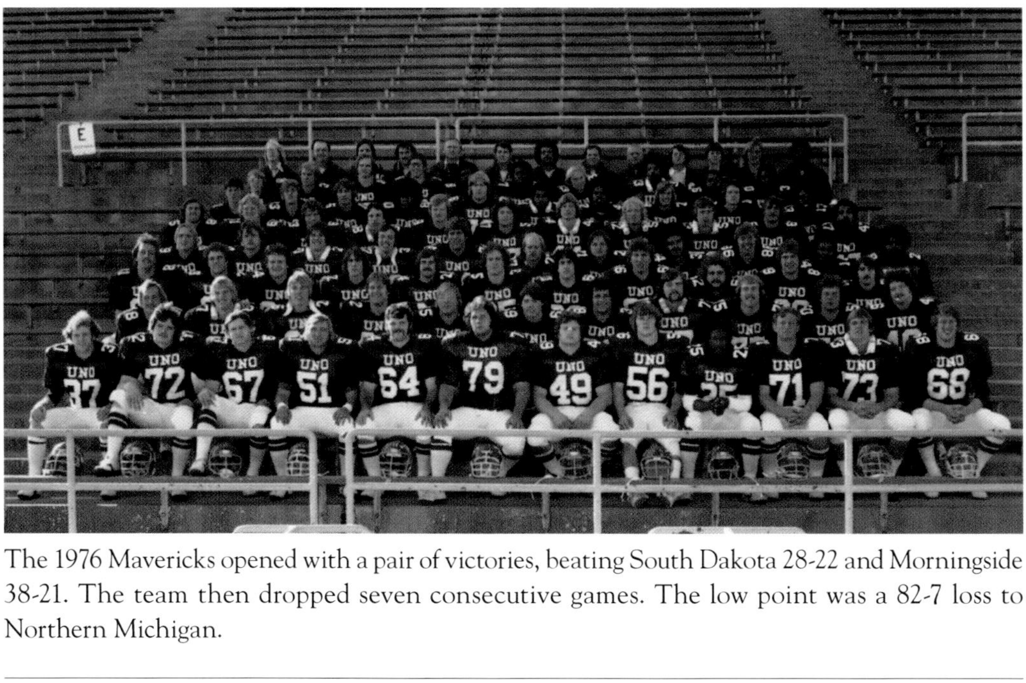

The 1976 Mavericks opened with a pair of victories, beating South Dakota 28-22 and Morningside 38-21. The team then dropped seven consecutive games. The low point was a 82-7 loss to Northern Michigan.

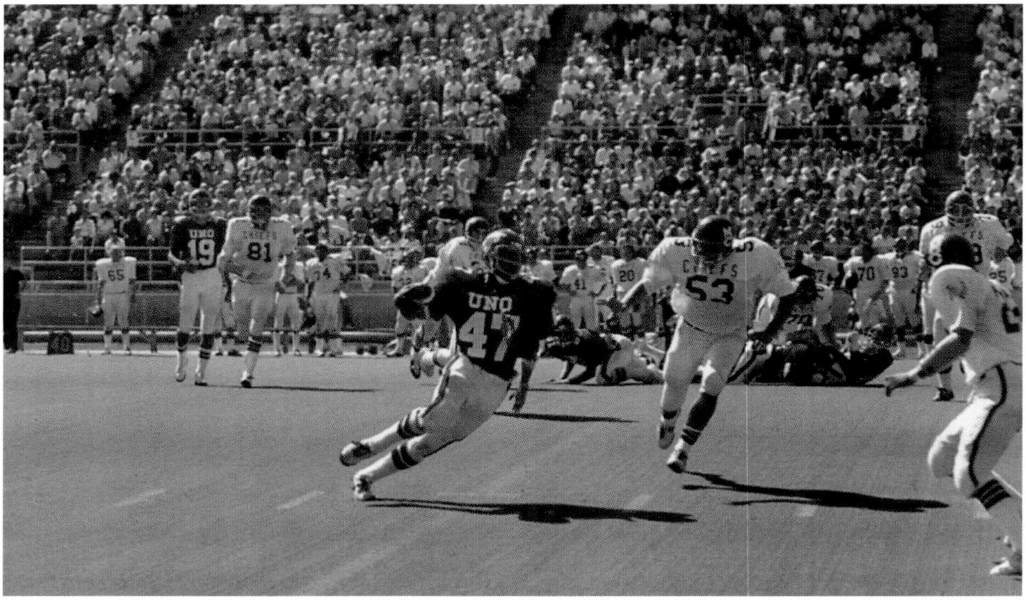

Clarence Elliott carries the ball for the Mavericks against Morningside College. Elliott led UNO in rushing in 1975 with 302 yards and five touchdowns and in 1976 with 852 rushing yards and six touchdowns.

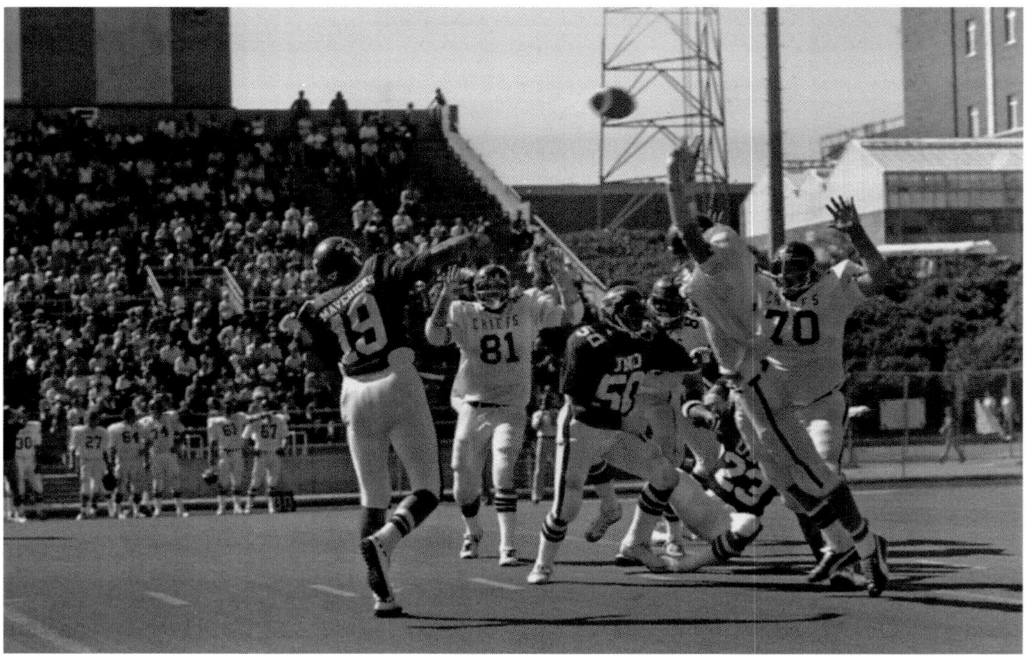

Quarterback John Smolsky delivers a pass against Morningside. Smolsky threw for 2,682 yards, which ranks second all-time for a single season at the school. He also threw 22 touchdown passes, which ranks third at UNO. Smolsky amassed 2,477 yards of total offense, including 371 against UNLV. His 3,903 career passing yards and 31 touchdown passes rank eighth all-time on the career charts.

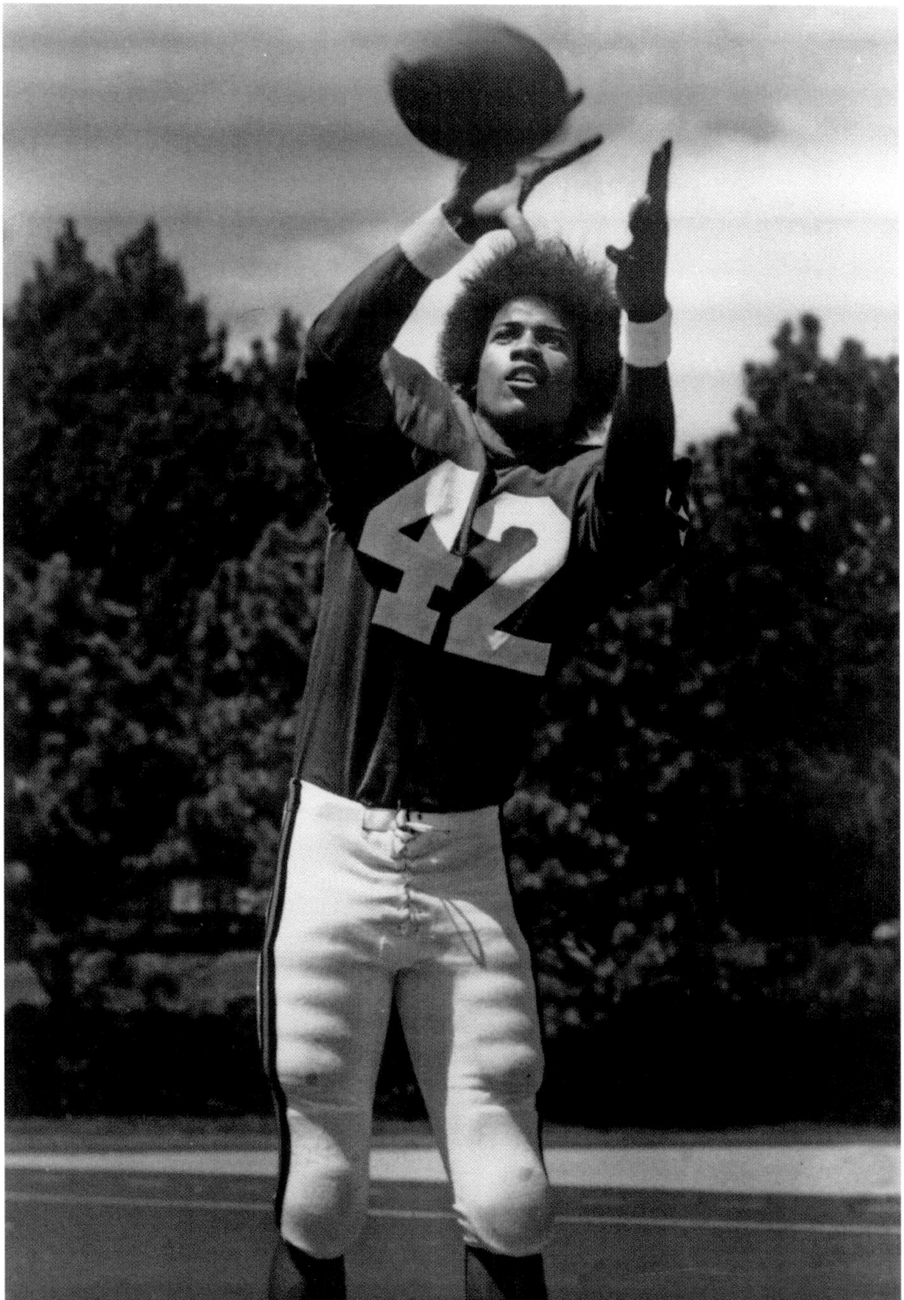

Danny Fulton was a favorite target of Smolsky, as he hauled in 67 catches for 1,581 yards and 16 touchdowns in 1976 to earn All-American honors. Fulton also led UNO in receiving yards in 1975 with 554 yards and six touchdowns. In 1977, he had 604 yards and four touchdowns. Fulton is UNO's all-time career receiving yards leader (2,739) and receptions leader (152), and he is second in career touchdowns (26). Fulton's top receiving game came in 1976, when he had a school-best 317 receiving yards on 10 catches against South Dakota.

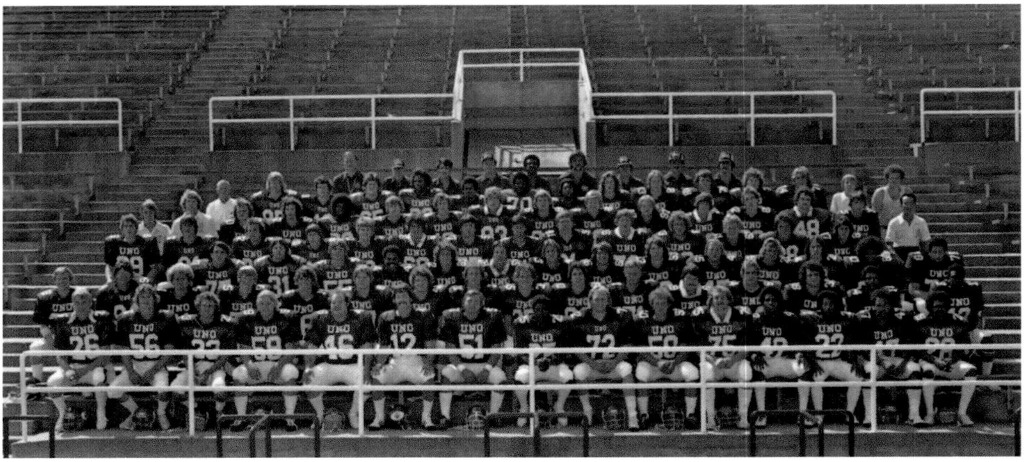

The 1977 UNO football team was more competitive. The school rejoined the North Central Conference, but the team finished 3-6-2, and Danenhauer was let go. In Fulton's final game, against Northern Arizona, he had a school-best 13 receptions. He was drafted in the third round in 1978 by the Buffalo Bills.

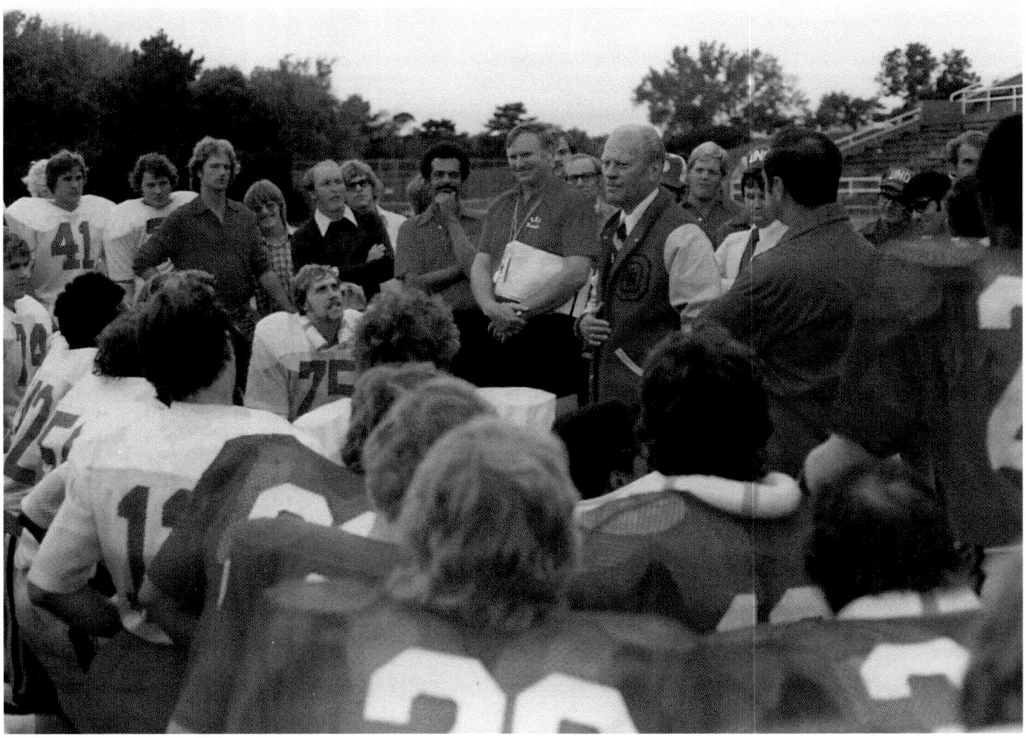

Shortly after leaving office in 1977, Pres. Gerald Ford, who was born in Omaha, visited Coach Danenhauer and the 1977 Maverick football team.

7

Coach Buda's Teams

Players had experienced an array of turmoil when Sandy Buda took the reigns as the head football coach in 1978. The Mavericks were five years into being an NCAA school again, and only the late Al Caniglia, in 1973, had been able to lead the program to a winning season against the tougher competition. "We lost all incentive to play," fullback Clarence Elliott said of the 1977 team.

Buda, a 1963 Omaha Creighton Prep graduate and former recruiting coordinator for coach Pepper Rodgers and the Kansas Jayhawks, immediately brought respectability back to the program with a pair of 8-3 seasons behind quarterback Mike Mancuso, running back Bobby Bass, and wide receiver Kurt R. Anderson.

The 1980 Mavericks were ranked no. 1 as they raced out to a 7-0 start, but they lost their final three games of the season. Buda compiled an 84-49 record from 1978 to 1989 and captured North Central Conference titles in 1983 and 1984. His teams advanced to the NCAA Division II playoffs twice, in 1978 and 1984. In 1984, the Mavericks lost in the national semifinal game. The Omaha native ranks second all-time in wins at UNO.

Buda says that some of his former players include his orthopedic surgeon, his dentist, lawyers, businessmen, fire chiefs, and engineers. "You name it, they all played for me," Buda said. "They got a great degree here, [and] came for the right reason—to get an education first, then have fun playing an extracurricular activity, football."

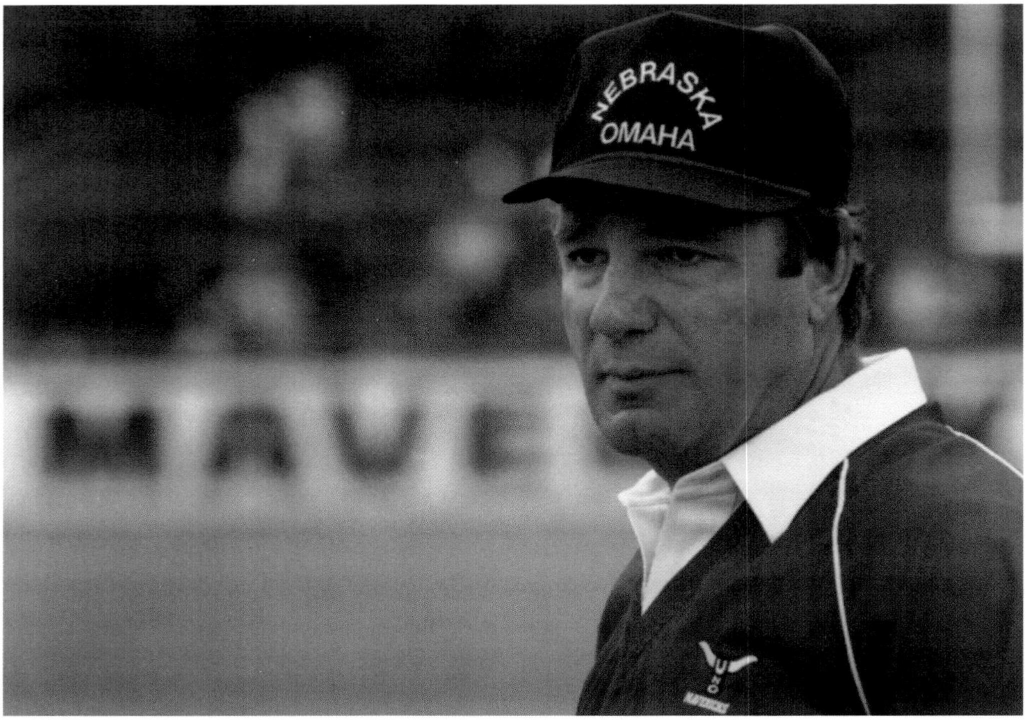

After serving as an assistant coach in the Big Eight Conference for 12 years, Sandy Buda spent the next 12 years as coach of the Mavericks. He was three times named the North Central Conference coach of the year. Buda, a great promoter of the program, had his own television show for all 12 years of his tenure.

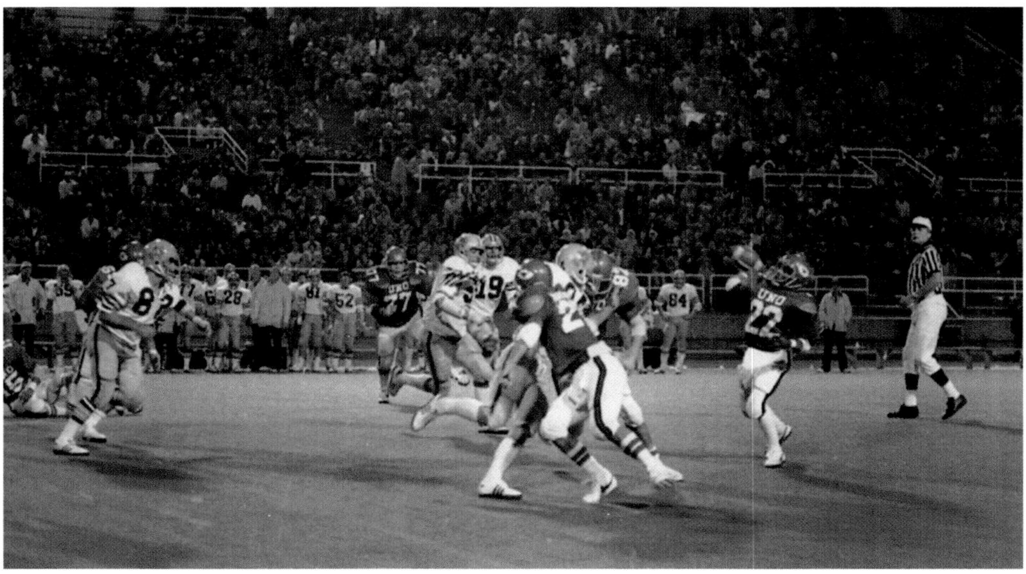

Running back Bobby Bass throws a halfback pass to Kurt R. Anderson during a 19-12 victory over North Dakota State in 1978. Bass was the leading rusher for the Mavericks from 1977 to 1979, totaling 748, 780, and 899 yards, respectively. He also scored 16 touchdowns.

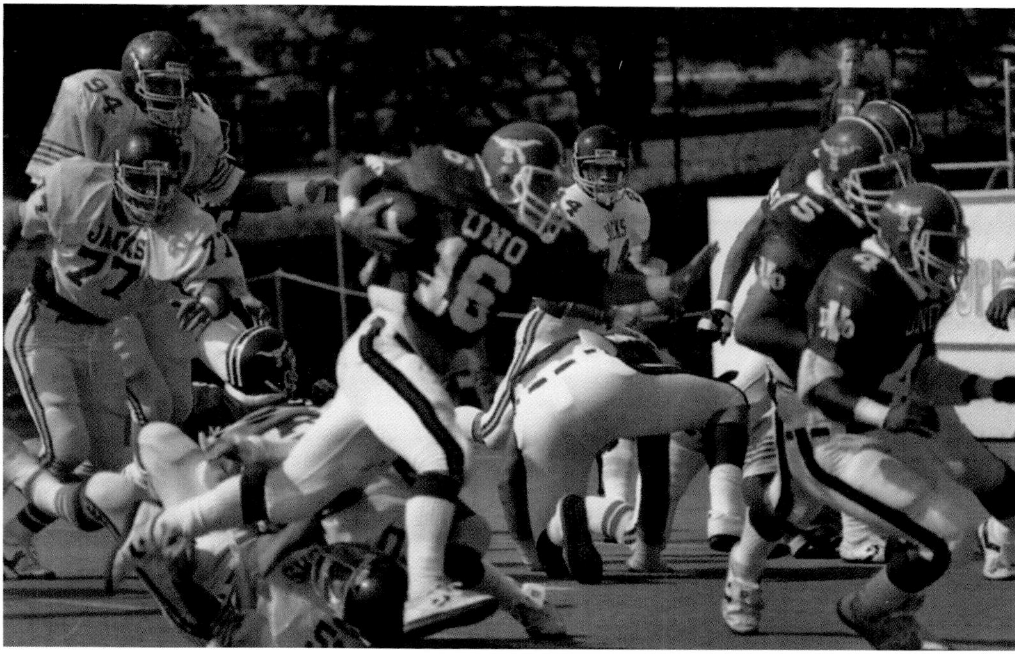

Mark Gurley carries the ball against South Dakota State in 1983. Gurley was the Mavericks' leading rusher in 1982, with 480 yards and three touchdowns.

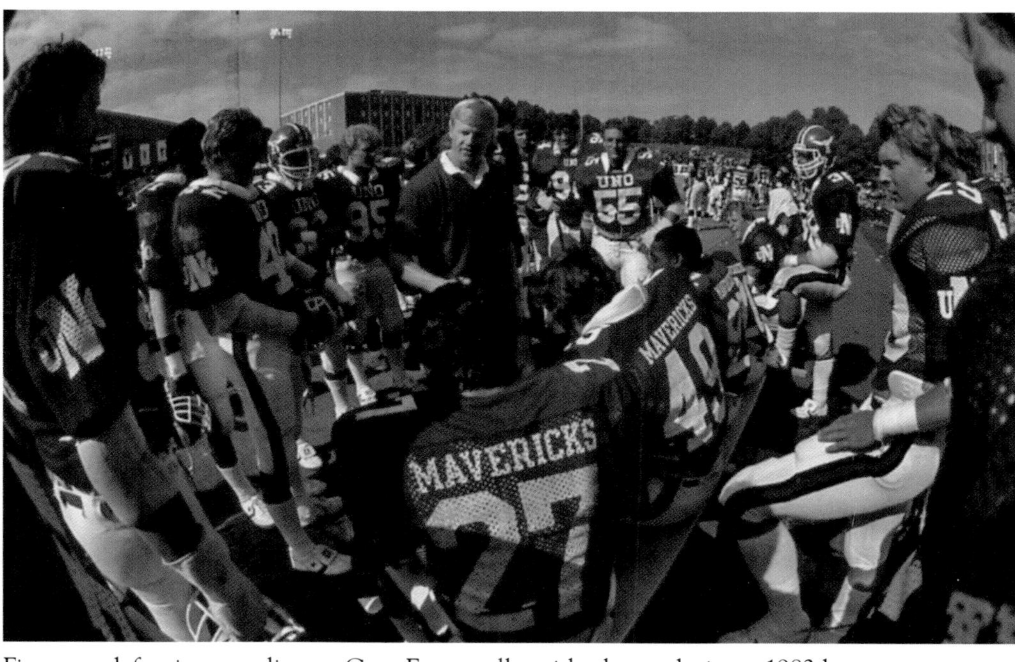

First-year defensive coordinator Gary Evans talks with players during a 1983 home game.

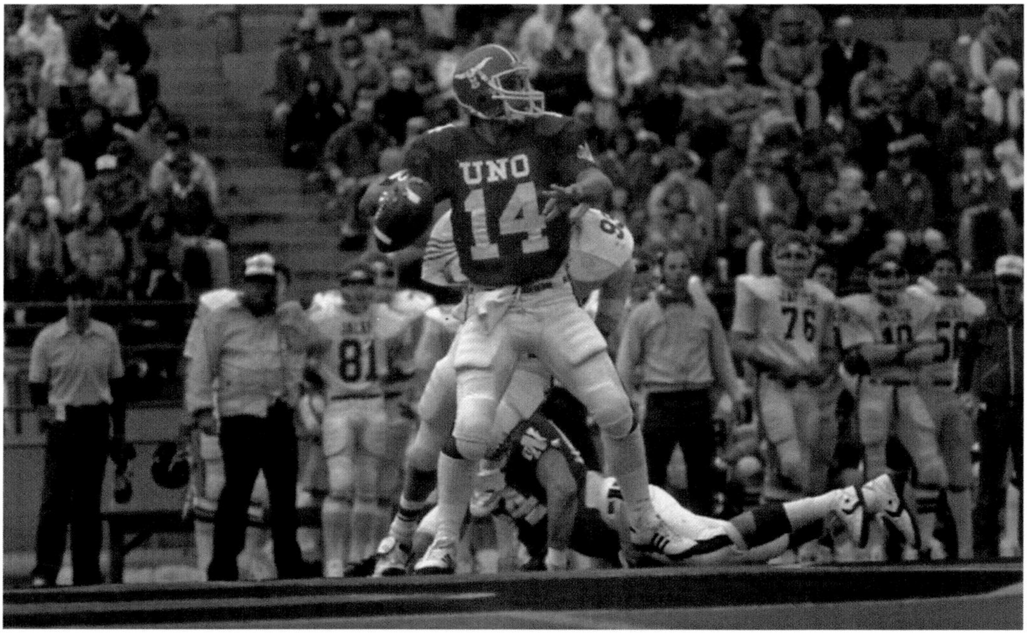

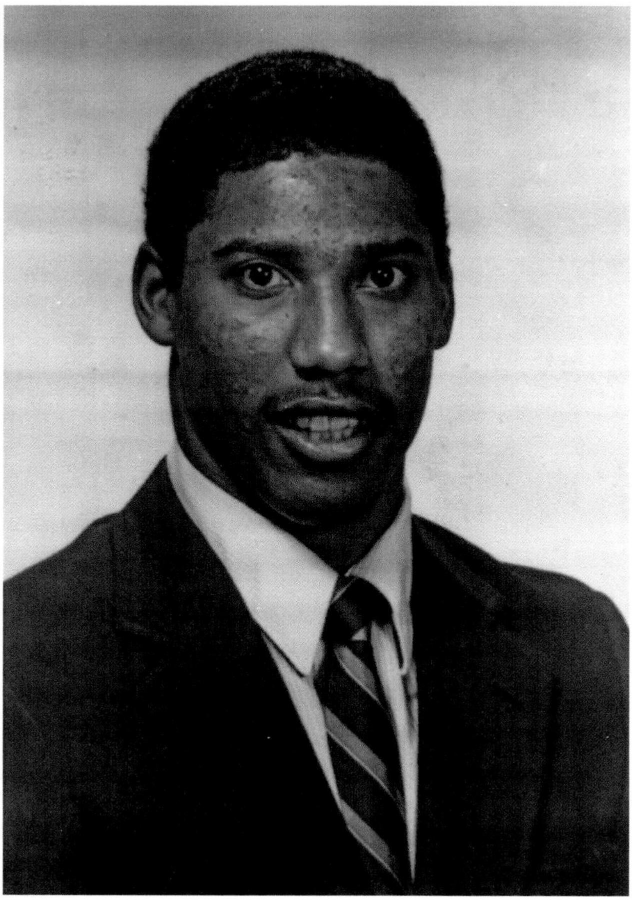

Randy Naran left UNO as its all-time career passing leader, with 5,814 yards. That total ranks second all-time. His 40 touchdown passes still ranks third, as does his 22 touchdown passes in 1984. His 451 completions and 800 pass attempts both rank second all-time. He was the NCC Most Valuable Player in 1984.

Keith Coleman left UNO as the all-time leader in sacks, with 16.5 from 1983 to 1986. He earned first-team All-American honors in 1986. He was first-team All-NCC in 1984 and 1986 and second-team All-NCC in 1985.

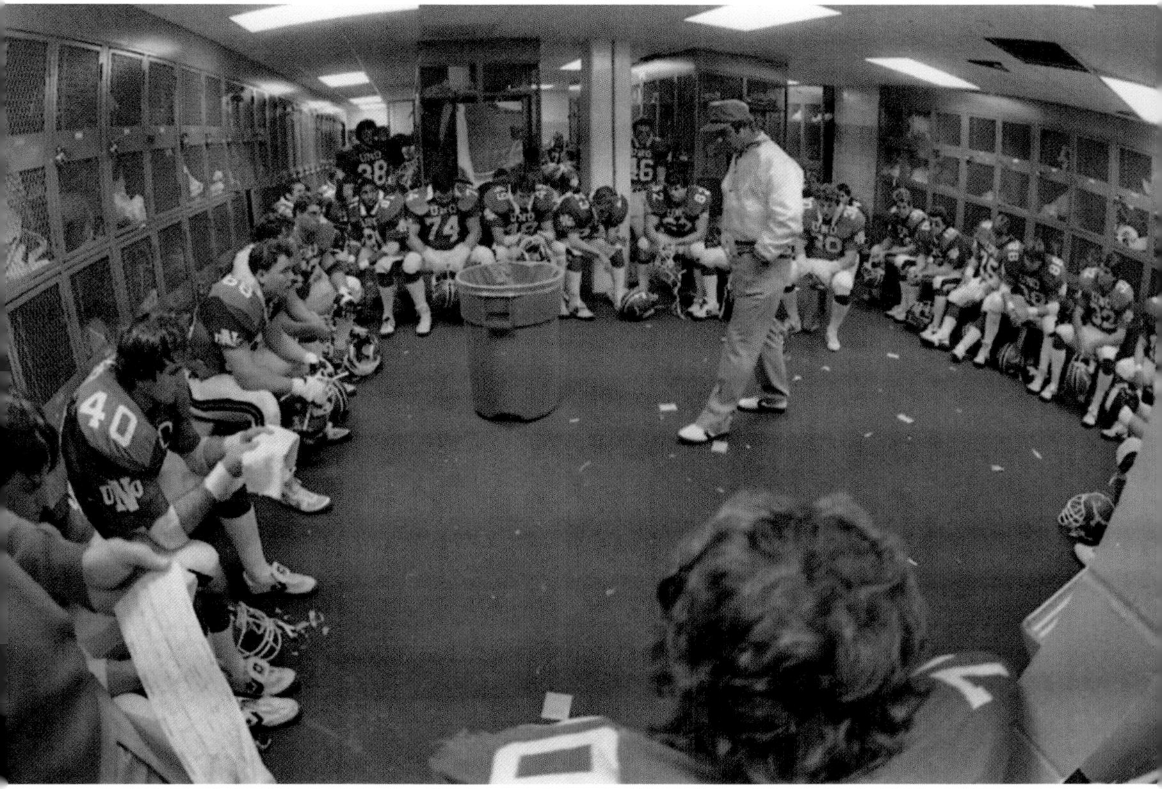

Sandy Buda addresses his players during halftime of a game in 1984. Buda coached at UNO until 1990, when he retired at the age of 44. His decision was influenced by his having undergone two heart operations. He told the *Gateway*, "I have decided now is the best time to retire and look for other opportunities, pursue other interests and spend more time with my family."

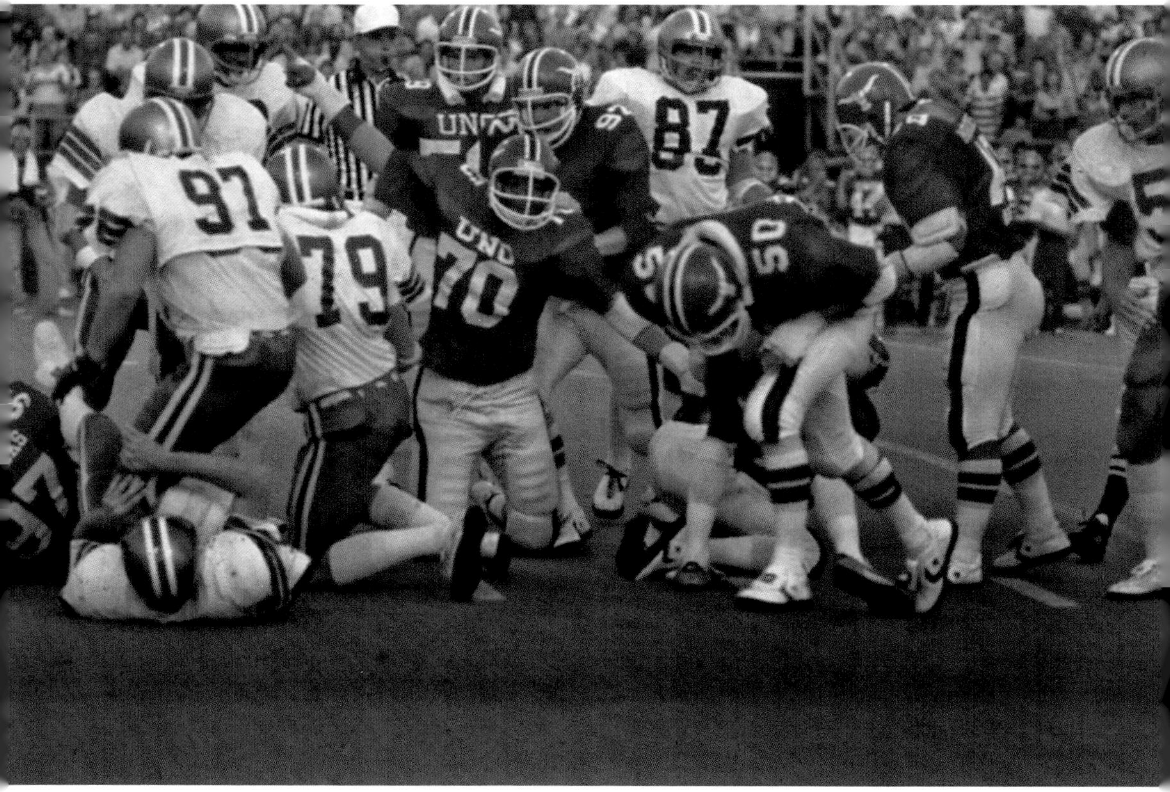

Defensive tackle John Walker signals that it is UNO's ball. Walker was a first-time All-American in 1982 and a three-time NCC first-team selection from 1980 to 1982. He was drafted in the fifth round in 1983 by the New York Jets.

8

COACH BEHRNS'S TEAMS

After Sandy Buda went 30-25 in his final five seasons at UNO and retired, defensive coordinator Tom Mueller was promoted to head coach. Mueller had joined the UNO program in 1983 as a linebacker coach after serving as the defensive coordinator at Morningside College for two years and as offensive coordinator at Upper Iowa University. He was promoted to defensive coordinator at UNO in 1987 before being elevated to head coach in July 1990. Following three 2-9 seasons and a 6-4 mark in 1991, Mueller resigned and was replaced by veteran coach Pat Behrns in 1994. Behrns was selected from among 50 candidates.

It took Behrns a couple of years to rebuild the program, going 1-10 in 1994 and 3-8 in 1995. But then came a breakthrough 10-2 season in 1996, when the Mavericks won the North Central Conference title for the first time since back-to-back titles in 1983 and 1984. The squad also qualified for the NCAA Division II playoffs. Including that season, Behrns helped the Mavericks to 14 straight winning seasons. The team went 5-6 in what turned out to be UNO's final season in 2010. The school captured seven NCC titles under Behrns, including four in a row (2004–2007) before joining the Mid-America Intercollegiate Athletic Association Conference in 2008.

Behrns finished as UNO's winningest coach, with a 124-68 record in 17 seasons. His teams made the NCAA playoffs eight times, including a quarterfinal effort in 2000.

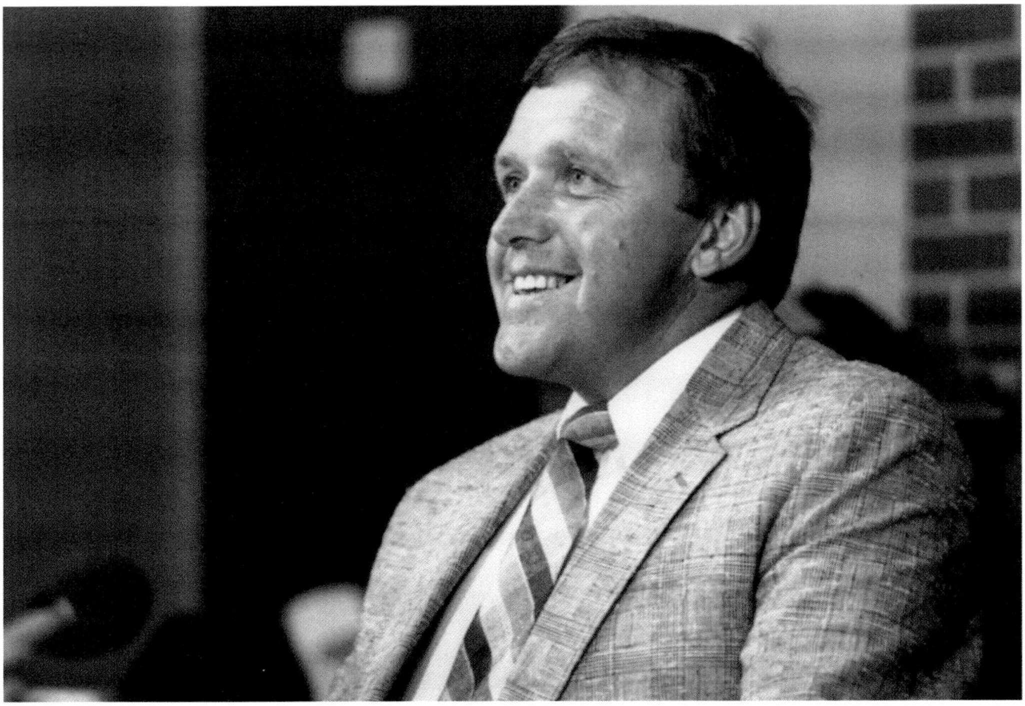

Iowa native Tom Mueller served as the head coach of the Mavericks from 1990 to 1993, compiling a 12-31 record. He had been with the Mavericks program since 1983 as an assistant coach under Sandy Buda.

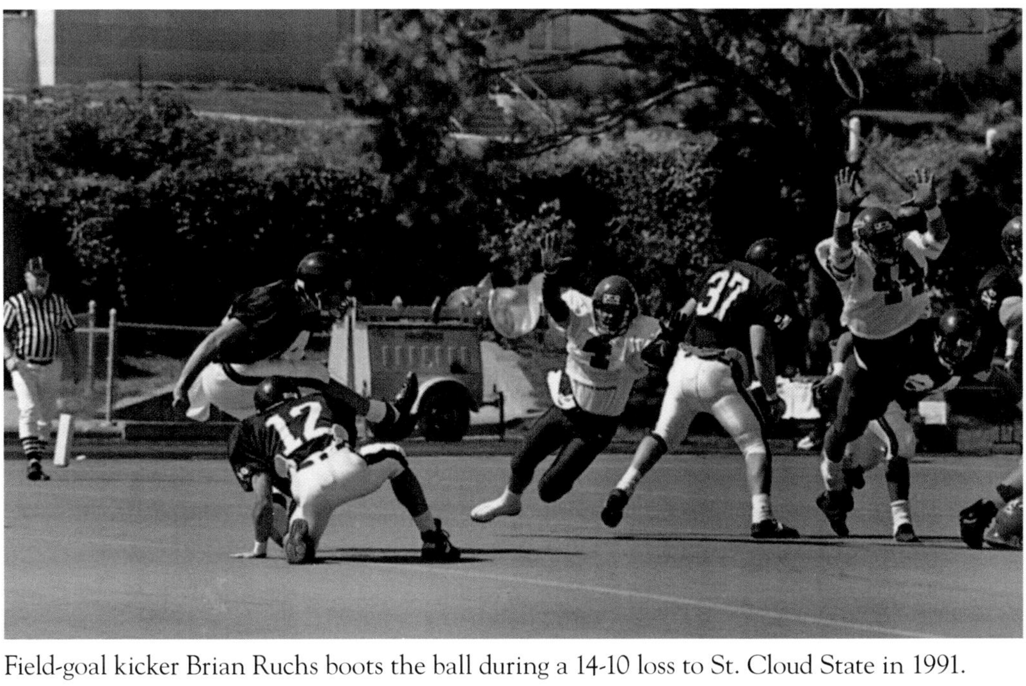

Field-goal kicker Brian Ruchs boots the ball during a 14-10 loss to St. Cloud State in 1991.

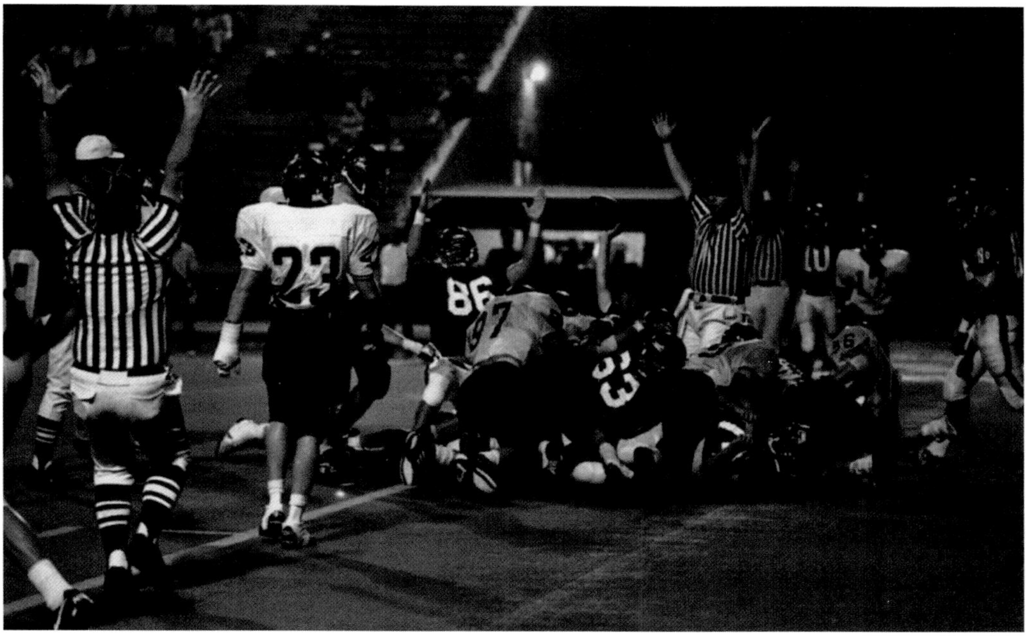

Jeff Jennings (86) signals a touchdown in a 28-0 opening-game victory over Wayne State University in 1991. Jennings led the Mavericks with 19 catches for 227 yards and four touchdowns in 1991.

Pat Behrns returned to the North Central Conference in 1994, when he was hired as the head football coach at UNO. Behrns, the head coach of North Dakota from 1980 to 1985, also served five years as an assistant coach at Utah State and two years as an offensive coordinator at the University of Nevada–Las Vegas.

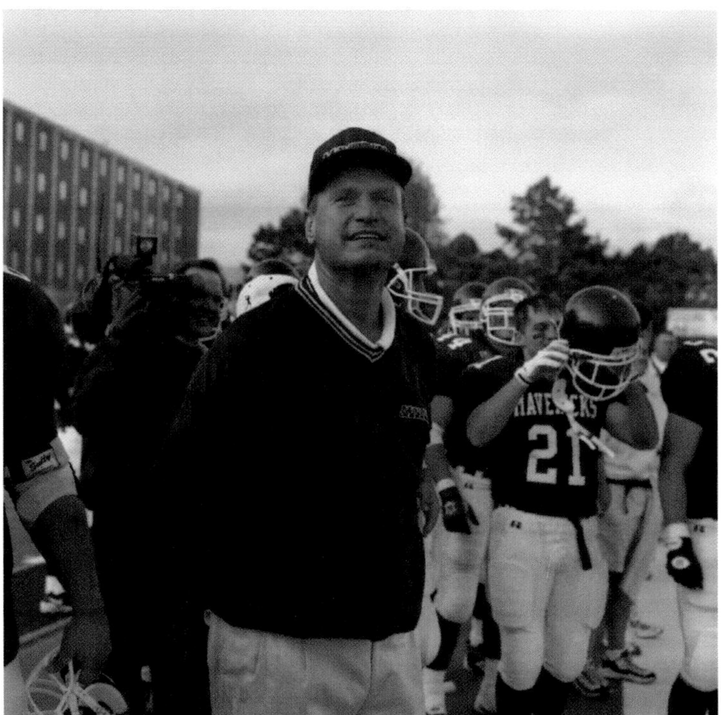

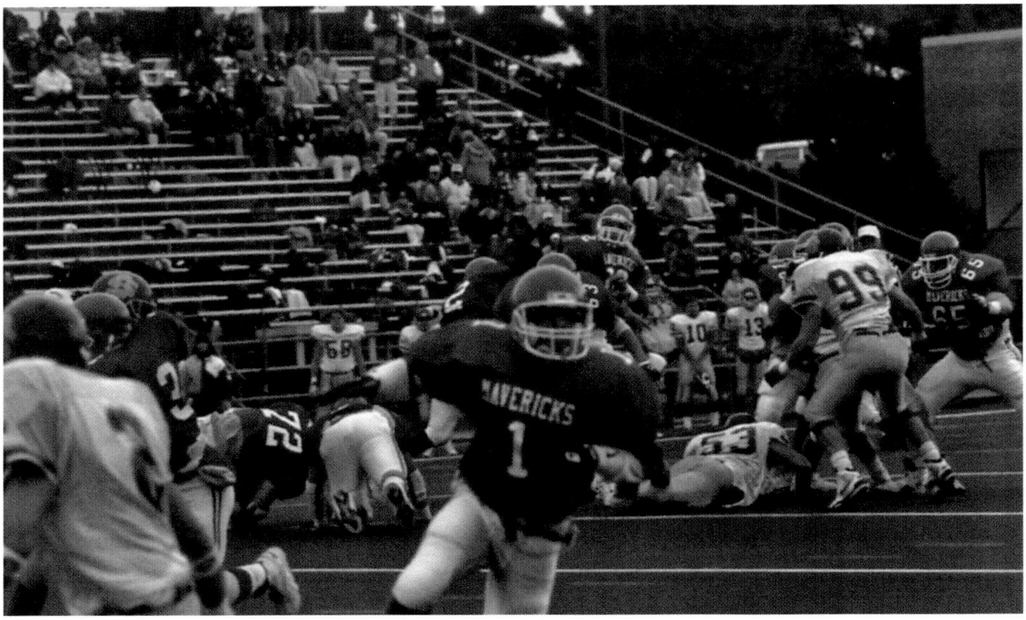

MarTay Jenkins (1) led the Mavericks in receiving in 1996, with 848 yards and eight touchdowns, and again in 1998, with 540 yards and three touchdowns. The Dallas Cowboys chose Jenkins in the sixth round of the 1999 NFL draft.

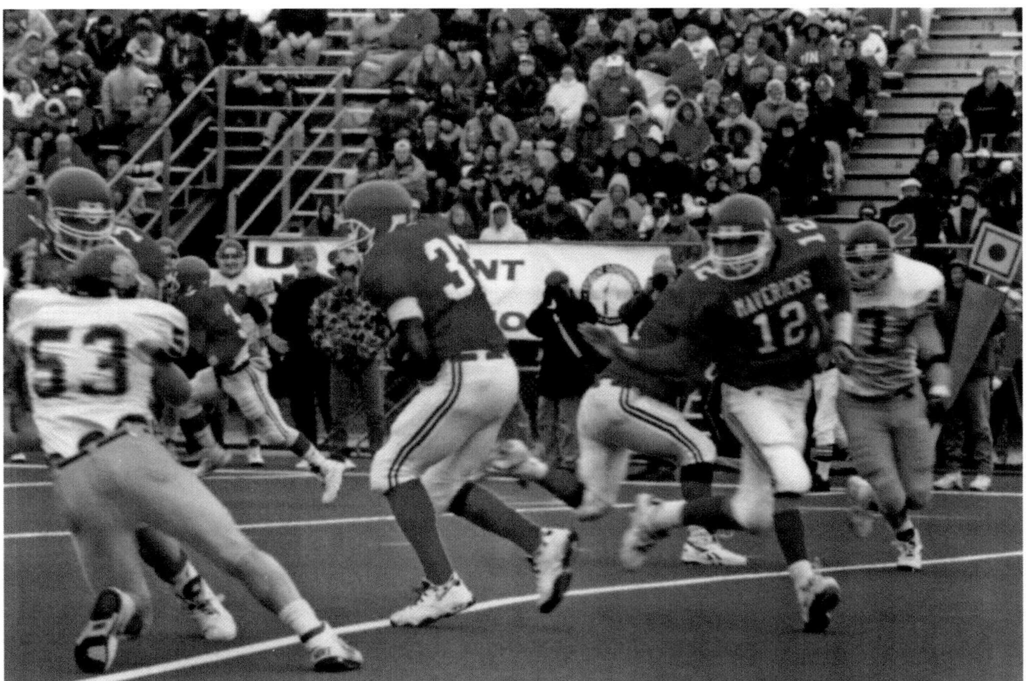

Quarterback Ed Thompson hands off the ball to Lionel McPhaull in a 31-21 win over South Dakota State in 1997. Thompson led the Mavericks in passing from 1996 to 1998, compiling more than 1,000 yards each season. His mark of 36 career touchdown passes is tied for fourth all-time.

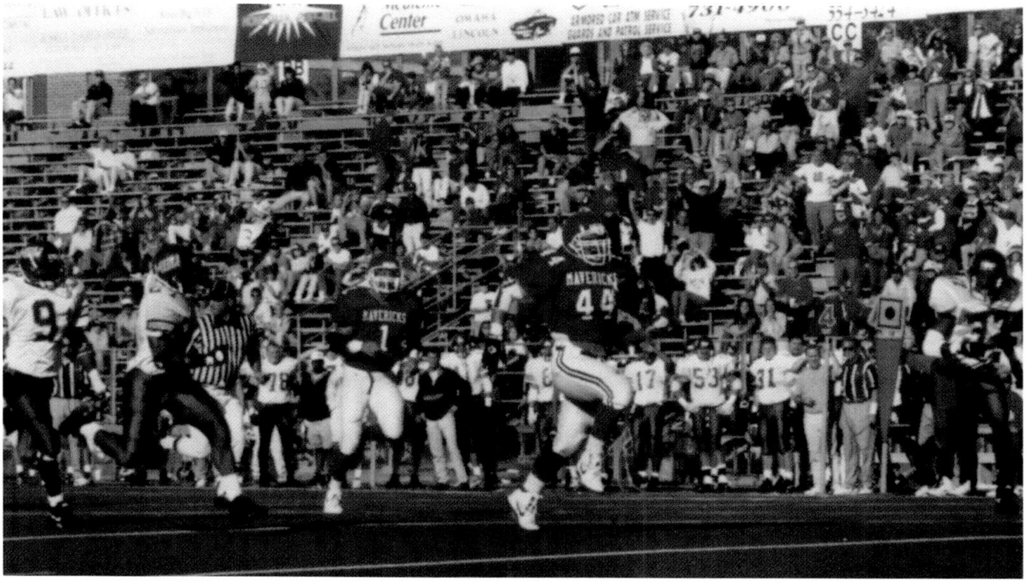

Mickey Koory (44) goes in for a touchdown against Minnesota State as MarTay Jenkins (1) looks on in 1997. Koory had 77 carries for 293 yards and 10 touchdowns in 1998.

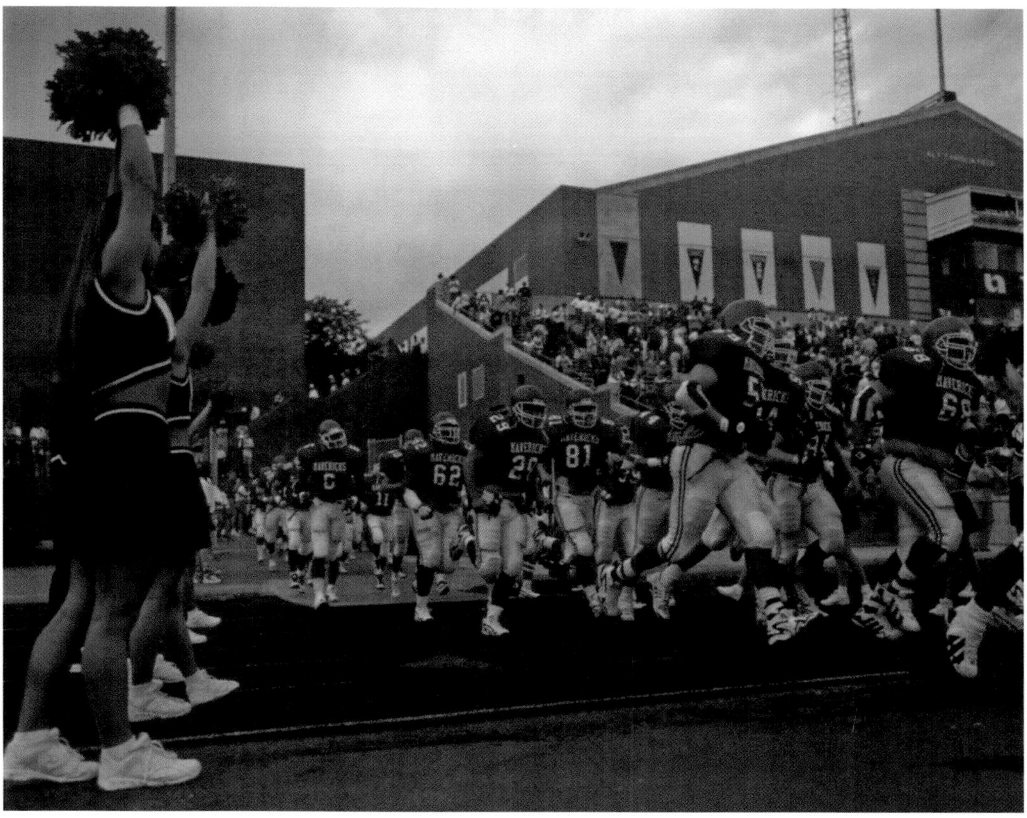

Players enter Caniglia Field during a 1997 game. The Mavericks went 8-3 that season, including a 5-0 record at home.

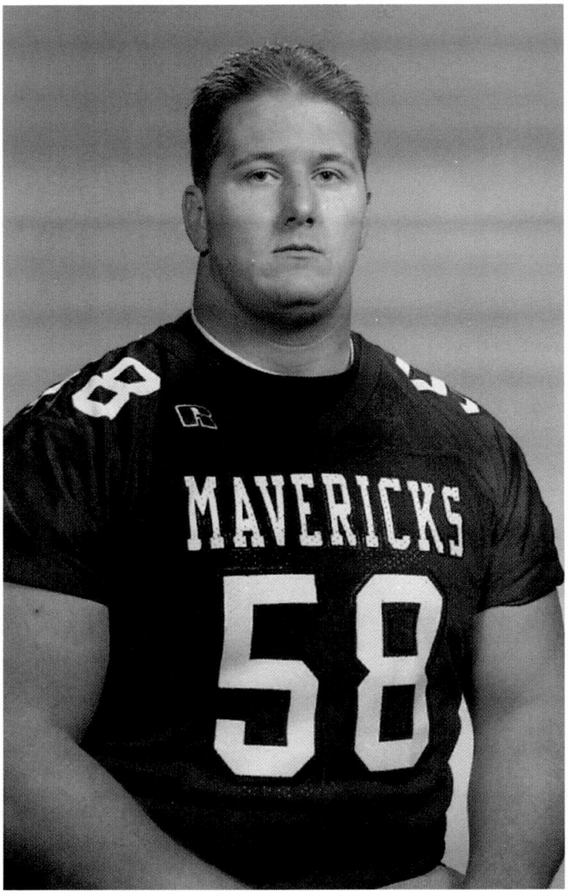

Chris Bober earned first-team All-American honors as an offensive lineman in 1998 and 1999, becoming UNO's first two-time first-team football All-American since Bill Englehardt in 1955–1956. An outstanding blocker and pass protector, Bober redshirted in 1995, played as a part-time starter in 1996, then started full-time for three seasons. UNO won two NCC titles and made three NCAA II playoff appearances during his career. He was all-NCC twice, each time being named most valuable offensive lineman. Drafted by the New York Giants, he became a starter in the NFL and signed with the Kansas City Chiefs in 2004.

Chris Cooper (94) comes up to make a tackle against Pittsburg State in 2000. Cooper ranks at the top of UNO's career charts for tackles for a loss (53) and sacks (31) during his career at the school, from 1997 to 2000.

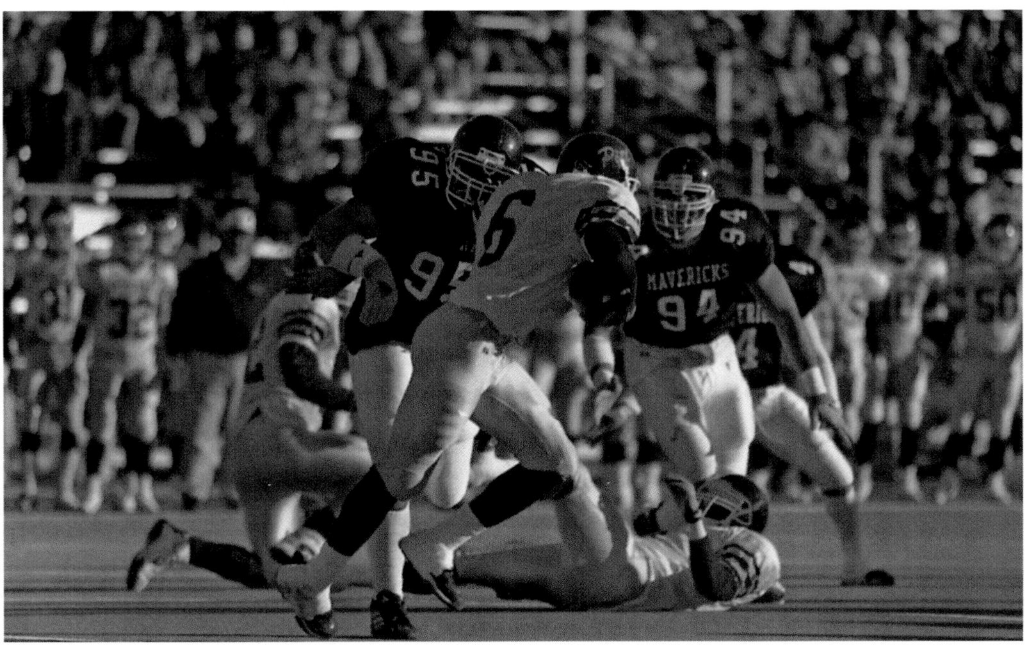

Defensive tackle Chris Cooper was taken in the sixth round of the 2001 NFL draft by the Oakland Raiders.

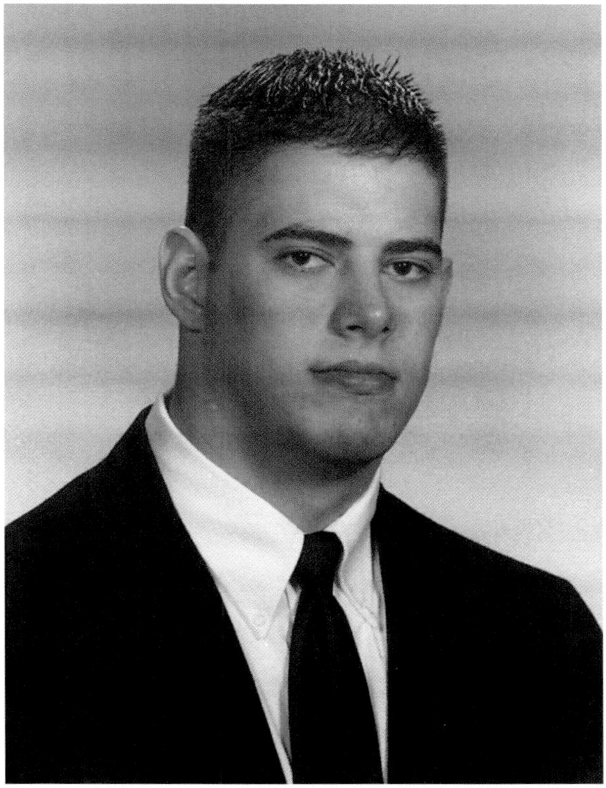

The 2000 team won the NCC conference title and advanced to the quarterfinals of the NCAA Division II playoffs before losing 43-21 to North Dakota State. Earlier in the season, the Mavericks (11-2) had beaten North Dakota 6-3. The 11 victories tied for the most in school history.

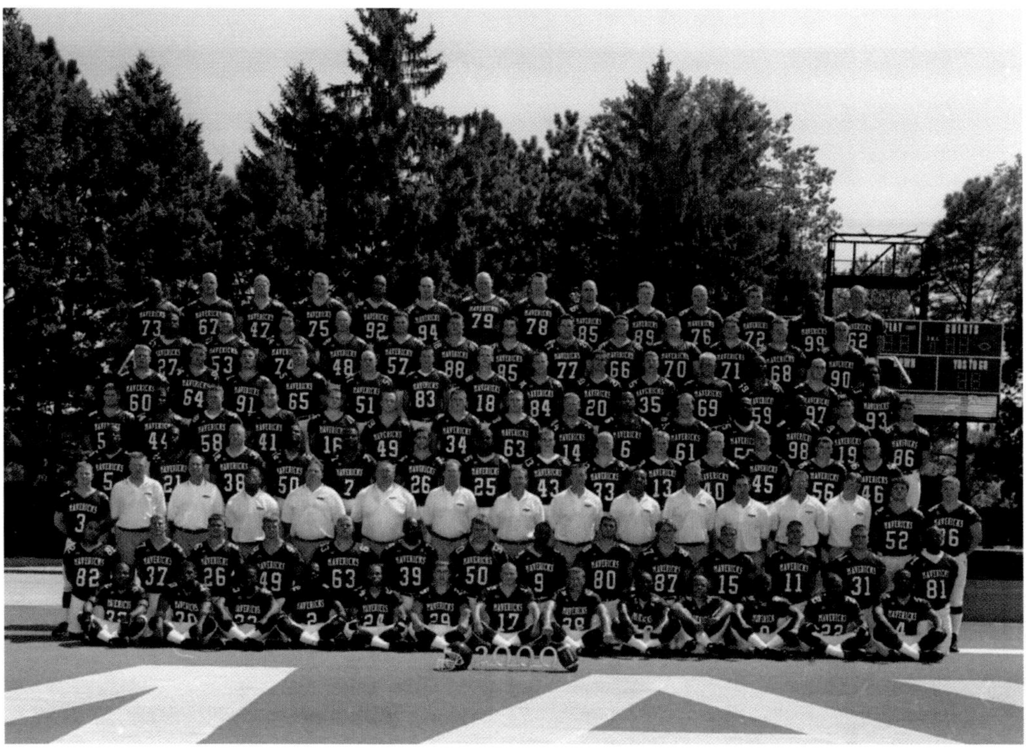

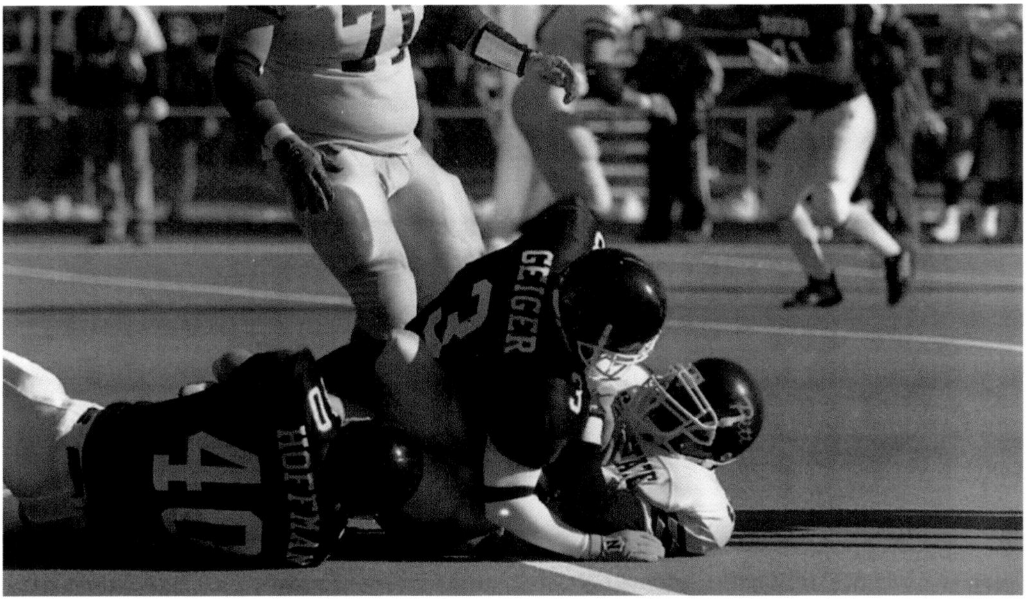

Chad Geiger makes a tackle against Pittsburg State in 200. Geiger was a two-time first-team All-American as a defensive back in 2000 and 2001.

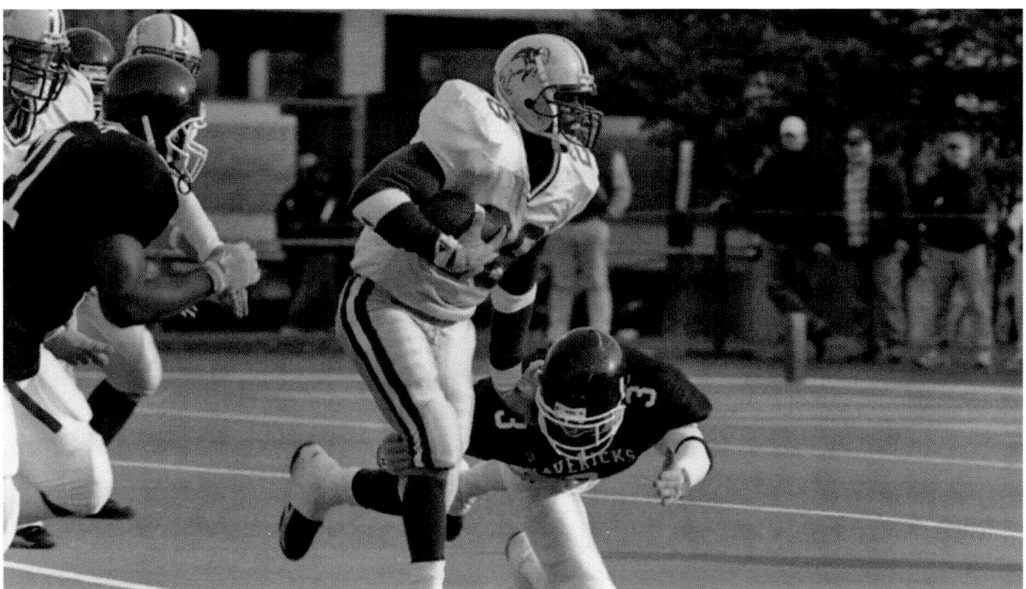

Chad Geiger makes a stop against North Dakota State in 2000. Geiger is tied for fifth all-time at UNO with 11 interceptions.

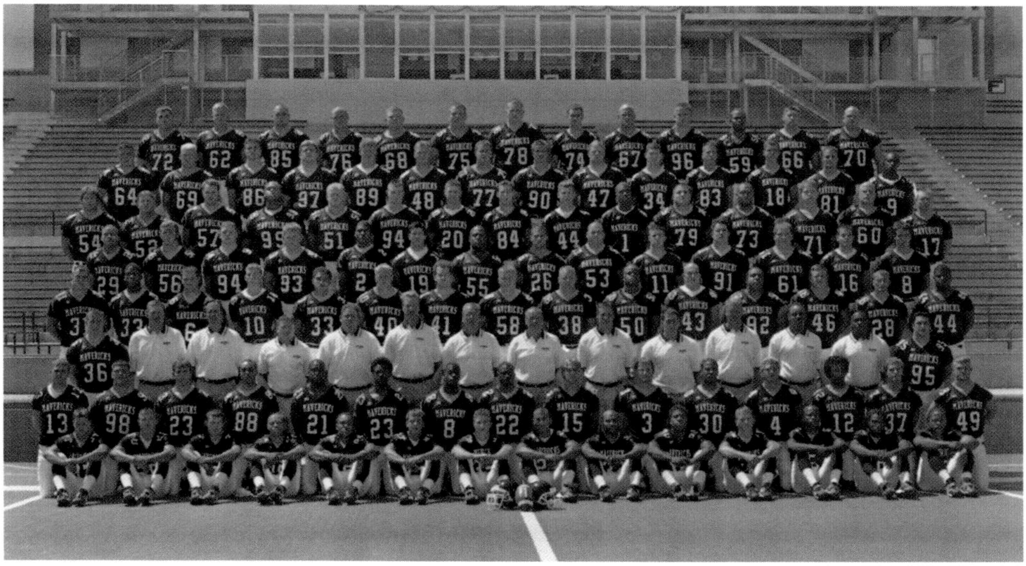

The 2001 team won its first eight games to start the season. The Mavericks ended with a 31-22 setback at North Dakota State and a 38-21 defeat at Augustana College. Still, UNO made the NCAA Division II playoffs, where they were eliminated in the first round by Pittsburg State 20-7.

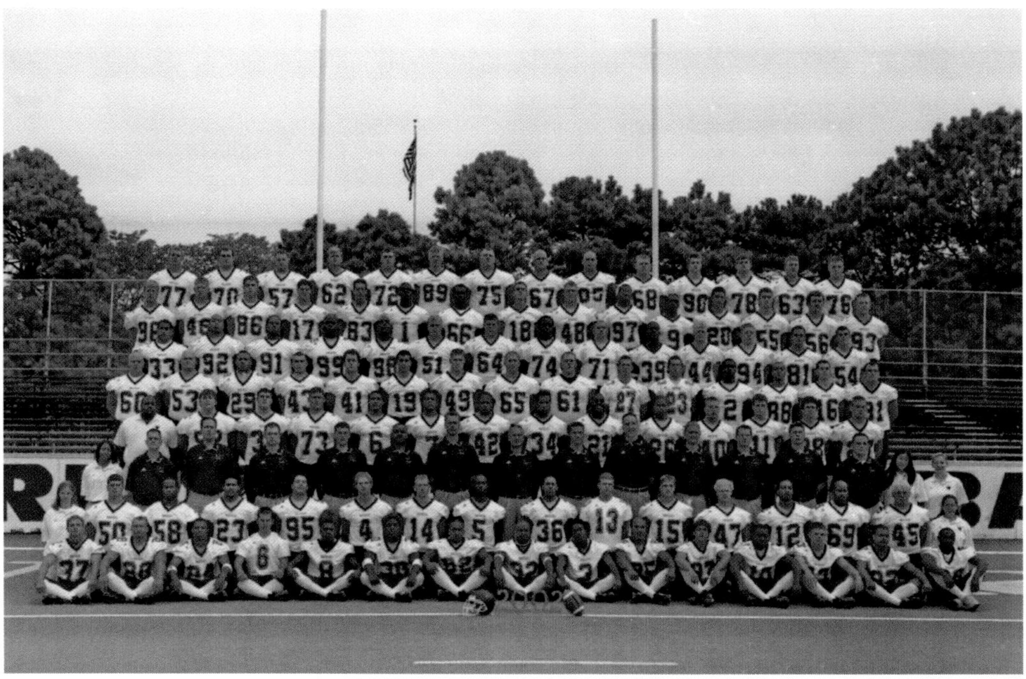

The 2002 team lost three of its first four games and finished with a 6-5 mark. Offensive lineman Connor Riley earned first-team All-American honors that year.

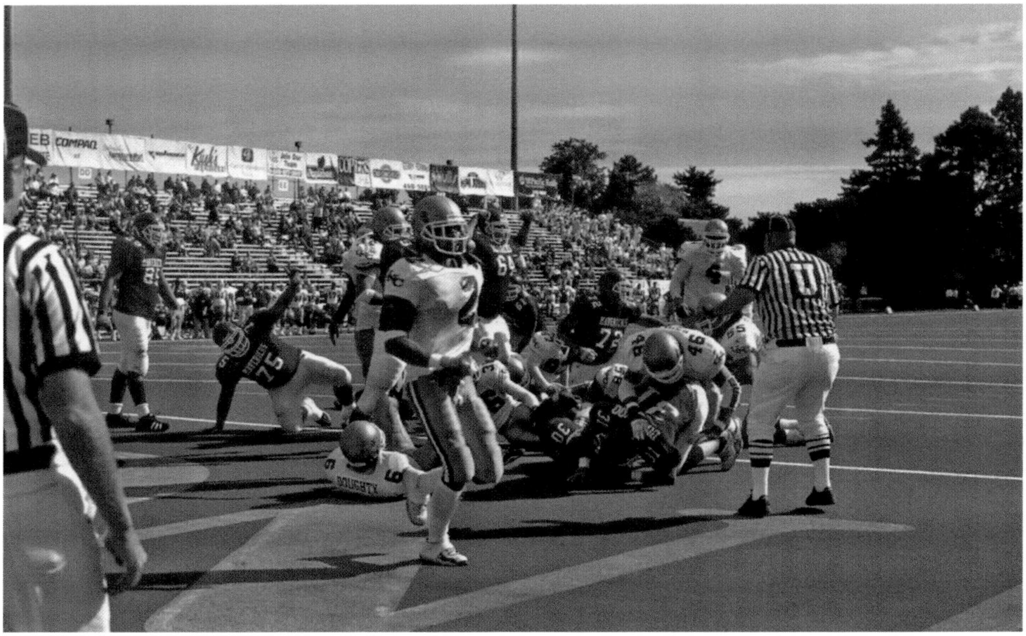

James Johnson (30) scores a touchdown against Northern Colorado in 2002. Despite his efforts, UNO fell 30-25. Johnson was the school's leading rusher in 2002, with 216 carries for 1,074 yards and four touchdowns.

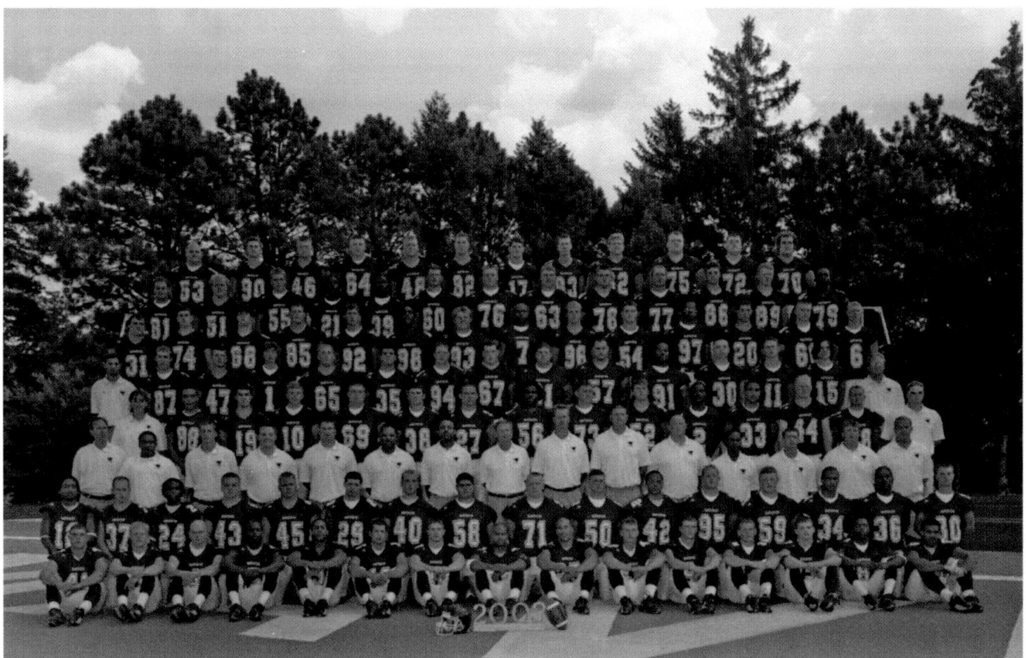

The 2003 team finished 8-3. Some of the leaders of this team were quarterback Brian Masek, who threw for 2,336 yards and 24 touchdowns, and Ryan Krause, who had 1,066 receiving yards and 11 touchdowns.

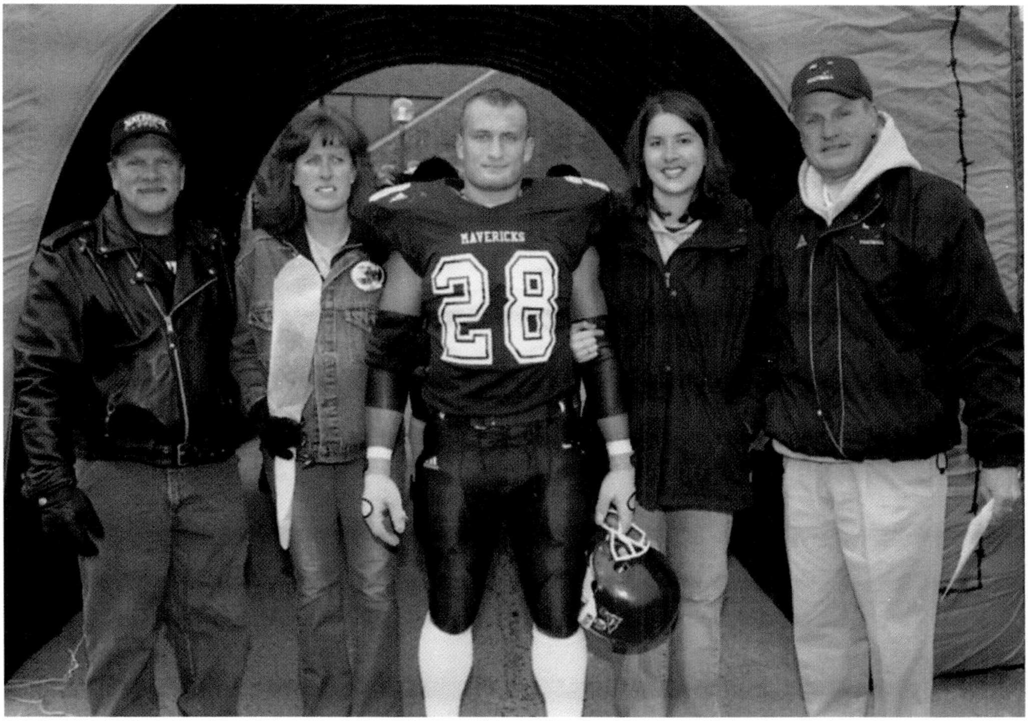

Justin Kammrad poses for a photograph on Senior Day. Kammrad led the team in scoring in 2003, with 14 touchdowns and 86 points. He earned first-team All-American honors that year, following a season in which he led NCAA Division II schools with 1,866 rushing yards.

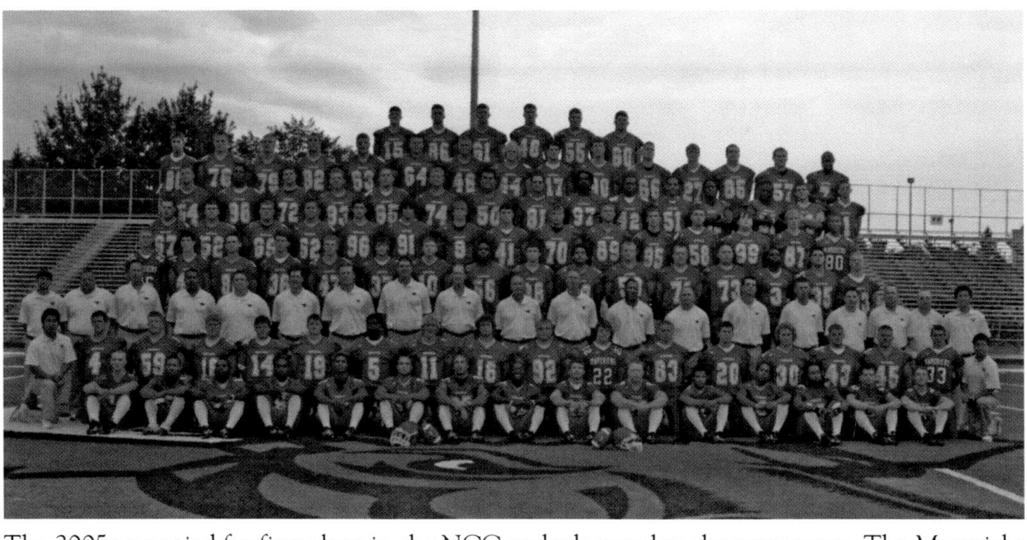

The 2005 team tied for first place in the NCC and advanced to the postseason. The Mavericks (8-3) were unable to get past Saginaw Valley State, losing by a 24-21 margin.

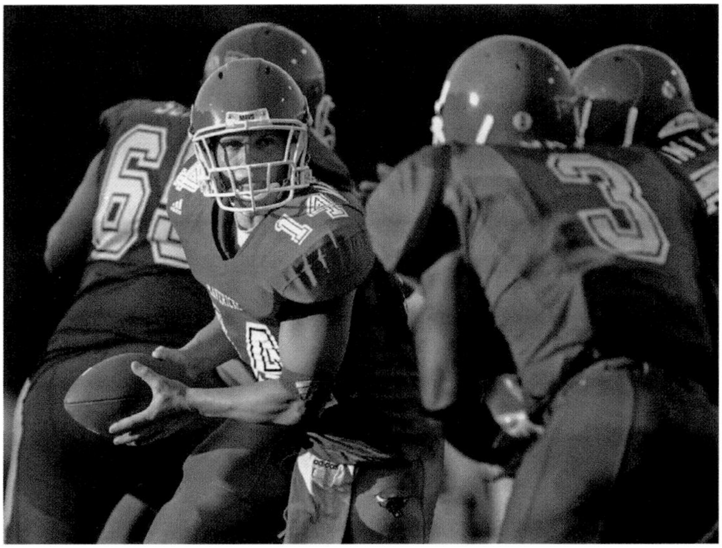

Brian Masek (14) hands the ball to Jamar Day during a 2005 game. Day led the Mavericks in scoring in 2004, with 17 touchdowns and 104 points. Masek is UNO's career passing leader, with 7,155 yards from 2002 to 2005. He also is the career passing touchdowns leader (70), career completions leader (500), and career attempts leader (879).

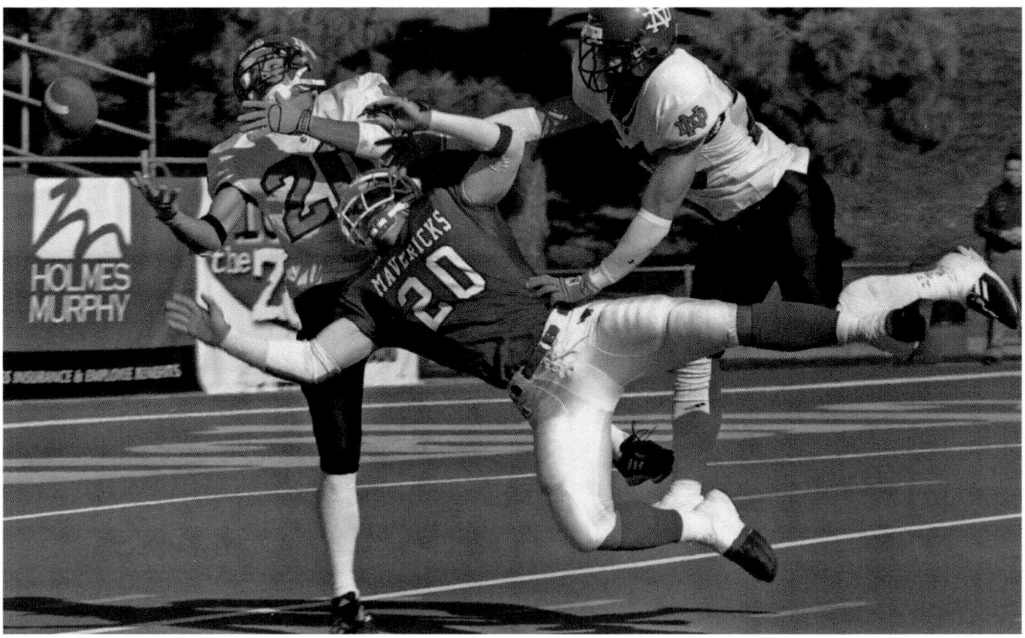

Tight end Ryan Krause tries to make an acrobatic catch against North Dakota in 2004. Krause led the Mavericks in receiving in 2001 (468 yards and three touchdowns), 2002 (893 yards and eight touchdowns), and 2003 (1,066 yards and 11 touchdowns). Krause was taken in the sixth round of the 2004 NFL draft by the San Diego Chargers.

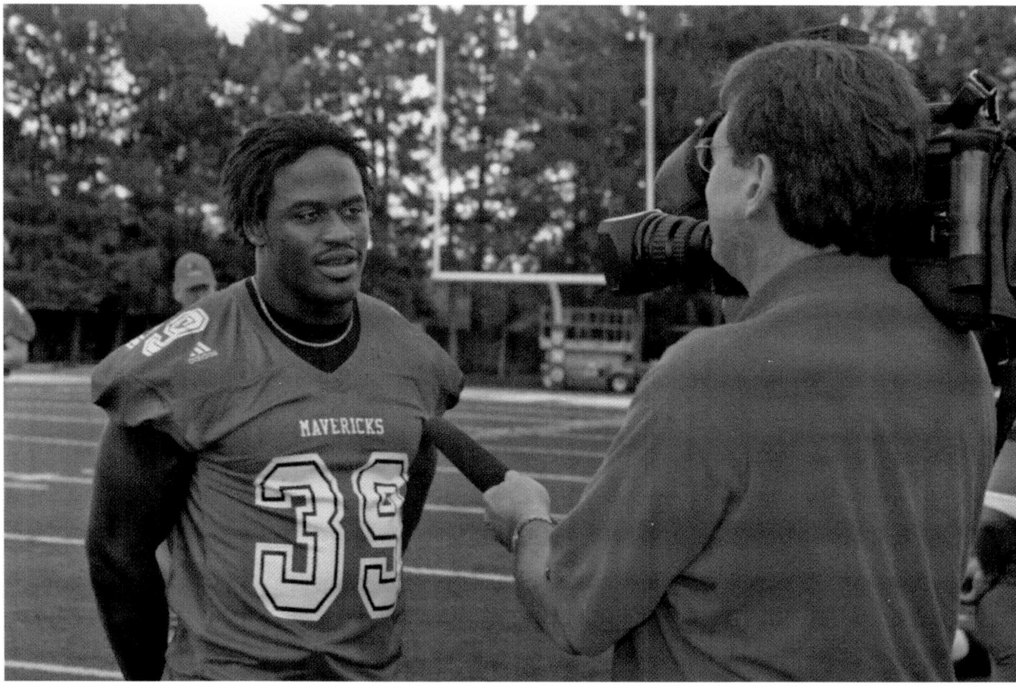

Taiwo Onatolu is shown here being interviewed in 2005. Onatolu was UNO's second-leading all-time tackler, with 371 tackles. He also had 12.5 sacks, ranking seventh all-time for the school.

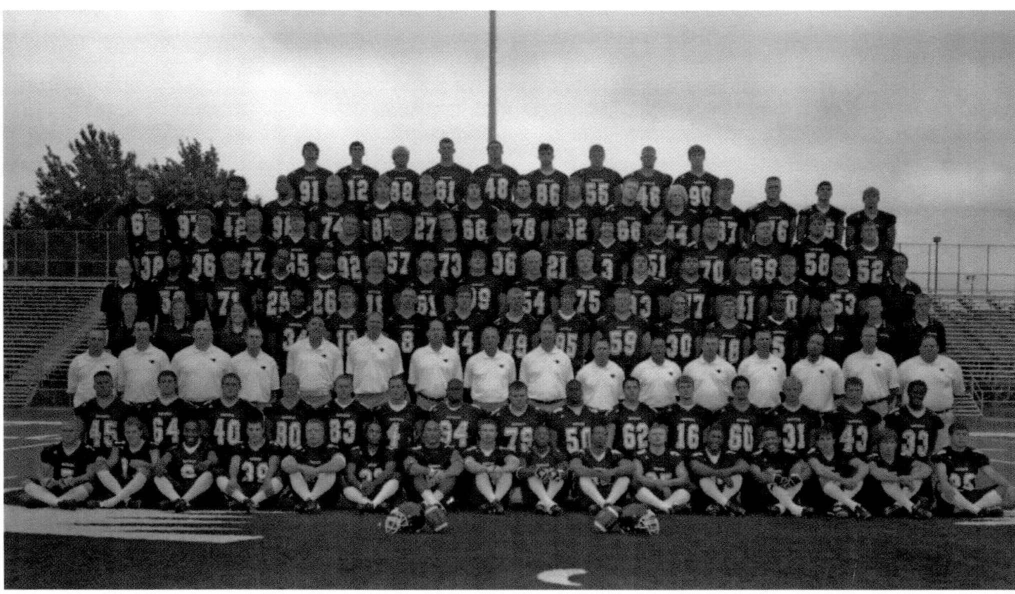

The 2006 Mavericks went 8-3 and were North Central Conference champions. UNO suffered a heartbreaking 38-35 loss to North Dakota in the NCAA playoffs. Troy Kush led receivers as a sophomore in 2006, and he continued to be the top receiver in 2007 and 2008. Sophomore quarterback Zach Miller was the leading scorer, with 19 touchdowns.

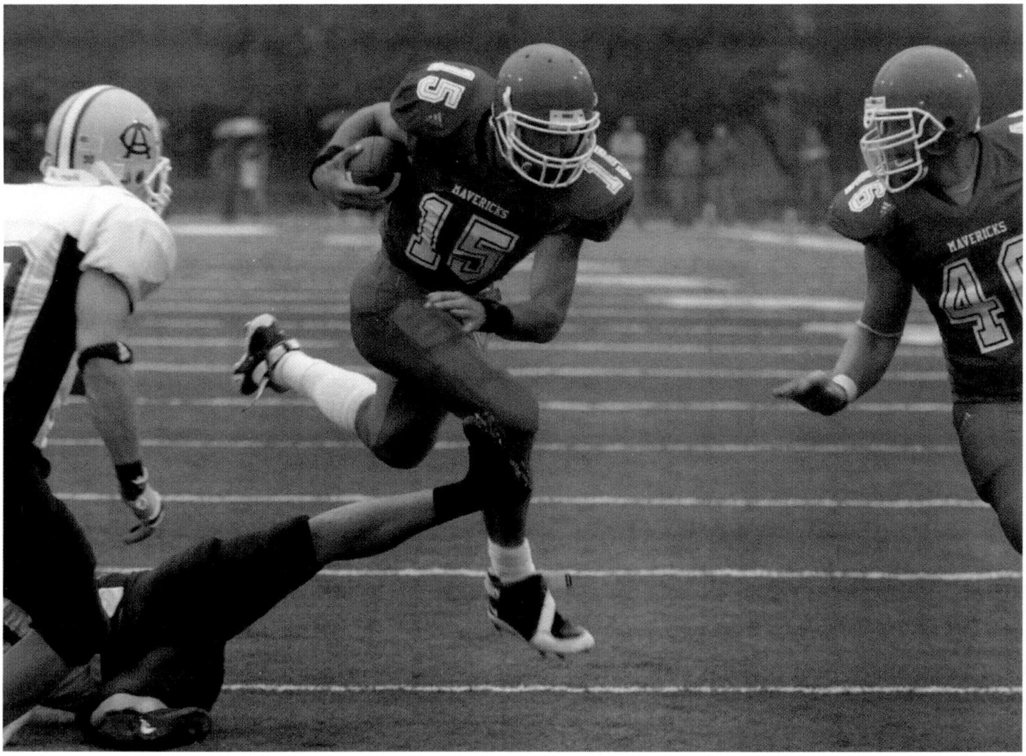

Quarterback Zach Miller runs against Augustana College in 2006. For the season, Miller completed 54 of 97 pass attempts for 713 yards and four scores. He led the Mavericks in scoring in 2006 (114 points) and 2008 (108) and finished his career as the all-time leading scorer (306). Miller was taken in the sixth round of the 2009 NFL draft by the Jacksonville Jaguars as a tight end.

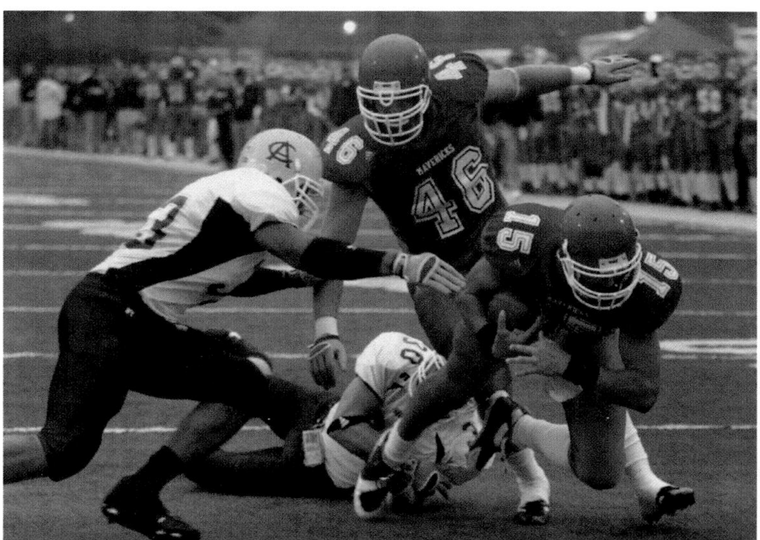

Zach Miller goes in for a touchdown in a 59-28 rout against Augustana College in 2006. Zac Herold (46) helps spring him with a block.

Tight end Zac Herold goes airborne to avoid a tackle against St. Cloud State in 2006. Herold was an All-American in 2005 and 2006.

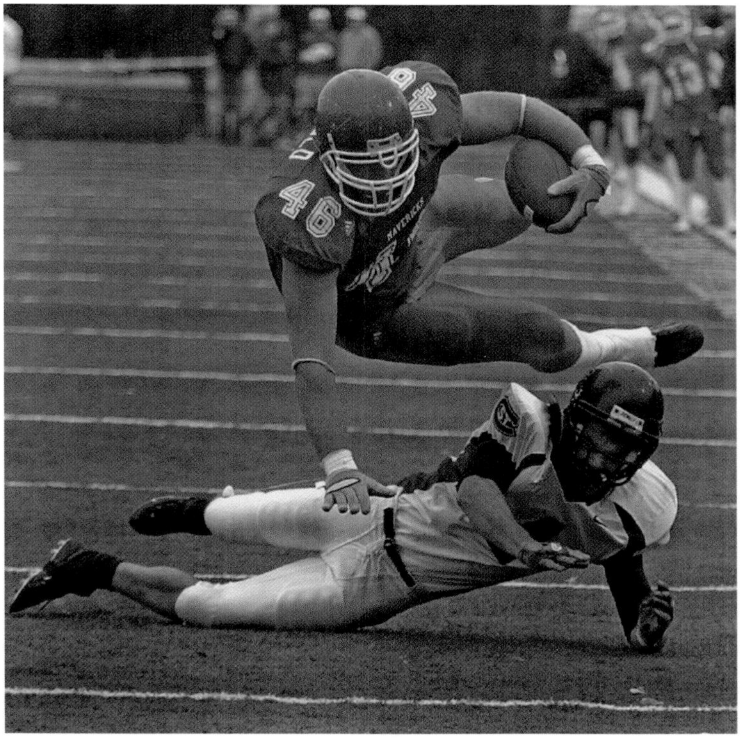

Sophomore linebacker Robert Lewis (55) makes a tackle against Minnesota State in 2005.

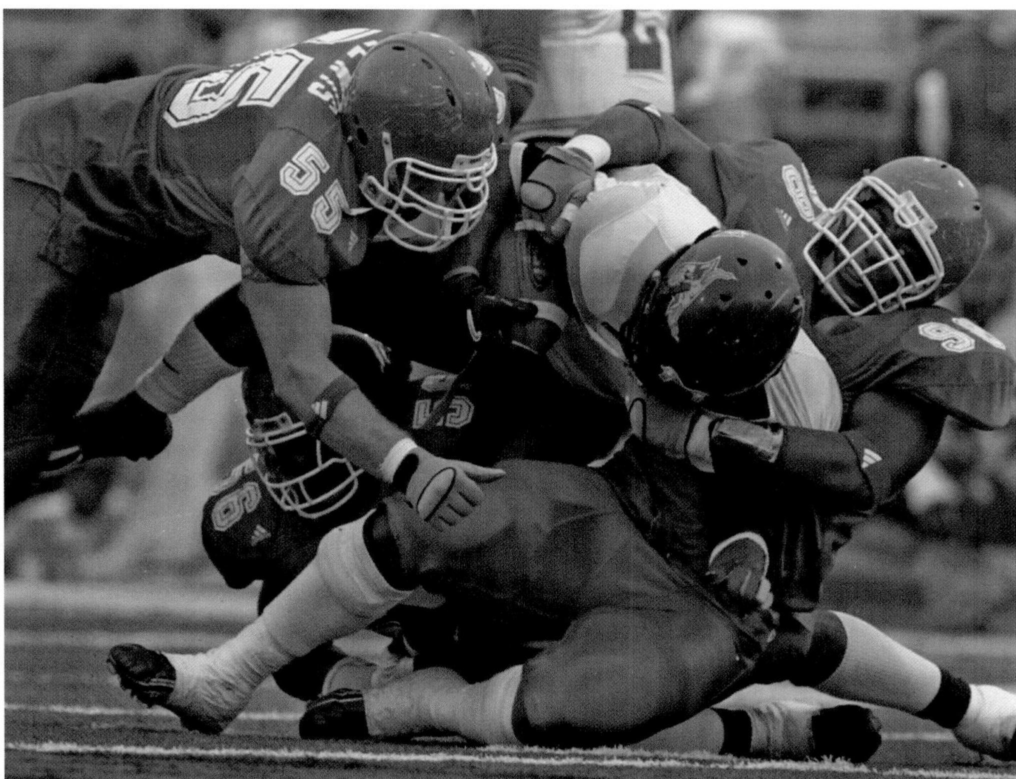

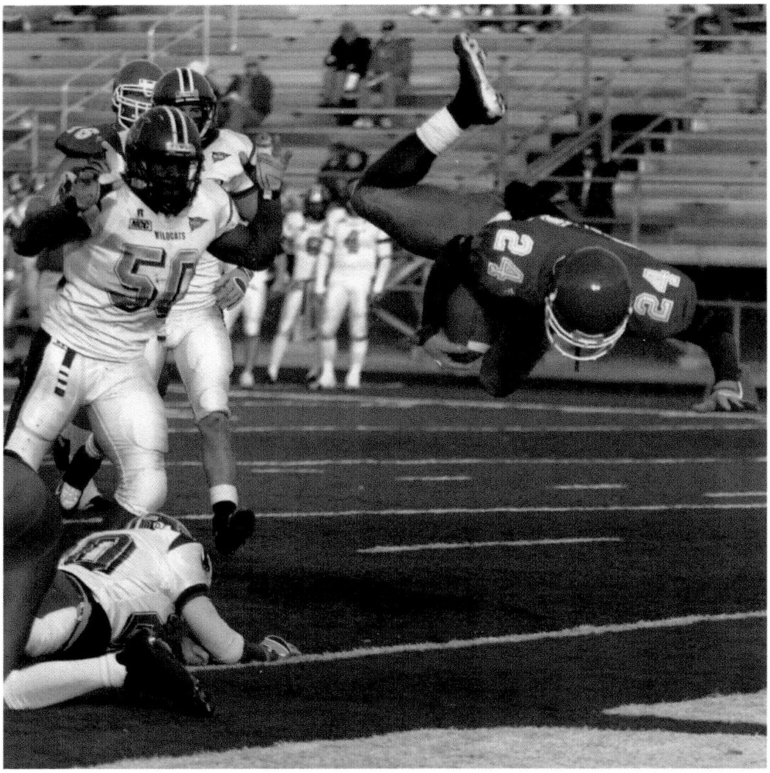

Pagel Williams (24) dives into the end zone following a 13-yard reverse for his first career touchdown, against Central Washington in 2006. He also scored on a 14-yard pass in the 48-14 victory that assured UNO a share of the NCC title.

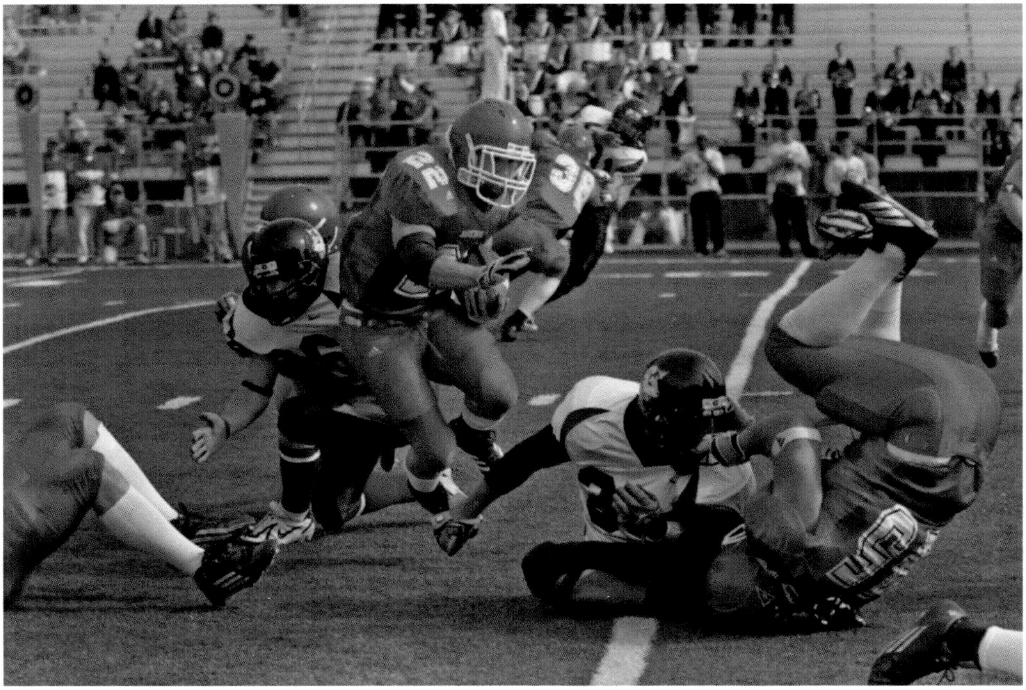

Kyle Kasperbauer (22) carries the ball during the 2005 season. He was the Mavericks' leading rusher in 2006, with 222 carries for 1,288 yards and 10 touchdowns.

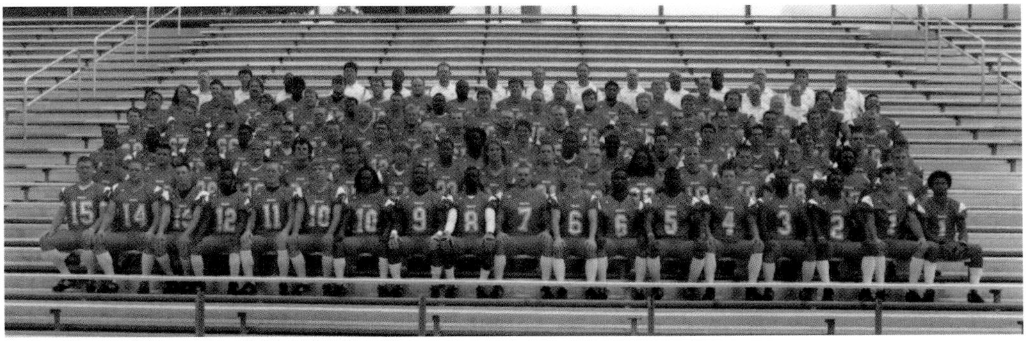

In 2009, the Mavericks competed in their third and final bowl game, the Kanza Bowl in Topeka, Kansas. The Mavericks (7-5) suffered a 31-25 loss to West Texas A&M, despite Greg Zuerlein booting four field goals in five attempts and Greg Wunderlich going 26-44 for 252 yards with one interception and four sacks.

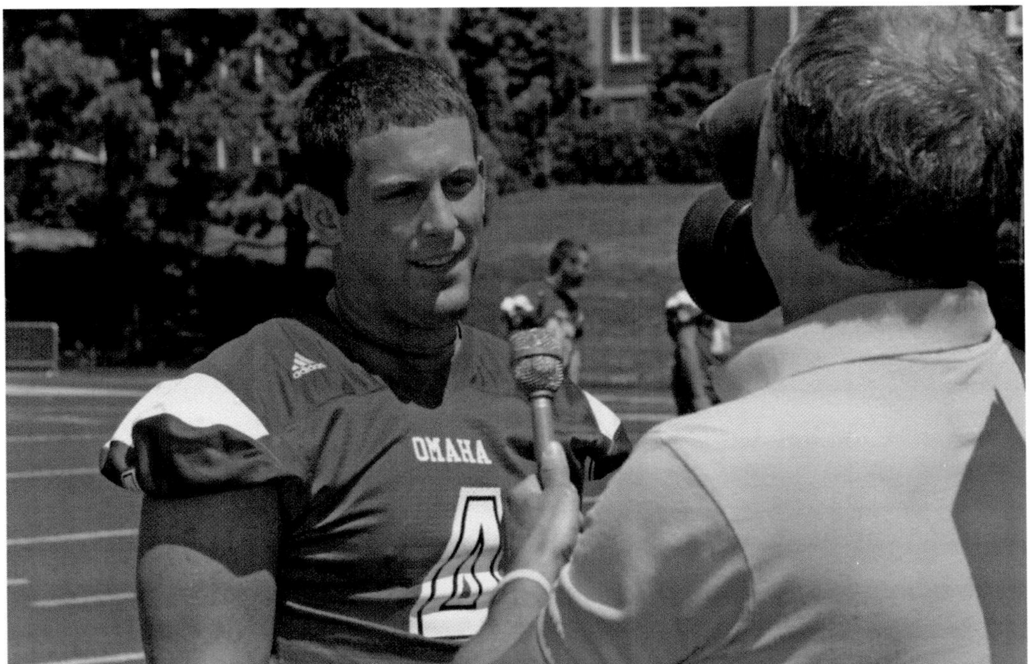

Quarterback Greg Wunderlich is interviewed in 2009. Wunderlich threw for 2,492 and 21 touchdowns that season. That yardage is the best single-season total in school history. Wunderlich's 321 pass attempts in 2009 ranks as the second most in UNO history.

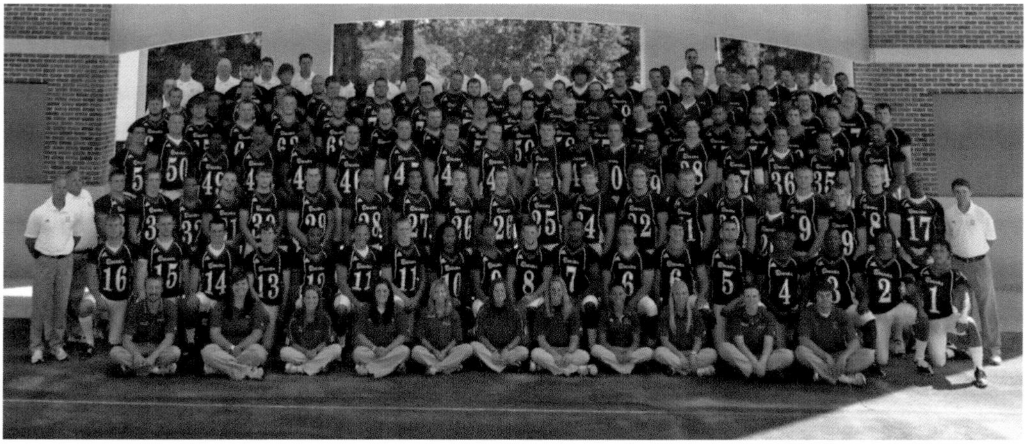

The 2010 football team did not realize it at the time, but when the season ended, this would be the final Maverick football team. The group can find some solace in the fact that it won the final game, 62-61 over Truman State on November 13, 2010. Sophomore running back Levi Terrell scored three touchdowns and rushed for 226 yards. Quarterback John Teigland connected with Mike Higgins on the game-winning touchdown with 30 seconds left.

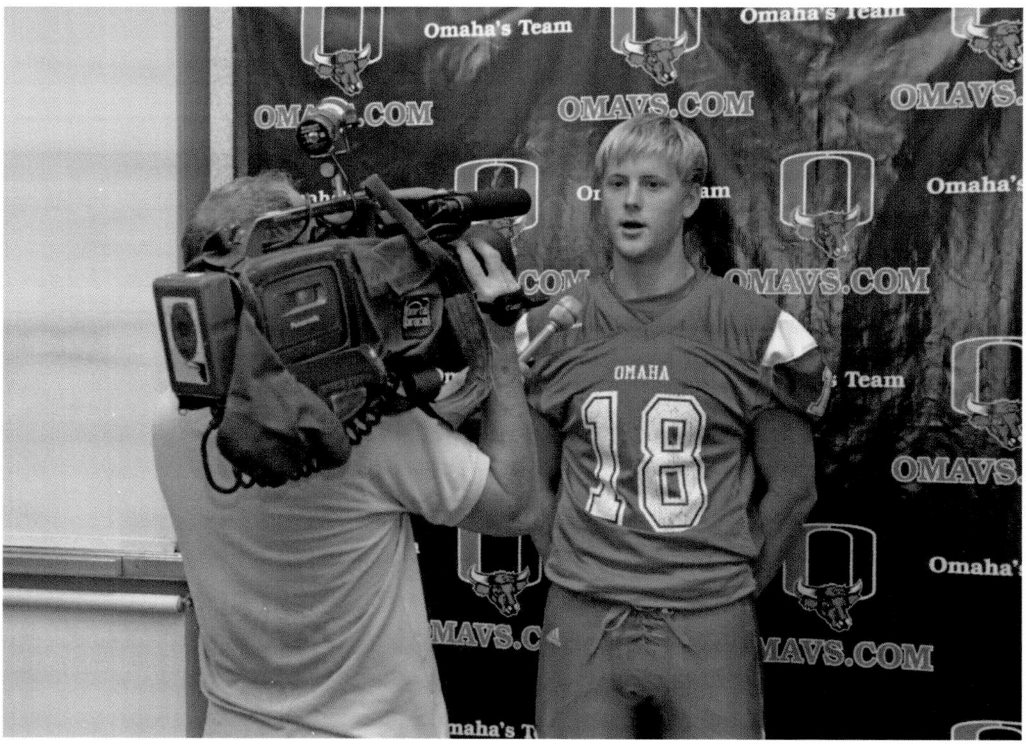

Quarterback John Teigland threw for 1,870 yards and 16 touchdowns in 2010. His 62.2 pass completion percentage ranks best all-time for UNO. Teigland threw five touchdown passes against Truman State, which is a Maverick single-game record.

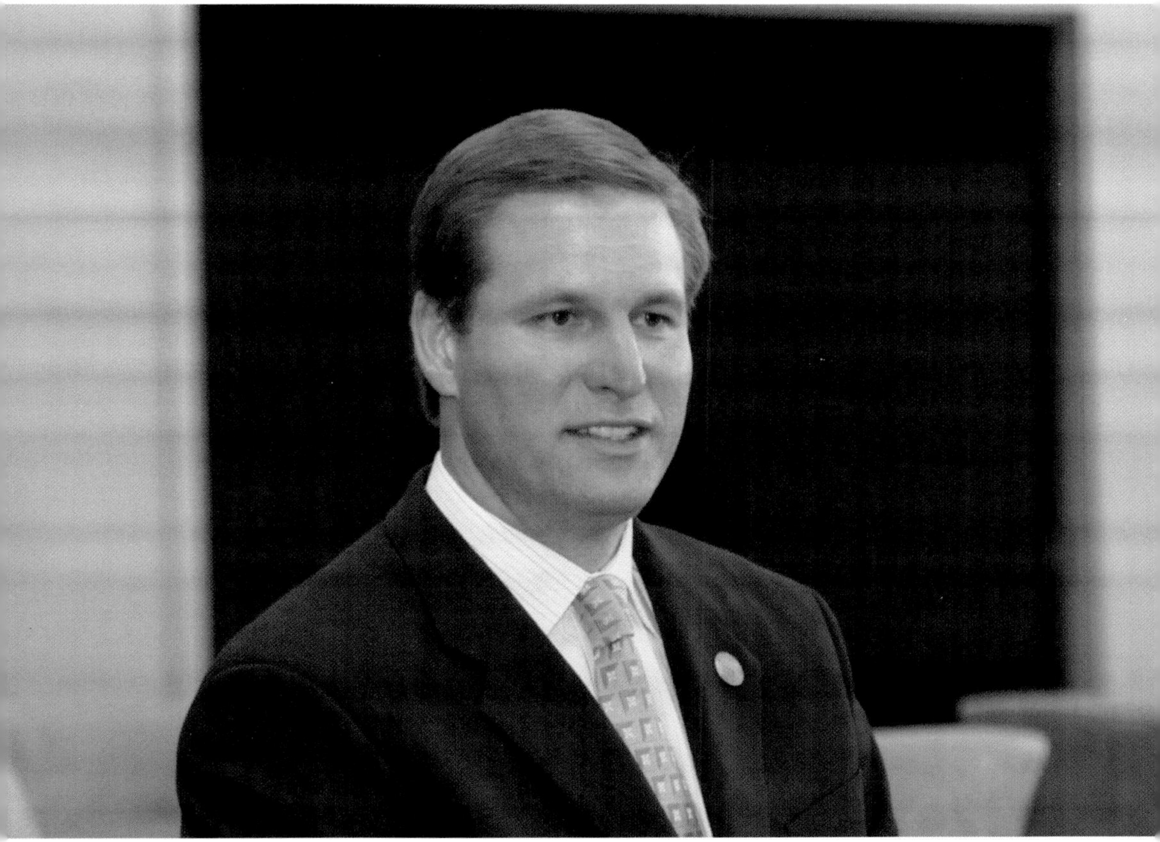

At a March 13, 2011, press conference, former Nebraska All-American football player and current UNO athletic director Trev Alberts made the announcement that the school would be ending its football and wrestling programs as it completed its move to Division I in the Summit League. Alberts, who had been hired in April 2009, was a former Butkus Award winner and All-American at the University of Nebraska. In the end, it came down to money and business considerations—football could no longer continue.